Baltic Sagas

*Events and Personalities
that Changed the World!*

Karl G. Heinze

"Baltic Sagas: Events and Personalities that Changed the World," by
Karl G. Heinze. ISBN 1-58939-498-4.

Published 2003 by Virtualbookworm.com Publishing Inc., P.O. Box
9949, College Station, TX, 77842, US. ©2003 Karl G. Heinze. All rights
reserved. No part of this publication may be reproduced, stored in a
retrieval system, or transmitted in any form or by any means, electronic,
mechanical, recording or otherwise, without the prior written permission
of Karl G. Heinze.

Manufactured in the United States of America.

To Marja –a daughter of the Baltic

To the reader

Marauding Vikings, fierce armored knights on horseback, strong willed women, one of the world's great cities built by the iron will of one man, and much more, are all part of the heritage of the Baltic.

Unlike the Mediterranean Sea area, about which much has been written and is familiar, the Baltic Sea area, particularly as a whole, has not received as much attention. The Baltic Sea is less than twenty five percent of the Mediterranean in size. On its southern shore are Germany and Poland; to the east, Russia and the Baltic States of Estonia, Latvia, and Lithuania; to the north, Finland and Sweden; and Denmark to the west. In addition to these countries, we include nearby Norway, because of its Viking heritage and close geographic association with the other Scandinavian nations.

A few years ago, I took an automobile trip around the Baltic Sea to see the people and places of this part of the world for myself. I found an almost limitless number of palaces, preserved medieval towns, museums, fortresses, cathedrals and much more. These places were connected with events of courage, murder, greed, seduction, and intrigue–every human vice and virtue.

Although most of my life has been spent in the northeastern United States, family ties to the Baltic area added to my curiosity and interest. Over the years, I visited most of the places about which I've written, and took all the photographs in the book.

Let me say a few words about my procedure. I have included several scenes throughout the book that are based on historical events, but to which I have sometimes added reasonable assumptions as to dialogue and incidents. This is not a comprehensive history of the region, but I have selected events and personalities that were important to the area and had an interesting story.

Spellings of places and the names of people vary, often due to translation differences. I have usually selected the simplest spelling and used it throughout. Until 1918, the Julian calendar, which added a day each year, was used in Russia. I use these local dates. In Europe, a legislative body is usually called a Diet or Parliament, so I use the local term.

A map of the Baltic, showing today's names of countries, is on the next page. In the text, I cite the name in use at the time.

The places I saw and the events and personalities I learned about, traveling around the Baltic, inspired me to return again and again, and finally to write about them.

Karl G. Heinze
Cranford, New Jersey, 2003

Map of the Baltic Sea

Baltic Sea Countries

Sweden, Finland, Russia, Estonia, Latvia, Lithuania, Poland, Germany, Denmark, and Norway

The boundaries and names of many of the countries and cities around the Baltic Sea have changed over the years. Kaliningrad at one time was Konigsberg. It is now owned by Russia. St. Petersburg became Petrograd, then Leningrad, and then went back to St. Petersburg. Southern Latvia was once Courland. Tallinn, Estonia was Revel. There are many more examples.

Table of Contents

V. Catherine the Great

VI. Rasputin and the Prince

VII. Communism Triumphs in Russia

VIII. Space Age Begins

IX. Winter War 1939

X. Soviet Communism Fails

Baltic Sagas
Events and Personalities
that Changed the World!

Viking Ship Museum
Roskilde, Denmark

I
The Vikings Are Coming!
They Came for Four Hundred Years and
Changed the Course of History Forever!

Raid on Lindisfarne Monastery

Holy Island
Off Northumbria Coast
England
June 8, 793 AD

The three, shallow draft vessels came up on the beach of Holy Island just as the sun was rising behind them. As the sand crunched under their wooden keels, the crews flung themselves over the sides into the surf and stormed ashore. Each man carried a shield and brandished a club, ax, or sword. Most had belts around their waists with an attached knife in a leather sheath. Some wore metal or leather helmets. As soon as their feet touched solid ground, they ran toward the nearby buildings of the Lindisfarne Monastery,

It was just before breakfast time. In the church the monks had their heads bowed and were saying their morning prayers before going to eat. After breakfast, the brothers would disperse into the fields, barn, craft shops and library to begin daily tasks. This was one of the Benedictine Order's most prosperous outposts.

There were no guards posted at the church, or anywhere else for that matter. The monks felt secure knowing they were doing God's work. They enjoyed the respect and gratitude of their neighbors, along with the entire Christian world. The monks were deep into their prayers and silent meditation when they heard a sharp, unfamiliar crash. The large church doors were suddenly flung open.

The monks jumped up to see large, fierce looking men with long unkempt hair storm through the doors swinging weapons wildly. For many monks, it was the last sight they were to see; they were killed immediately. But the younger ones were herded outside. These men were roped together and taken to the beach near the ships. They would be taken back to become slaves, or perhaps used as trade goods.

Some of the invaders rushed to the altar at the front of the church and scooped up silver and gold crosses, cups, and anything else that looked valuable or caught their eyes. Others ran to the kitchen and storerooms directing monastery workers to bring everything to the ships. They took pots, pans, knives, cooking implements, and the grains and cereals in the storerooms.

Among those found working in the kitchen were several women. They were members of three families that had been allowed to spend the winter at the monastery. They had been driven from their homes in a dispute with their manor lord. When it was discovered that two of the women were young and comely, they were both thrown to the floor and their garments ripped off. Both were raped. Although roughly treated, these women were not injured seriously–they were too valuable.

The invaders continued ransacking the rooms of the monastery taking anything of interest or value. The old and infirmed they found were clubbed to death or their heads split by an axe or sword. Those who looked capable of a day's work were rounded up and sent off to the ships with the others.

There were cows and horses in the barn, and outside were pigs, sheep, and chickens. Most were sent to the ships. What couldn't be carried was used as target practice. Statues, tables, workbenches and troughs all fell under an axe or sword as the attackers indulged their desire to take away what they wanted and destroy everything remaining.

After satisfying their lust for killing and booty, the attackers settled down to eat the breakfast the brothers had expected to enjoy. There was hot cereal, warm bread, honey, butter, and milk. To this, the invaders added a great many freshly slaughtered chickens and two pigs that were promptly roasted. They also found the mead supply and a quantity of wine in casks, probably received in trade with a French Benedictine monastery. The raiders had traveled by water from what is today's Norway, with nowhere to stop and build a fire. At sea, a fire couldn't be risked aboard the wooden ships; so only cold, dried fish or meat was eaten. Now they feasted to satiate their hunger and to celebrate a satisfying expedition.

After a few hours, the raiders slowly returned to the beach area where the captives and stolen treasures were gathered. The stragglers set fire to the wooden structures and the roof of the church. There were so many prisoners, animals, and other plunder that it was difficult to find room for everything. Disagreements broke out about what should be taken and what should be left behind. A fight broke out between two of the raiders leaving one with a nasty knife wound in the shoulder. The leader of the raid, a huge man, menacingly brandished a large axe thereby calming things down before a general melee could erupt. The knife wound was the only raider casualty of the day.

The leader directed the captains of the other two vessels to supervise the distribution of the spoils. The two young girls were separated and each put on a different ship. The larger farm animals were put aboard one of the vessels that was deeper and wider than the other two. When the prisoners got closer to the ships, they saw that large dragonheads, skillfully carved from wood, decorated the bows and sterns.

The invaders were the *Vikings*. The raid on Lindisfarne Monastery was one of their earliest reported attacks outside the Baltic area. Who were these Vikings? How did they come to leave their native, northern waters? Why did they have no respect for God's servants?

Unleashing the Dragon Ships!

The Viking Age depended on superior ships. The vessels that brought the Viking raiders to England were the result of centuries of developing shipbuilding skills. The early inhabitants of the western Baltic Sea region now called Norway, Denmark and Sweden, enjoyed lands with long seacoasts and many rivers and lakes. When spring melted the winter ice, the people ventured out on these waters in small boats to fish, hunt walruses and whales and to get to nearby villages to trade, or sometimes to conquer them, plundering their goods and making slaves of the inhabitants.

In the beginning, the means of water travel were dugouts. These canoe-like boats were made by scooping out the center of felled trees. Side planking was later added so that the dugout could hold more goods and prevent water from coming in over the side. The next step was to add more overlapping planks or lapstrakes, securing them to the lower plank with ropes inserted through holes and lined up plank to plank. A bottom plank eventually replaced the dugout.

Later a true keel was added to provide the base for better shape and stability than a bottom plank permitted. There were bow and stern stems to secure the planking. Iron rivets eventually replaced the lapstrake's ropes when iron ore was discovered and metalworking began. This type of ship construction is called building a "shell."

The boats were now getting longer as well as higher. Paddles replaced oars. Holes were bored so that the oars could fit into the top laptrake. These boats were shaped the same front and back with dragonheads often decorating each end.

The increased number of rowers and the use of oars made it necessary to provide benches. Benches for the rowers were equally spaced, providing added strength for the hull and uniform propulsion on both sides. The benches evolved into cross beams further strengthening the boats as they grew in length.

The hull was now strong enough to support a mast and sail, adding the power of wind to the manual power of the oars. Sails were long used by sailors in the Mediterranean but came late to the north. Now sail power would allow greater range and speed. However, one characteristic of the Viking ship that didn't change was its shallow draft. These ships didn't need to come alongside a wharf or pier but could ride right up onto a beach. They could also navigate in shallow lakes and rivers. Because they rode high in the water, gliding along on the surface, the shallow draft also made them swift.

Finally, the growing size of the ships resulted in a rudder being introduced on the ship's right side. Although a ship no longer could go in either direction, its design still enabled it to turn swiftly and rapidly change direction. Some grew to a size that required 80 rowers on a each side.

By the eighth century the Viking ship was the swiftest and most agile vessel afloat, and, in addition, could go into places other ships couldn't maneuver. They also didn't need a dock when they got to their destination. The Vikings held this advantage for over three hundred years. During this "Viking Age," the superiority of these ships gave them a decisive military advantage.

We are adding to our knowledge of these vessels by studying the remains of ships unearthed by archeologists. Although the design of Viking ships was very consistent - shell construction, oars through holes in the upper lapstrake, similar shaped bow and stern, and a starboard rudder - they came in a variety of dimensions.

Two of the first ships found were named the "Gokstad" and "Oseberg" ships. They are now in a special museum in Oslo, Norway. A greater appreciation of these ships has also resulted from modern reproductions that are being successfully sailed long distances, including across the Atlantic Ocean. Some reproductions can be found at Roskilde, Denmark. There is also a museum in Roskilde of actual Viking ships that were uncovered and salvaged from where they were sunk, hundreds of years ago, to block the entrance to the city.

We have also added to our knowledge of these vessels from the Bayeux Tapestry in Bayeux, France. It accurately depicts many aspects of Viking ship construction in the eleventh century. It is particularly helpful in understanding their sails and rigging, the remains of which no longer exist.

These ships finally lost their preeminence to taller ships with more freeboard and offering the comfort of cabins. In sea battles, these taller ships could rain down destruction on the lower, open Viking vessels.

Vikings Terrorize Europe

The Lindisfarne Monastery raid in England in 793 AD was only the beginning. For the next few hundred years the inhabitants of what is today Denmark, Norway and Sweden would set out in their swift ships to make sudden and daring raids throughout Europe. These adventurers would strike terror into the hearts and minds of the people of any city, particularly those on rivers or near the coast.

At the start, raiding parties were made up of gangs of well-armed men, perhaps twenty or thirty, who rallied around a leader considered to be the best fighter or who had proven successful in finding booty for his retinue of followers. These men might be relatives or members of his village, or villages nearby. If a particular leader didn't do well and his group heard of another leader whose raiding expeditions were more successful, they might switch groups.

If a planned target promised rich booty but was too large for one group, several groups might join together to attack the prize. The interest of these men was in treasure portable enough to be seized quickly and taken away in their ships.

In the beginning, the Vikings often directed their raids against church properties, which had few defenses. Vikings had no respect for Christianity, and the booty was abundant. Churches contained bejeweled crosses, chalices, and statues of silver and gold. A gold or silver cross was valuable to the Vikings for the gold or silver it contained. The cross had no significance as a symbol of Christ's sacrifice.

They also slew, or took as prisoners, monks, priests and nuns, because their dedication to Christ and their vows had no significance to the Vikings. Vikings were pagans. They had no regard for the Christian religion, its symbols and followers, but believed in their own pagan gods.

The pagan gods had a variety of attributes associated with them.
The most powerful and popular of the gods was Thor, the god of thunder, who was usually depicted with a hammer. Legends have him using his hammer to fight giants, the enemies of the gods. The Vikings, who attributed to him strength and determination, recounted many stories of his feats and passed them down the generations. They gave his name to places throughout the Viking world and in personal names, such as Thorgrim and Thorstein.

The father of all gods was believed to be Odin, and he was said to ride an eight-legged horse named Sleipnir. He was also the god of war. When Vikings in battle let loose a volley of arrows from their bows, they often referred to them as "Odin's Wind." His symbol was the raven, and is sometimes depicted with a raven on each side of his head. They may have been mistaken for horns and this may be how the idea got started that Vikings wore horned helmets.

Frey was the fertility god. His symbol was the sickle. He made sure the sun shone, the rain fell, and there was a good harvest.

Three Viking gods- Odin, Thor, and Frey- are recalled today in the following days of the week- Wednesday, Thursday, and Friday.

Ferry was the goddess of love and war. She was the most beautiful of all the gods and could also turn herself into a bird. Associated with prosperity, she was the sister of Frey and daughter of Njord ("earth"). Tyr was another god of war. He was depicted wearing a bearskin clock and a bear's head over his helmet. The Viking word for bearskin is "berserk." Sometimes, a group of Vikings would dress in bearskins and work themselves into a rage before going into battle. This became the origin of the term "going berserk."

The Vikings also had legends about their gods. One of the most important Viking legends concerned the Valkyries. These were women sent by the gods to choose the warriors who were to die. They kept watch over battles and selected the bravest warriors to die and then escorted them to Valhalla. Here the Valkyries attended to their needs. At Valhalla, these brave warriors were received by Odin, who welcomed them with goblets of wine. The warriors feasted the nights away. Valhalla was the drinking hall of heroes where brave Vikings went who were slain in battle. The slain warriors remained here until called upon by Odin to fight alongside the gods.

When these pagan warriors began raiding, they looked first to the places closest to their homelands. In the coastal area between southern Denmark and today's Holland, there are a number of islands and a low coastline. This was the part of Europe nearest to the Vikings. For a number of years, the Vikings had sailed into this area and traded their iron, leather, and ivory products for the glass vessels, cloth, and jewelry of the local people. During these trading sessions, the Vikings were aware of the variety of valuable goods produced in these lands. They became discouraged by the paucity of luxury goods they could trade for in return. In the Nordic homeland, the Vikings didn't have the resources to produce goods of similar value. They decided to correct the imbalance by seizing more and trading less.

This area was part of the Carolingian Empire ruled by Charlemagne (c. 768–814 AD). He had established a great empire that included today's France, Germany, Switzerland, Austria, Holland, Belgium and parts of Spain and Italy. This domain was ruled from Aachen, Germany. Charlemagne's throne and casket can still be seen in the cathedral there today.

The first record of an attack for plunder in this area called Frankia was in 799. These attacks became more numerous after the death of Charlemage's son, Louis the Pious (c. 814–840 AD). His death brought a disorganized political situation to the Empire. He had three sons each of whom controlled a different area of the Empire. Lothar had the Italian area, Louis, the German, had the lands east of the Rhine, and Charles the Bold controlled France and the Low Countries. Nobles, and others loyal to them, supported their different claims and even the church took sides.

The situation was very beneficial to the Vikings who took advantage of the chaos. The Vikings sometimes took sides in the disputes and made themselves available to serve as mercenaries. There was also fighting between factions of Vikings hired by one group or another.

The Vikings were meeting with so much success that many decided not to return to their northern homeland after raids. Instead they would establish a strong base in their raiding area, often an island, and then move down the European coast and sometimes over to Ireland, Scotland and England.

One such early island base was in Walcheren, now in Holland, and another was in Normoutier, near the mouth of the Loire River. Here the Vikings gathered enough forces to become known as the "Army of the Loire." A second Viking army known as the "Army of the Somme" was established at Walcheren. A third Viking army concentrated its activities on the Seine River and became known as the "Army of the Seine." These three Viking armies camped in Europe for many years. Paris was attacked in 845, 856, and 885. Hamburg was raided in 845. The Vikings raided Cologne on the Rhine River in 862 and 863.

Sometimes the Vikings conquered and took what they wanted, but at other times, they were paid tribute to prevent their attacks. After a century of Viking raids, fights and looting, the locals organized their defenses, and the Vikings were sometimes beaten or held off, bringing about a new phase of Viking activity.

Starting in 911, the Frankish King, Charles the Simple, and the Viking leader, Hrolfur, known as Rollo, acknowledged that their battling had come to an impasse. To establish peace, the Vikings were granted land around Rouen in return for ceasing further raiding and for securing their protection against other attackers. The land they were granted became known as Normandy "the land of the Northmen." These Normans will reappear in our story later.

Vikings were also trying to establish a foothold in the province of Brittany to the southwest of Normandy. Raids started here in 843 when a large Viking fleet raided Nantes and killed the bishop and priests. This began a series of Viking raids in Brittany, which weren't checked until a Brittany ruler, Alain of Vannes, defeated them and kept them at bay until his death in 907. After his death, the Vikings started again raiding Brittany and in 914 a band of Vikings stayed and ruled for four years. In 919 a new Viking commander, Rognvaldur, arrived. Many Britons fled and took refuge in England, including the grandson of Alain.

Finally, after about twenty years of occupation, the exiles returned, led by Alain II. With the help of troops and a fleet of ships provided by the English Anglo–Saxons, he took the Vikings by surprise. Aided by local Britons who joined the liberating army, the Vikings were expelled from Brittany in 939.

Some Vikings sailed farther south down the coast of Europe and penetrated the Mediterranean through the Straits of Gibraltar. A raid on Moorish-held Seville was recorded in 844. However, the Moors, which are what the Muslims were called in Spain, were fierce fighters themselves. These followers of Mohammed had swept west across North Africa and crossed over to Spain in 711. The Vikings fought fiercely because they believed that an honorable death in battle meant a quick and certain trip to their version of heaven, which they called "Valhalla." The Moors matched this with their similar; belief; Allah's special reward for those who die in battle. After holding Seville for a week, the Vikings were routed and sent packing.

A major expedition to the Mediterranean by two Viking leaders, Bjorn and Hastein, was mounted in 859 from the Loire and consisted of 62 ships. They raided the southern coast of Spain and went upriver in today's France to raid Nimes, Arles, and Valence. They went on to Italy to raid Pisa and Luna, which they may have mistaken for Rome. They then returned to Spain and captured the prince of Navarre, holding him for ransom. The Viking fleet had been reduced by two-thirds when they finally left the Mediterranean. Their booty, however, must have been considerable.

At same time Vikings were raiding the coastlines of mainland Europe, Britain, and Ireland, other Vikings were assaulting Scotland and her outlying islands, Shetland, Orkney and Hebrides. As usual, the first raids were of churches and monasteries, for their rich and portable treasures. After these were seized, they sailed off.

After a while, the Vikings stopped returning north to their homes, just as they did while raiding mainland Europe. In 840, for the first time, they stayed in Ireland during the winter, and Dublin became a center of Viking trade activity.

In 866, a large Viking army arrived in East Anglia in England, and then moved north to establish a base at York. Eventually, an area was defined: the Vikings would control the land in the east, and the Anglo-Saxons, under King Alfred, would rule the land to the west. The dividing line was known as the Danelaw Boundary.

The Viking influence in York was substantial and can still be noted today. In modern times, extensive archeological excavations have revealed a large settlement of that time. It became a trading center and an area for producing craft items.

In Scotland, and the islands of Orkney and Shetland, many Vikings reverted to the same farming activities of their original homelands. They came to these islands last, settled the land, and stayed longer than they had in other places.

Norman Invasion of England – Battle of Hastings

The invasion of England in 1066 is generally accepted as the last major event of the European Viking era. The invasion's leader William, Duke of Normandy, was heir to the Viking lands that resulted from the peace between Rollo, the Viking leader, and the Carolingian King, Charles the Simple, in 911. William was a direct descendent of Rollo and the illegitimate son of his father, the Duke, and a tanner's daughter. He was known as William the Bastard.

William invaded England after the English king, Edward the Confessor, died and Harald II, Edward's brother-in-law, stepped in to claim the crown. During a visit to England, William insisted he had obtained Edward's agreement that he would succeed to Edward's throne. He further strengthened his claim by marrying Matilda of Flanders, a descendent of the former English King, Alfred the Great.

William thought he also had Harald's promise that he would inherit the English crown. William had ransomed Harald, who was Edward's brother-in-law, when a boating accident off the Normandy coast had left Harald ashore there in 1064. William claimed that Harald had agreed to support his claim to the English crown when he returned to England. William decided he needed to enforce this agreement on the battlefield.

Before facing William's invading forces, Harald had to subdue his brother Tostig and Norwegian King, Harald III, who had invaded Yorkshire in support of William. Harald II marched north and at the battle of Stamford Bridge on September 25, 1066 he defeated this northern threat. His brother Tostig and the Norwegian King Harald III were both killed. He then turned south to meet William's invading force, which had landed at Sussex.

Karl G. Heinze

William had organized a strong invasion force of mounted knights and crossbowmen. Men and horses went aboard nearly 700 ships, including William's flagship, the Mora, at the French port of Dives-sur-Mer on September 27. After landing in England, these forces marched up the road to engage Harald's army, just over six miles away on the road to London. Harald's 7000 infantry defended Senloc Hill in a strong, interlocked shield line. Harald's orders were to stand firm against the Norman cavalry charge. They did this successfully, but when the Normans were repulsed, the English got excited, broke their shield line and ran after them. The Normans surrounded these groups and annihilated them. Another feigned retreat by the Normans led to a further break up of the no-longer disciplined shield line and further slaughter of the English. During the melee, an arrow hit Harald in the eye mortally wounding him and further demoralizing his troops. In the end, the Norman cavalry rode down and killed the rest of the defending army in what became known as the Battle of Hastings.

William and his Norman supporters now ruled England. He became known to history finally as "William the Conqueror" instead of "William the Bastard." One of his early edicts was ordering a survey of his subjects' wealth to guide tax collection. This became known as the Domesday Book.

An illustrated, historical record of the conquest of England by William the Conqueror is preserved in a tapestry known as the Bayeux Tapestry. By recording this event in embroidery on linen, it also shows us the clothing, arms, ships and customs of these descendants of Vikings. As mentioned earlier, it is also one of the best records available today of the sails and rigging of Viking ships since, unlike a few of the wooden shells, rope and sails have not survived. The 70 meter long Tapestry is displayed in a special room in a building across from the Cathedral of Notre Dame in Bayeux, France. The Bishop of Bayeux, Odon de Conteville, half-brother of William, commissioned it. It is a "must-see" when traveling in northwest France.

Vikings in Russia

The extensive river network and lack of a central governing authority made the great Russian landmass a very desirable target for Viking plunder, trade, and settlement. With their shallow ships, the Vikings penetrated the large Russian landmass through the rivers emptying north into the Baltic Sea. Important cities were later established on these rivers. The Dvina River now has Riga, Latvia on its bank, and at the delta of the Neva River sits St. Petersburg, Russia. From the Neva River, the Vikings sailed east a short distance to Lake Ladoga and then down the Volkhov River to Novgorod and on to Lake Ilman. From the headwaters of the Dvina or the southern shores of Lake Ilman, they could haul their ships on land and portage to the headwaters of the Dnieper River, which flowed south.

After a long journey south, the Dnieper River empties into the Black Sea. There were river rapids and hostile tribes to overcome, but the rich prize for making this long journey was the immensely wealthy and ancient city of Constantinople (now Istanbul). It was just beyond the southern shore of the Black Sea through a passage that became known as the Bosporus. Here the Vikings would trade their furs and captured slaves for silk, spices and silver.

Southeast of Lake Ladoga were the headwaters of the Volga River, one of the world's longest rivers to which the Vikings would portage. The Volga empties far to the south into the Caspian Sea. The Vikings would trade with cities along the shores and even travel farther by land to Baghdad and its riches.

Viking travel to the Russian heartland to raid and take slaves, extract tribute, and later trade and settle, must have gone on for a long time before the Viking raids took place in Europe, first recorded in 793 AD. The distances were shorter, the Baltic Sea and river shorelines were always visible, water was near, and food could be hunted and cooked on shore.

A trading center was established near the mouth of the Volkhov River named Aldeigjuborg and now called Staraia Ladoga. A settlement was also established where the Valkhov River begins its journey from Lake Ilmen, called Holmgard, and now called Gorodishche.

The early Vikings in Russia were called Varangians. At some point the local tribes near Novgorod refused to pay them any further tribute and drove them off. However, the local tribes couldn't agree among themselves who was to rule. Consequently, there was dissention and strife among them. Finally, in 862, they decided to invite three Viking brothers to establish order and rule over them. The oldest brother, Rorik, located himself in Novgorod and the other two brothers were sent to other cities. These Varangians were known as " Rus" and the area around Novgorod became known as Rus.

When Rorik died, his son Igor was too young to rule, so his cousin, Oleg became the leader. He extended his power south and gained control of Kiev, a great center of trade and the gateway to the Black Sea. He established his ruling center in Kiev and united the entire region, which became known as Kievan Rus. He attacked Constantinople with two thousand ships, extracted tribute from the Byzantiums, and negotiated a trading treaty with them. The Vikings made such a fearsome impression on the Sultan that he employed a troop of Vikings as his personal guard, and they became known as the"Varangian Guard."

The Rorik dynasty continued to rule Russia for hundreds of years. During this time the power shifted to Moscow. The Moscow ruler, starting with Ivan IV (known as the Terrible), began using the title "Tsar."

Canals, reservoirs, and lakes now link the extensive rivers of Russia. Large and extensive locks control the water level. You can travel the entire distance from St. Petersburg on the Gulf of Finland to Odessa on the Caspian Sea by water.

* * *

I recently took the St. Petersburg to Moscow trip on a river cruise ship. The land is so vast that much of the shoreline landscape probably remains as earlier voyagers saw it. There is still a lot of eager trading and selling when the ship docks along the way.

Vikings Journey West
to Iceland and Greenland

In 870 AD, the Vikings put their skills, and ships, to an important and peaceful use. That was the year Viking settlers began arriving on a large island in the middle of the Atlantic Ocean. This island, given the name "Iceland," was larger than Ireland and uninhabited, except perhaps for a few hermit monks, who fled when confronted by large numbers of heathens.

Three men, Floki, Ingolf, and Hjonlief are recorded as being the first Icelandic explorers. Floki is credited with naming "Iceland" because of the harsh climate and the drift ice to the north. Ingolf and Hjonleif, who came together in 860 for the first time, each came back separately in 870. Ingolf, who came from Sunnfjord, Norway, built a large farm on a bay overlooking the sea in a location that became the capital, Reykjavik. Hjorlief went farther east along the southern coast.

About four hundred families were among the first Viking settlers to arrive in Iceland following the initial explorers. During the next sixty years, the first settlers were followed by thousands of other immigrants. They brought what they needed to start their lives in a new land–farm animals, tools, cooking and weaving implements, clothing, sturdy ponies (famous for their gait), even slaves.

Many of these immigrants were relatives, or close friends, of the earliest settlers, those who had staked out the best land for themselves. The early arrivals wanted close neighbors who would be friendly and known to them. Soon the land that was suitable for sustaining a comfortable living was occupied. Few settlers came after 930.

This sudden rush to a new land came about for a number of reasons. One was the increased power and tyranny of local rulers in Scandinavia, especially the Norwegian King, Harold Haarfagri. Another reason was the lack of land in Scandinavia, particularly in

Norway, where only the coastal areas would provide a living, and not enough was available for the growing population.

The swift and sturdy Viking ships now available made it possible to leave Norway and embark on the hazardous journey across the north Atlantic, carrying whole families and their household goods.

The society that these immigrants set up was unique for that time. The early settlers were mostly from Scandinavia, but there were also Irish and Scots. In 1871, the "landnam" (recording of land claims) had established the initial claims to the ownership of most of the best land. For the most part, it was a stable and peaceful society. Families who lost their property to fire or other misfortune were helped. This era is referred to as the "early, happy time."

At the beginning, a set of laws was established and recited orally each year at a designated site. An assembly (Althing) was established at Thingvellir, a natural amphitheater. The Iceland Althing is the oldest parliament in the world. At the annual meetings, the leaders were elected. The Althing had no military power of its own to enforce its decisions, and this caused problems later.

Although trade with Scandinavia was brisk, the land and social environment allowed the people of Iceland to develop what was largely a self-sustaining society.

Christianity was proclaimed in Iceland in 1000 AD after years of pressure from the Norwegian King, Olaf Tryggnoson. However, heathen practices were tolerated, at first. The coming of Christianity brought with it two new influences. The Bishop became an important new factor in Iceland's power structure. The Church also reduced reliance on oral tradition and substituted the written word. The law book kept by the bishop now replaced the "law-reader." Unhappily, the peaceful course of events began to unravel when rival chieftains began using the annual meetings of the Althing to promote greater power for themselves.

At about this time a new immigrant to Iceland arrived, Erik the Red. Red was a hothead who had trouble getting along with his neighbors. Even so, he was able to retain a following that was loyal to him. Those personal characteristics indirectly resulted in his colonizing the lonely and isolated island of Greenland, a place that served as the gateway to

North America. It was far to the west of Erik's original home in Jaeren, Norway. He and his father were forced to leave Norway because of some altercations with neighbors that resulted in people being killed. Around 980, the family left and traveled west to set up a new home in Iceland.

Erik's son, Leif Eirikson, was born in Iceland and is proudly claimed there. However, his father, Erik got into a scrape in Iceland, as he had in Norway, and people were killed. Once again, he was banished.

Erik gathered some of his followers and headed farther west. He was looking for land that had been sighted 60 years before by a man named Gunnbjorn. Gunnbjorn had overshot Iceland while traveling from Norway and spread the word of a land farther west.

Erik found the new land and stayed there for three years. When he returned to Iceland, he called the new land "Greenland." He thought this sounded more inviting than "Ice" land. In 985, as a result of his tales and enthusiasm, twenty-five ships set off from Iceland for Greenland. However, only fourteen arrived in Greenland, the rest were lost at sea or turned back.

Settlements were set up in Greenland in the only two areas that would support colonies, Julianehab Bay (Eastern Settlement) and Godthab Fjord (Western Settlement). Only these areas had enough grazing land to support the livestock - cattle, horses, sheep, goats and pigs- they had brought. There were no trees. Although there was no timber from trees, driftwood was occasionally found. The settlers constructed buildings of stone and sod, as they had learned to do in Iceland. They hunted for reindeer, hares, and game birds, and from the sea they harvested seals and fish. They traded furs, sealskins, and ropes of hides, walrus and whale ivory for timber, iron and corn.

It was a hard life, but eventually about three hundred farmlands were established.

Vikings Encounter
Native American Indians

Sheltered Bay
South and West of Viking Base Camp
North America
Spring, 1000 AD

Four, tall men came out from behind the trees with their forearms extended and hands open. They walked slowly toward the strangers that had brought a large ship up on the beach the night before. It was an hour after sunrise and a clear day. The four men had ruddy, light brown complexions and hair that was dark and long. Two had decorated their hair with feathers and seashells. They wore very little, just a small, square covering in the front that tied around their waists. Two of them wore leather vests. They had serious expressions on their faces, but carried no weapons.

The strangers on the beach were Vikings from Greenland who had sailed down the coast from their base camp in Newfoundland. The leader of the Vikings, Leif Eirikson, was a large and imposing man, known as Leif the Lucky. He and two of his companions walked forward to meet the approaching men. They carried no weapons. The other twenty-six men in the company stayed near the campfires close to the ship. Their weapons were on the ground nearby, but they didn't hold them.

The Shaman, or leader of the four natives, had sent them ahead. He wanted to be sure these powerful looking strangers, with their long red or blonde hair and fair complexions, would not be a threat to them, their women or their children in the nearby village. Also, he wanted to learn how many there were and how they were armed. Finally, he wanted to find out what they might have to trade. The Shaman had decided that four of their largest and strongest looking warriors should approach the strangers, but with empty hands, in order to avoid any misunderstandings or hostility. Watching from behind the trees, there were many more warriors armed with spears and other native weapons.

The Vikings also wanted to be cautious and avoid any immediate trouble because they needed water and food. They also wanted to see how many people were in the area and if they had goods to trade. The Vikings were few in number and, until coming this far, they had not met any large groups of people. A particular need that brought them this far south was timber. In their Greenland colony, there were no trees. Trees were sorely needed for building homes and repairing ships.

As the three Vikings and four natives got closer to each other, the Vikings put their open hands in front of them just as the natives were doing. At this, all broke into smiles and everyone felt immediately better. The Vikings cupped their hands and placed them to their mouth, gesturing that they wanted water. By further gestures, with their hands directed to their mouths, they indicated they wanted food. The Vikings then took the natives to their campfire and showed them their empty cooking pots. The natives also noticed the nearby weapons–swords, axes, iron studded clubs, and shields.

The Vikings then walked them over to their beached ship, which had its bow and stern decorated with fearsome dragonheads. The ship was much bigger than any vessel the natives had seen. Dugouts, and birch and leather-covered canoes long enough to hold six to eight men, were small compared to this vessel. The ship had twelve oar holes on each side, a large mast and a sail tightly wrapped around a spar.

The Vikings also showed them small metal pendants, animal figures carved from stone, and bracelets and necklaces made from beads. They gestured they wanted to trade these in return for food and anything else the Indians had to offer. The natives nodded they understood. Before leaving, the Indians pointed in a northeasterly direction and indicated water could be found there. They returned to the forest after waving farewell and exchanging smiles all around. The Vikings called these native Americans "Skrnelings." We refer to them as Indians.

This was the third landing the Vikings had made since sailing south from their Newfoundland base camp where they sometimes spent the winter. As they traveled south, they encountered a more hospitable climate with plentiful supplies of game and timber and the opportunity for a longer growing season for crops. But there were also more natives. In an earlier journey he had led farther north, Leif's brother, Thorwald, had been slain by a hostile native arrow during an encounter. The Vikings were hopeful that the long coastline they had been sailing past would enable them to find a place with good supplies and few inhabitants.

Later in the day, in the early afternoon, about a dozen Indians returned, accompanied by an older man elaborately dressed and wearing a headdress made of feathers. The Indians carried ducks, turkeys and geese; they brought hampers and leather sacks with dried corn, beans, clams, and eggs. They also offered large, dark brown shellfish, which when placed in boiling water, turned bright red. They soon discovered upon breaking the shells, succulent, delicious, pink meat.

The arriving Indians were greeted with friendly smiles and whoops of appreciation for the food, which was quickly cooked on the open campfire. The natives also brought for trading, fur pelts, leather moccasins, and jewelry made of seashells.

The Vikings made all the Indians feel welcome but lavished particular attention on the older man, clearly their leader. Leif made him a gift of a metal pendent depicting one of their Gods, Odin, holding a sword overhead. The chief gave Leif a beautiful pair of soft, leather moccasins decorated with tiny seashells and a purse made from leather and decorated with snakeskin. Their leader, called "Qunnoune" by the natives, was very interested in the Viking weapons. Metal swords and metal axe heads were closely examined, generating animated discussion among the Indians. They knew nothing of swords and had no metal to make them.

The Vikings didn't want to trade their metal swords or metal-headed axes since they were much stronger weapons then the stone axes and wooden spears carried by the Indians. Leif wanted more experience with these Indians before arming them with metal weapons, remembering what had happened at other places. However, the natives received some metal pots, flax and wool clothing, combs, decorative metal and stone carvings in trade, and seemed content. The Indians proved to be shrewd traders, often trying to improve the trading to their advantage.

After eating together, Leif gestured to the chief that they wanted to cut down some of the nearby trees. The chief nodded in agreement. The natives left, returning to the forest. That night, the Vikings heard the sound of many drums from across the water to the west and the north. In the morning, the Vikings chopped down and trimmed about a dozen trees, putting the trunks in their ship.

About noon, a larger group of natives returned, this time with a few older women. They brought a number of large pots containing vegetables and meat, added water and hung the pots over the campfire. The resulting stew was flavored with local herbs, nuts, wild onions and salt. The Vikings learned that salt could be extracted from brine prepared by cooking clams. While two of the women were preparing the stew, two other women had crushed dry corn kernels to make a fine cornmeal, which they mixed with hot water and wild strawberries to form dough. They heated round mounds of this dough on hot stones at the campfire.

While they were waiting for the food to be cooked, two Vikings jumped up and began demonstrating their wrestling skills. After much clutching and pushing, one wrestler was pinned down. Immediately, two Indians got up to show how they wrestled. Before this went any further, a woman got up who had accompanied the native group. She hadn't participated in the cooking, but now she chanted and circled the food in a rhythmic dance, which was accompanied by drums and flutes played by the natives.

The Vikings noted the special respect she was accorded by all the natives, who called her "Mag-nus." Leif decided it would be good to recognize her special status among the natives and presented her with a metal brooch. He showed her that by attaching it with a small metal bar it could be used to decorate her blouse. She smiled, acknowledging Leif's generosity. From the nods and smiles of all the natives, Leif was satisfied he had done the right thing by making this friendly gesture. After the food was cooked the women served it to the entire company in carved wooden bowls. The dough had baked into a filling and delicious bread. This meal was the best the Vikings had eaten in a long time.

After eating, the Chief brought out a long, hollow earthenware rod with a rounded bulb at the end. Into this bulb he pressed some brown plant fibers and lit them with a flame from the campfire. He then began to suck on the other end of the rod and exhaled smoke. The other natives smoked similar "pipes." The pipes were offered to the Vikings, but when they inhaled they gagged and got dizzy.

While resting, a few of the Vikings started talking among themselves that it might be nice to take the women with them when they left, and if some younger ones could be found, so much the better. When Leif heard this talk, he immediately became worried and on guard. From the number of drums they heard the night before, and the large number of natives now in the camp, he realized his small band would be overwhelmed if the present good feeling in the camp were forfeited. He was called Leif the Lucky, but his good luck often resulted from applying his wisdom and experience.

After some more trading, the women collected their pots, and all the natives started to leave. Leif took the chief aside and, with gestures, made clear they would be leaving in the morning. The chief nodded for he was also apprehensive that his warriors were becoming overly interested in the strangers' metal weapons. Both leaders were also concerned that what started out as friendly wrestling demonstrations might get out of hand. Although the Chief knew that in a general melee the Indians would prevail by sheer weight of numbers, he didn't want a lot of dead warriors, widows, and fatherless children.

After the Indians left, Leif announced to his men that he planned on leaving in the morning at first light. Although some of the men grumbled, he insisted that they would not risk their successful meeting going wrong over any incident, real or perceived. They had replenished their supplies, taken on a good supply of timber, and conducted some rewarding trading. The men finally accepted the wisdom of this decision and, early the next morning, they departed. Native men in the nearby forest watched them depart.

This meeting between the Vikings and Native American Indians had gone well. On other occasions, mutual suspicion, native concern for home and families, and trade misunderstandings erupted into sudden violence.

First Known Europeans in North America

Up until recently. the names, places, and events related to the Vikings' activities in North America have depended upon written stories, or sagas, recorded in Iceland a few hundred years after they reportedly happened. These are known as "The Vinland Sagas." Because these writings were not reported directly from the source, they may very well reflect bias accumulated over the years.

Today, we can add to these sagas substantial archeological evidence found at L'Anse aux Meadows, Newfoundland that supports the belief that Vikings came to America centuries before Christopher Columbus. The Vikings didn't appear to penetrate inland very far or stay very long. Unlike Columbus, they didn't motivate other Europeans to visit, colonize, and eventually rule over what they found.

The archeological evidences at L'Anse aux Meadows, Newfoundland was first discovered in 1961 by Helge Ingstad and excavated under the direction of his wife, Dr. Anne Steine Ingstad. It confirms a Viking settlement occupied the location for a period of time. Apparently, these early explorers sailed over from both Greenland and Iceland. We can only guess they were looking for supplies, first and foremost, probably timber, which wasn't available in Greenland. They needed timber for building and repairing ships. Although they built homes in Greenland from stone and sod, this wouldn't work for ships. They might have been considering the area also as a site for future colonization.

We can't be sure why they didn't stay long, but we can speculate. It may have been too far west from the settlement in Greenland, even farther from Iceland and from their primary base for supplies in Norway. Also, the local people who used the area for hunting and fishing may have resented the newcomers. These attitudes probably became obvious leaving the Vikings, small in numbers, quite concerned. We can't be sure the builders of the settlement weren't killed or captured, or taken away somewhere.

A damaged silver coin was found in Maine 1957 that was identified as a Norwegian penny minted 1065–1080. It had a small hole drilled on one edge indicating it might have been on a necklace or an ornament. The coin was found on a site, owned by DeWitt Goddard and then named after him, on Penobscot Bay, Maine. This place had been an important Indian trading center at one time. Perhaps there will be new discoveries in the years ahead that corroborate the existence of early Vikings in North America so that more can be learned about their activities.

According to accepted historical records, Bjarni Herjolfsson, was the first person to sight the coast of North America. On his way to Greenland in 985 with supplies, he journeyed too far west. Recognizing his error, he turned around without landing. When he finally arrived in Greenland, he told the people there of his discovery of new land to the west.

The son of Erik the Red, Leif Eirikson, Leif the Lucky, heard Bjarni's story and decided to see this new land himself. Leif bought Bjarni's ship, enlisted a crew of thirty-five men, and set sail westward from Greenland to see this new land. Their first landfall revealed only rocks and glaciers. They named it Helluland (stone slab land). Leif sailed farther and landed on what is today probably Baffin Island. He continued going south to what is today's Labrador. He called this new land "Vinland" and stayed the winter.

It's likely that Leif returned at some later date and established the L'Anse aux Meadows base. It seems to have been used regularly as a place for making repairs, gathering timber, skins, and food supplies to help sustain the colony in Greenland. The established camp enabled those who came there to extend their stay. An expedition could be organized, using the base, to hunt and gather (from the surrounding area) goods that couldn't be obtained in Greenland. When a ship was loaded, it returned to Greenland.

Other Vikings followed Leif to North America. Leif's brothers, Thorwald and Thorsten, came. Thorwald was killed by an arrow in a skirmish with natives. Another Norse explorer to be tempted by the tales of green fields and trees was Thorfinn Karlsefni, a prosperous merchant from Iceland. He came to Greenland and married Erik's daughter Gudrid, sister of Leif and Thorstein and widow of the slain Thorwald. He made a number of trips to the North American continent. On one trip his wife, Gudrid, gave birth to a son, Snorri, the first European known to be born in North America

Freydis, daughter of Erik, and sister of Leif was also reported to have made a journey to the North America continent. The report relayed information about a ship arriving in Greenland one summer from Norway by way of Iceland commanded by two brothers, Helgi and Finnboggi. They had heard the talk about land farther to the west. They met Leif's sister, Freylis, who proposed she combine her resources with theirs to journey there together. She persuaded Leif to let them use his base camp.

The expedition set off in two ships. The two brothers and their group, which included five women, arrived first and unloaded their belongings at the camp. When Freylis arrived, she was annoyed by their presumption of using the camp in her absence. A quarrel erupted. The brothers set up their own camp. Over the winter, the brothers made an attempt to restore harmonious relations but their effort proved unsuccessful.

In the spring, goods for the return journey had been gathered and the two ships were readied for departure. Suddenly, Freylis ordered her band to kill the brothers and their entire group. Her companions refused to kill the five accompanying women, so she took an axe and killed them herself.

She then led the expedition, including the brothers' boat with cargo they had gathered, back to Greenland. She seems to have been "her father's daughter" in temperament. You may recall that Eric the Red had been banished from both Norway and Iceland for being in more than one fracas in which men had been killed.

We can only speculate as to why the Vikings stopped using the base camp at L'Anse aux Meadows. Items found at L'Anse aux Meadows suggest ships came in from both Iceland and Greenland. We presume that Leif, who inherited the leadership of Greenland from his father Eric, collected revenues from all goods taken from there since it was subject to his claims of discovery.

The base at L'Anse aux Meadows was substantial. It consisted of three main halls and a number of smaller buildings. The three main halls probably provided a social center and accommodations for a leader and his community. It's likely that each hall was the support center for a single ship and its crew. The nature of the living quarters suggests a cross–section of social classes was here, including slaves. The entire base represented a substantial investment of time and effort. It never developed into a permanent settlement. It may never have been intended to be more than a base for tapping the resources of this New World and perhaps acting as a springboard to an even more hospitable place. The lure of much needed timber and other supplies probably continued to entice the Vikings from Greenland to North America. Perhaps it occasionally drew some adventurers from Iceland. It's likely the distance and hostility of the natives gradually made the trip counterproductive.

When Europeans came to America again after the voyage of Columbus, their weapons included firearms, and their numbers and resources were substantially greater. The natives this time were overwhelmed. Even so, the first isolated colony of Europeans in Virginia disappeared.

The difficulties of sustaining the isolated Greenland colony got worse later on when the climate grew harsher. Eskimos began coming further south to compete for the seals and walruses both groups needed to survive. The Godthab colony was visited by a priest, Ivar Bardarson, in the mid-1350's when they had not been heard from for a time. He found the settlement abandoned. The buildings were still there but no signs of people, alive or dead. Julianehab colony had a wedding recorded there in 1408 and it is estimated that it survived until 1415. The Viking era in Greenland had ended.

Iceland fared better, although it went through difficult times after rival chieftains fought among themselves, resulting in a civil war. This stopped when the Norwegian King Haakon intervened in1262, ending Iceland's independence. Denmark took Iceland from Norway and ruled during the years 1380–1944.

The years before 1944, when Iceland again became independent, were difficult for the island nation. Because distant rulers regulated Iceland's trade, the economy suffered. Severe volcanic eruptions that occurred regularly caused further hardship. These volcanic eruptions are caused by Iceland's position between two tectonic plates of the North Atlantic and Europe. When they shift, volcanic activity occurs. Since its independence in 1944, however, Iceland and its people have made great strides. The country enjoys a high level of economic well being today, and the people enjoy one of the world's foremost education systems.

Viking Sites and Heritage

There is considerable evidence of Viking lifestyle and customs. Burial sites and the remains of towns and fortifications are not only in Scandinavia but the many other places where their voyages took them, as well. From all this evidence we have learned that Viking pagan, burial rites involved providing the dead with everything they would need in the afterworld. The chiefs and the wealthy were sometimes buried in ships. Slaves and horses were slain to accompany them, along with their dogs, clothes, pots, pans, and furniture. The poor might be buried only with a favorite personal article–a bracelet, axe or a kitchen pot. The burial site was covered with earth or set on fire.

The Oseberg and Gokstad ships were used as burial sites. Burial sites, not always including a ship, are continuously being found and are a rich source of information about Viking life.

Large memorial stones, runestones, were carved by Vikings to commemorate important events or people. They contained both writing and pictures. The Viking alphabet had 16 runes. The monuments were placed in public places where many people could see them.

The most famous runestone is the Jelling Stone. King Harald Bluetooth had it raised, about 965 AD, between two mounds in which it is believed his parents, King Gorm and Queen Thyne, were originally buried. When Harald became a Christian, he built a church near the mounds and there he reburied the remains of his parents. He then raised the eight-foot tall solid granite, runestone as a memorial and to recount, as well, his own exploits. The runestone has pictures on two of its three sides–on one side is Christ with his arms outstretched and on the other is a great beast encircled by a snake. There is also a saying in the rune alphabet, "King Harald commanded this memorial to be made in memory of his father, Gorm, and Thyre, his mother. It was this Harald who won for himself all Denmark and Norway and made the Danes Christians."

The reference to Christ indicates that as their interaction with Christianized Europe increased, the Vikings converted to the Christian religion. This interaction included both travel to Christian countries by the Vikings and visiting missionaries traveling to Scandinavia. Sometimes inhabitants in an area would include both Pagan and Christian worshipers. Often Viking monarchs led the way to acceptance of Christianity for commercial or political reasons. By the second millennium the conversion of Scandinavia to Christianity was virtually complete.

In 2000, a reproduction of the Jelling Stone was shown at the Metropolitan Museum of Art in New York as part of a touring exhibit about the Viking culture.

Two of the best-known Viking sites are Birka, near Stockholm, and Hedeby, formerly Danish but now German. Also, in York, England substantial archeological work has revealed well-preserved outlines of former Viking streets and houses. The archeological site at L'Anse aux Meadows in Newfoundland attests to the wide range of Viking exploration. The thriving country of Iceland is testimony to their successful colonizing exploits. Today, the remains of Viking ships can be seen in museums in Oslo, Norway and Raskilde, Denmark.

The Viking spirit of adventure and their interest in trading also brought them east to the rivers that flowed into the landmass of Russia. Here they could portage to the rivers that flowed south. Their leadership and fighting prowess enabled them to help pull this large territory together and united the scattered tribes to help establish Russia as a nation. Their commercial activities extended as far south as Constantinople where their fighting qualities secured them employment as guards to the ruler.

The Viking ability to explore, trade and colonize was based, to a large extent, on their craftsmanship, particularly in shipbuilding. Their swift, shallow draft dragon-ships, enabled them to sail and put ashore everywhere that was accessible by water. When they arrived, they would trade their carefully crafted household items, combs, pots, weapons, and artfully made figures made from silver, bone, iron or wood. Sometimes, when conditions were right they seized what they wanted, instead of trading, and contributed once again, to their fearsome reputation as raiders.

The spirit of adventure and exploring the unknown represents the Vikings' most enduring legacy. They seemed driven to see what is over the horizon; what's beyond the next bend in the river; when will the next landfall be reached; can we trade with the people we encounter; or will the meeting be hostile? It was this enterprising and courageous spirit that made many Vikings leave their homes on the shores of the Baltic Sea. No fear or concern about falling off the edge of the world for them. They braved the unknown, the cold climates and harsh environments to colonize Iceland and Greenland and to reach out to a new continent.

Perhaps some of this same spirit was passed on and absorbed in the many parts of Europe in which they settled and became assimilated. After all, the entire world for hundreds of years was colonized and influenced by the colonial empires of Europe and very much in the "Viking Spirit."

Today there is a great interest in the Vikings and their exploits. Museum exhibits, books, Viking ship reproductions, and visits to burial and other historic sites, attest to a new appreciation of their spirit and culture.

Seeing Iceland for Myself

I had had the opportunity of seeing Iceland briefly, thanks to the U.S. Navy. It was the spring of 1955, and I was serving as a junior officer on a destroyer, the U.S.S Samuel B. Roberts DD823, operating out of Newport, Rhode Island. On the weekends, the ship's crew was divided into three sections. Two sections were allowed to leave the ship from late afternoon Friday until Monday morning. The third section had the duty and stayed aboard.

I wasn't on duty that particular weekend in July, so I took the bus to Providence and then the train to New York's Grand Central Station. From there I would catch another bus to my parents' home in New Jersey. This time, however, when I got off the train, my father met me on the train platform. He told me I had to go back to the ship immediately. Someone from the Navy had telephoned him to tell me that all members of our crew had to report back as soon as possible. I caught the midnight train back and was aboard ship again by 8 a.m. The duty section, the men living in the Newport area, and those of us who had been contacted and returned, got the ship underway almost immediately. While underway and steaming out of the harbor, late crewmembers climbed aboard from a small craft sent out to the ship before it cleared the harbor.

The sudden departure of our ship was caused by an order for us to station the ship between Greenland and Iceland. We were one of four destroyers to be strung out across the northern Atlantic while President Eisenhower flew to Europe for a Summit conference in Geneva with the Soviets. Our ships were to be positioned nearby in case the President's plane was forced down into the ocean for any reason. We made a brief stop that evening in Argenta, Newfoundland for fueling. More of our crew, who had been flown there, joined us.

We then steamed to our designated position between Greenland and Iceland and later watched as the President's plane flew overhead on its way to Europe. After the President's plane disappeared over the horizon we steamed to Iceland for supplies and fueling.

We were sent to a remote pier where a fuel line came aboard. It was early morning and chilly. A few of us walked over to where a gang of men on a nearby dock was cutting up a black whale that was about 40 feet long. They were using long poles with sharp, large cutting blades at the end. What a smell! It was absolutely gut-wrenching. I can recall it to this day.

After fueling, we were sent to a dock near Reykjavik. It was around noon when we tied up to take on supplies. We were to leave early in the morning to be back on station for Eisenhower's return trip. Four officers were to go to the U.S. Air Force base at Keflavik to take care of required formalities and collect any mail that might have been sent to the ship. I was among the four selected to go. We were to be back by early afternoon.

We took a cab to the base where, after attending to our duties, we planned to visit the commissary, a small department store restricted to military personnel, and the Officer's Club. On our way, we saw some homes with a hammer and sickle painted on the door. The driver explained that the inhabitants were "Communists" who were making their viewpoint known. He said they were a small but significant influence in Iceland.

The limited scenery we saw on the way consisted of widely scattered houses and a mostly barren landscape. The local people we met, besides the cab driver, were the people working on the base. The young girl who waited on me at the commissary was a statuesque blonde. While I've since learned not all Scandinavian women are tall, blonde and attractive, there are enough to keep fueling this perception.

We then went to the Officer's Club where we were told refreshments were available, but only by the bottle. I don't recall what we ordered. I was drinking scotch in those days, but since I had the lowest rank at the table, my preference wouldn't have carried much weight.

We had a drink and maybe one or two of us had another. Finally, and reluctantly, we left the rest of the bottle and returned to the ship. As soon as we boarded, we received the order to get underway. "Set the special sea detail," was immediately announced. The European conference had ended sooner than expected, and we were ordered back to our mid-ocean station. I was the Junior Officer of the Deck for getting underway, because of my navigation duties, and went to the bridge.

In a few minutes, another officer, who was the Officer of the Deck for getting underway and had been with us at the club, came into the pilothouse. He wasn't wearing shoes or socks and didn't have on his hat. I told him to get below quickly before the Executive Officer saw him. While he was arguing with me, the Executive Officer came in, took one look at him and ordered him below. The Exec then looked me over very carefully while I held my breath. I apparently passed muster. The orders for getting underway came in quick succession.

"Single up all lines"
"Rudder amidships"
"Take in number 1 line"
"Port engine ahead one-third"
"Starboard engine back one-third"
"Take in number 2 line"
"Take in number 3 line"
"Take in number 4 line"
"All engines ahead one-third"

We steered through the channel buoys as the water under our keel increased. We were now in a wide bay with a straight line to the open sea. I gave the Captain a recommended course, and we were on our way.

"Secure the special sea detail!"

At sea, the regular watch took over. My short visit to Iceland was over, but it had been memorable.

Baltic Sagas
Events and Personalities that Changed the World!

Teutonic Knights' Fortress
Marienburg (Mary's Town) Castle
Molbork, Poland

II
The Teutonic Knights and Queen Jadwiga of Poland
A Young Woman Brings Down a Mighty Empire

Pope Urban II Calls for Crusade

Large Field
Outside Eastern Gate
Clermont, France
November 27, 1095

Pope Urban II arrived in France in August 1095. He spent the time until November in various towns and cities conducting church business. He also called for general Church Council to be held in Clermont, in southern France, the middle of November. Three hundred clerics attended the Council of Clermont and passed various reform degrees and heard many petitions. The Pope also announced he would make an important speech on Tuesday, November 27 to which the public was invited.

The weather was chilly that morning. A large, curious crowd came from many miles around to hear what the Pope, who had been born in France, had to say. The crowd was so large the Pope had a throne set up in an empty field outside the town's eastern gate so that all could see and hear him. The throne was placed on a platform under a gold cloth canopy. Church dignitaries, many dressed splendidly in silk and brocade ecclesiastical raiments, attended him on his right and left.

Pope Urban II was a tall man and dressed this day in white. He took his position between two crosses, and, after a brief prayer, moved to the front of the platform and began speaking. He spoke in the language of the crowd, not in Latin, so that all who heard him would understand. The Pope was a powerful speaker and made a moving and memorable speech that drew attention to the plight of Christians in the east. Among the things he said were: "Jerusalem is held by the Muslims, and Christian pilgrims are being prevented from going to the Holy Land. The West - rich and poor, commoners and noble - must go to the aid of our eastern Christians. Internal wars and squabbles among Christians must stop and hostilities should be directed against the heathens instead! There will be absolution and remission of sins for all who die in Christ's service! God wills it!"

Many men in the audience raised their swords and repeated, "God wills it!"

A number of reports were later made of the Pope's remarks. Harold Lamb's book, "The Crusades," written in 1930, gives a lengthy account.

Although there is some disagreement, many authorities cite two reasons why Pope Urban II may have announced a call for a crusade to free the Holy Land from the infidels. The first was a call for help from the Emperor, Alexius Comnenus, of the Eastern Roman Empire at Constantinople. He was being pressed hard by the nearby, fearsome Muslims, whose prophet, Mohammed, had already inspired substantial Islamic conquests.

The second reason may have been a desire by an active and reform-minded Pope to harness the interest of many in military glory and the religious zeal then existing in the hearts of numerous Christians. A crusade to the Holy Land would serve these two aims very well.

How did the call for a crusade to the Holy Land, by a Pope in a French city, result in the conquest of the entire south shore of the Baltic Sea by a knightly order? After ruling with a heavy hand for 200 years, how were the Knights finally subdued by the personal sacrifice of a young queen?

The Crusades and the Knightly Orders

The response to the Pope's appeal for a Crusade to free the Holy Land from the infidels was swift and all but overwhelming. Just as the Pope may have expected, it appealed to two basic human traits of the time—religious fervor and a thirst for adventure and military glory. The Council quickly agreed to the indulgences that would be granted to crusaders and designated that a red cross was to be worn on their mantle as their sign.

All kinds of people in Europe responded to the call to journey to the Holy Land in search of God's work. Rich and poor, young and old, at every level of society, and in every line of work, wanted to share in this great enterprise. The church soon lost control of what it had started and pilgrimages east began spontaneously. Nobles were slower to respond because they had to make arrangements to have their affairs looked after while they were gone. The poor didn't have any such delays and were ready to leave immediately.

One of the first to begin attracting a following by preaching about going on crusade was a poor hermit in Flanders called Peter. He journeyed east with about 20,000 followers made up of all classes. They were mostly the poor although even some knights came along as well. After great hardships, they finally reached the Holy Land where they were met by a Muslim army that routed them. This didn't discourage new Christians who continued to arrive in the Holy Land, and in 1098 Jerusalem was captured!

In the Holy Land there was little established authority and few facilities in the hot and mostly primitive country to help pilgrims. This led to the formation of local organizations, which provided needed services. The Hospitallers of St. John, the Templars, and the Teutonic Knights became the best known and remembered.

The first knightly order established in the Holy Land is generally agreed to be the Hospitallers of St. John of Jerusalem. They were formally recognized in a papal bull in 1113. In the beginning, they provided care and hospitality to pilgrims. This expanded into protecting pilgrims. An armed escort was established. This armed escort gradually grew larger and became a significant fighting force. They wore black mantles with a white cross. The Order continued to add new recruits from among arriving Crusaders. As time went, on the Order's work included both care of pilgrims and military service against the Muslims. They received donations of money and estates from all parts of Europe in gratitude for their efforts and to support their work. They used these revenues to build protective castles in many conquered parts of the Holy Land.

In contrast to the Hospitallers of St. John, the Order of the Knights Templar was a military order from the beginning. After the capture of Jerusalem by the Crusaders in 1098, there was the problem of defending the city against the Muslims who surrounded it. Nine Knights pledged themselves to do this and were assigned a portion of the Jerusalem palace next to the temple. They derived their name from being close to the "temple." Each wore a white mantle with a red cross. Members also took strict vows and accepted austerity in their daily lives.

Recruits flocked to this new Order. They became a great favorite of the Pope, which led to some conflict with the local clergy. The Templars zeal in fighting the Muslims grew along with their reputation–first to attack and last to retreat! Many died in battle and when captured would be killed and martyred for refusing to deny Christ. The Order grew rapidly, built castles, and was in the forefront in fighting the Muslims.

The great Muslim leader, Saladin, recaptured Jerusalem in 1187. He destroyed a hospital that had cared for German pilgrims and that had been originally dedicated to the Blessed Virgin Mary. Later, a temporary hospital, using ships' sails as a tent, was erected for German pilgrims near the walls of Acre, which the Crusaders besieged. After Acre was captured, a permanent hospital was established in the city and German knights were assigned to give it protection. They set up rules similar to those of the earlier knightly orders and grew under the patronage of the German Emperor. In 1205, Pope Innocent III granted them the use of a white mantle with a black cross and they became known as the Teutonic Knights.

The most famous crusade was mounted in 1190, known as the Third Crusade. King Richard I of England, King Phillip II of France and German Emperor Frederick I Barabrossa led it. In 1212, there was a children's crusade, and later a shepherds' crusade. As late as 1309 there was a "people" crusade that reflected the failure of the nobles to retake Jerusalem. These crusades and their mixed results reflected the lack of a central organizing authority, the distance to the Holy Land, supply problems, and the strength of the Muslims in their home territory.

The Templars ferocity in battle lost them so many Knights that recruitment pressure caused them to become lax. The Order's secret rites, their zeal, their accumulated wealth and rivalry with the Hospitallers, finally subjected them to inquires by both Philip the Fair, King of France, who coveted their French possessions, and a weak pope, Pope Clement V. The Order's Grand Master along with many Templars were finally burned at the stake for heresy. The Templars' property, their duties, and some of the members were then given over to the Hospitallers.

When the fortunes of war turned against the Christians in the Holy Land, the Hospitallers conquered the island of Rhodes and ruled there from 1309 to 1522. They became known as the "Knights of Rhodes." When the Muslim leader Mahomet II conquered the Order in Rhodes, they went on to Malta. They then became known as the "Knights of Malta," but in 1798 they surrendered Malta to Napoleon. There are only four Malta religious houses today and are mostly known for providing ambulance service on battlefields.

When Acre fell, and the Holy Land became inhospitable, the Teutonic Knights moved to Europe, primarily the Baltic Area.

Teutonic Knights Arrive in Baltic Region

Between 1209 and 1239 the Order of the Teutonic Knights' Grand Master was Hermann Von Salza. Salza was a resourceful leader, successful in obtaining privileges for the Order from Pope Honorius III. He also enjoyed the favor of German Emperor Frederick II Barbarossa. Salza had been successful in expanding the Order into Sicily and to many other parts of Europe.

In 1211, King Andrew of Hungry invited the Order to establish a stronghold on the border of Transylvania to help quell attacks from his enemies. However, the Knights' demand for greater independence was unacceptable, and, in 1225, King Andrew ordered them to leave.

Just prior to the Knights' departure from Hungry, Pope Honorius III proclaimed a Crusade against the Prussians, tribes of pagans living on the southern shores of the Baltic. However, Duke Conrad of Massonia, who ruled the border area, didn't have the resources to subdue these tribes, and in 1225 he asked the Teutonic Knights to come to his aid. This invitation was timely, coming as it did when they were being asked to leave Transylvania.

Duke Conrad was so desperate for help against the Prussians, he immediately gave the Order two possessions, the areas of Culin and Dobrzin. Grand Master Salza accepted them and added that the Knights wanted to claim any Prussian territory the Order captured. The Duke agreed. The German Emperor confirmed this arrangement and the Teutonic Knights began the campaign of subduing the Prussian tribes and built castles as centers of their power.

In 1237, the Order was greatly strengthened by uniting with the Brothers of the Sword. The Brothers of the Sword was a military order of knights established by Bishop Albert of Burhorden. Bishop Albert arrived in the Baltic region in 1201 with a large group of German colonists and founded the city of Riga. The Brothers served as the military arm in subduing the local inhabitants. The Brothers had prospered since their establishment, but, in 1236, they were badly defeated in the Battle of Sauler, losing nearly a third of their knights and their Grand Master. Joining the Teutonic Order assured their survival. The Teutonic Knights were strengthened by extending their territories north and to the western borders of Russia. They now controlled the entire southern Baltic seacoast from Danzig to Narva, today's Estonian city on the border with Russia. However, the lack of access to the Baltic Sea was one of the reasons for strife between the Order and its neighbors, particularly Poland and Lithuania.

One of the benefits the Order gained by occupying the entire southern coast of the Baltic was the monopoly it gave them of the gemstone amber. Amber is one of the most desired and important trade goods from the Baltic region and has been sought and bartered for at least as long ago as the days of the Pharaoh in Egypt. Amber originally came from the submerged forests in the Baltic area. The semi-precious stones, called "Baltic gold," were first found on the shores of the Baltic Sea but are now found in other lands, as well. Their color ranges from almost white to dark brown. In size, they can be found in small pieces on up to several pounds. Amber can be both clear and, in other cases, may hold an object, an insect, a feather, or a piece of leaf or debris can be trapped inside. Amber is usually set off into necklaces, bracelets, rings and other jewelry and traded around the world.

The gem is formed from the resin excreted from a particular pine tree, Pinus Succinifera, that has fossilized for thousands of years. When the tree's surface was penetrated, wounding it, as it were, it would secrete a healing, sticky resin. Any object stuck to the resin would be trapped. After thousands of years a globe of amber would be formed. After a storm, the gems wash up on the Baltic beaches. The richest area for finding Baltic amber is the Samland Peninsula, the site of today's Kalingrad, and formerly the German royal city of Koningsberg.

Baltic amber found its way into many corners of the ancient world. Amber pieces were found in Pharaoh Tutankaman's tomb in Luxor and both the ancient Greeks and Romans prized it. Greeks associated it with the tears of a water nymph. Other legends were spun around it in Greek mythology. Amber also had healing powers attributed to it. The Romans believed in the healing powers of amber and developed a fondness for it as jewelry. It's likely that amber reached the Mediterranean area in ancient times through the Black Sea where traders who came down the rivers of Russia brought it from the north. Some amber also came south to the Danube River in central Europe, where the Romans traded for it in this farthest northern outpost of Rome.

In 1242, the Teutonic Knights attempted to add to their territories in the north by invading the Russian lands to the east, those ruled by Novgorod. The Order also wanted to block Russian access to the Baltic in order to continue their monopoly of the amber trade. These plans brought them into conflict with Alexander Nevsky, Prince of Novgorod.

Russia's great hero, Alexander Nevsky (1219–1263), Prince of Novgorod, successfully protected the western borders of Russia from the Lithuanians, Swedes, and Teutonic Knights during his lifetime. He had already defeated the Swedes near the junction of the rivers Izhora and Neva in 1240. It was for this victory he was given the name "Nevsky."

The Knights were aware that the Russians had defeated the Swedes, but expected that their superior battle prowess would give them victory. At the start of their campaign, the Knights burned some of the outskirts of the city of Pskov before the "Boyars" (the name used in Russia for nobles) opened the city's gates to them.

Alexander Nevsky was ready to aid the next target of the Teutonic Knights, the city of Novgorod, but the local leaders were divided as to a cause of action. It was even suspected that the Teutonic Knights had sympathizers in the city who wanted the Knights to seize Novgorod, and then submit claims for rewards from the conquerors. Meanwhile, Alexander Nevsky had withdrawn himself and his retinue to a location nearer his father, Grand Prince Yaroslav, at Pereaslavi.

After considerable discussion, the local leaders of Novgorod decided to call on Alexander Nevsky to return and save them in their time of danger. Nevsky returned with troops gathered from the surrounding area, enlisted all the able-bodied in Novgorod, and set off to the west to fight the Teutonic Knights.

Alexander Nevsky engaged the Teutonic Knights near Lake Peipus. The Teutonic Knights were clad in heavy armor and mounted on their similarly protected warhorses. They charged and drove a wedge between the less well-equipped Russians. The Russians retreated to the ice on Lake Peipus, where the Russians on both flanks attacked the pursuing Knights.

The weight of the mounted Knights broke through the lake ice. Many were unhorsed and drowned. Others fled but were relentlessly pursued by the more nimble Russians wielding clubs, spears, and swords. A large number of Knights were killed, fled, or taken prisoner and led back to Novgorod. Here they were displayed to the population and held for ransom. This decisive defeat of the Teutonic Knights was a turning point in preventing their farther move east.

Alexander Nevsky continued to fight and defeat Russia's other enemies, the Swedes and Lithuanians, but compromised and cooperated with the Mongols. The Mongols had conquered Russia but didn't interfere a great deal with local affairs or religion as long as they received tribute and their rule was acknowledged. Nevsky seemed to have judged the Mongols as too strong to defeat and that cooperation was the better choice. To some, this is considered a blemish on his record. However, to nearly all Russians he is a great hero. Russia's leaders, from Peter the Great to Stalin, have used his name and deeds to rally the nation.

Peter the Great, five hundred years later, recalled Nevsky's deeds in his own battles with the Swedes and named St. Petersburg's main street "Nevsky Prospect." After Nevsky's death, the Russian Orthodox Church, in 1380, declared him a Saint. Russian Orthodox Churches are named for him in many parts of the world. One of the most beautiful today is in Tallinn, Estonia. Peter the Great also built the St. Alexander Nevsky Monastery in St. Petersburg near the site on the Neva River where the famous battle against the Swedes was reported to have taken place.

Stalin used the memory of Alexander Nevsky's defeat of the Germans by having a famous epic film made of the event. Sergei Eisenstein, Russia's great film director, was given the resources in 1938 to make one of his most memorable films, "Alexander Nevsky." It also featured a musical score by the famous composer, Sergei Prokofiev. In the film, Germans are warned against hostilities against Russia, which served Stalin's purposes very well in 1938, although it failed to prevent the German invasion in 1941.

Karl G. Heinze

Later, in World War II, the German invasion of Russia also came to focus attention on Baltic amber. The most famous use of Baltic amber was an entire room paneled in amber presented by the Prussian King, Frederick William I in the early 1700's, to Peter the Great. It was later reinstalled in Catherine's Palace in Tsarskoe Selo (Tsar's Village). During World War II, the amber panels were stripped from the walls by the invading German Army and taken away. Where they are now and what might have happened to them is still a mystery. During the last few years, some pieces from the Amber Room have surfaced and been offered for sale.

The original Amber room is currently being restored by a group of Russian craftsmen. These same craftsmen demonstrated their skills at the American Museum of Natural History a few years ago as part of an exhibit called, "Amber–Window to the Past."

When I visited Catherine's Palace a few years ago, the former Amber room was still largely bare, but it is expected to be completely restored in the near future. A German company is financing the work.

Amber is found in many parts of the world today- Dominican Republic, Mexico and New Jersey, among other places.

Teutonic Knights' Power Peaks

In 1309, Grand Master Siegfried of Feuchtwangen transferred the headquarters of the Teutonic Knights from Venice to a castle built by the Order and located 36 miles south of Danzig along the Noget River. The castle was named Marienburg (Mary's Town) and dedicated to the mother of Jesus. Building the stronghold had begun a few years before when the Order had crushed the second uprising of the Prussian tribes. This ambitious new building program, and residence of the Grand Master, marked a transition in the Order from being a "crusade to Christianize the pagan Prussians" to becoming a permanent colonizing power. .

The first building was the High Castle and, in the following years, the stronghold complex grew to encompass 21 hectares. Its construction was of red brick; its three rings of defenses made it the most heavily fortified stronghold in Europe in its time. Since 1945, when it was badly damaged during World War II, it has been undergoing restoration. It is well worth a visit to see an outstanding example of medieval fortifications and to view its military and amber museums. The drive from Gdansk is about forty minutes.

The establishment of the Grand Master at Marienburg, in a significant way, signaled the period of the Order's greatest achievements in power and influence in the Baltic Region. The Order's success was the result of being superbly organized and enforcing rigorous discipline. Each castle stronghold had a commander, and strongholds were grouped into districts with an overall commander.

The Grand Master at Marienburg had a council of high officials to help him manage the affairs of the order. Only Germans were eligible for membership in the Order, and they had to be of legitimate birth, of noble ancestry, pure in morals, and unstained honor. The rules of the Order - unquestioned obedience, steadfastness in battle, and no intercourse with heathens - were enforced rigorously.

Christianity continued to be spread during this same time period. German peasants were brought in to establish farms under the protection of the Order's castles. The Order came to rule a vast area with a population of over two million in Prussia alone, but the local people were resentful, and bordering neighbors feared the constant expansion.

The Teutonic Order was the only Crusader Order that was able to establish a large, independent state after leaving the holy land. Upon subduing the Prussian heathens, and sustaining a rebuff when it tried to move east against Russia, the Order now turned more attention to the territories of its Polish and Lithuanian neighbors. Squabbles and attacks against nearby castles to the south, protecting the estates of Polish and Lithuanian nobles, became more frequent. Conflicts with Poland were difficult to justify because it was a Christian nation, but pagan Lithuania was a fair target for conversion and acquisitions. Due to mistrust of the Order, Poland and Lithuania tended to support each other and this made the Order's goal of conquest difficult.

In 1343, Poland and the Order finally arrived at a truce, freeing the Order to deal with Lithuania alone. The Order, and the Lithuanians under Grand Duke Guedemine, engaged in the fierce battle of Rudau in Sambia on February 17, 1370. The Lithuanians lost 11,000 men and were thoroughly defeated in spite of inflicting heavy losses on the Order.

After the defeat of the Lithuanians, the Order turned its attention to another adversary, the Baltic Sea pirates, and acquired a fleet of ships to combat them. The Order was now so powerful it attracted knights from all parts of Europe for periods of service, although they couldn't formally become members of the Order.

Queen Jadwiga of Poland (1373–1399)

While the Teutonic Knights were expanding their empire on the shores of the Baltic Sea, an event occurred in distant Hungry that would have a major impact on them in the future. A third daughter was born to King Louis of Hungry in 1373. King Louis named her Jadwiga (pronounced "yad VEE gah"), and she was destined to play an important role in Poland and with the nearby Teutonic Knights. Young Jadwiga's eventual position in Poland stemmed from King Louis's claim to the crown of Poland (he was the nephew of Poland's former King Casimir). King Louis spent a substantial amount of time and effort trying to find his three daughters husbands and kingdoms of their own to rule.

When Jadwiga was five years old, she was betrothed to a handsome German, Prince Wilhelm of Hapsburg. Betrothals of young royal children for dynastic reasons were not unusual in those days. Prince Wilhelm had been raised in Vienna and was destined to be a King, and King Louis was very pleased by the match. Jadwiga was growing up to be a beautiful young girl with a lovely smile and straightforward manner. She captivated all who met her.

Louis died in 1382 without fathering any sons. However, he had directed that Hungry and Poland both crown one of his daughters as ruler. The Polish nobles agreed to crown Jadwiga as their ruler in 1384 when she was only eleven years old. She traveled to Wawel Castle in Cracow, Poland to claim her throne, but there the nobles of Poland made every effort to convince her that she couldn't marry Prince Wilhelm. The nobles said Poland wouldn't accept an Austrian on the their throne. As this time, Poland's enemies beset Poland on all sides. The Teutonic Knights were attacking both Poland and Lithuania. The rulers of Moscovy were eyeing Polish lands and the barbaric Mongols and Tartars were a constant invasion threat.

To aid them in defense of Polish lands, the nobles proposed that the young queen marry Prince Jagiello, the pagan ruler of Lithuania, unite the two countries, and combine their strengths against their common enemies. In addition, the Lithuanian Prince Jagiello agreed to convert to Christianity. He would also convert his entire nation. This would deprive the Teutonic Knights of their reason for invading Poland in order to reach the "pagan" Lithuanians on the pretense of converting them to Christianity. The Order's drive to convert pagans always resulted in them annexing lands and the people on them.

The major stumbling block to this union, besides Jadwiga's previous commitment to the Austrian prince, was Prince Jagiello's age. He was 37 years old, a fairly old man in those days, and three times the age of young Jadwiga. Jadwiga was heartbroken at the thought of losing her handsome young Prince, and couldn't bring herself to agree with the Polish nobles. It's said she had misgivings, for a time, about Prince Jagiello's physical appearance so that he even agreed to have her representatives observe him bathing. Finally, she was persuaded, for the good of her country and the opportunity of converting an entire pagan nation to Christianity. Through her tears, the young queen dedicated her marriage to Jagiello to God.

After the marriage, the two rulers jointly presided over the combined kingdoms. The young Queen took her responsibilities to her people very seriously. She traveled on diplomatic business to help persuade Poland's enemies to remain at peace. She helped establish the Christian church in Lithuania by having churches built and establishing schools. She reconciled her husband with his cousin Witold, who was named Grand Duke of Lithuania and became its governor under Jagiello. She also was a great supporter of Cracow University, the oldest university in Europe, and established a college in Prague for Lithuanians.

Unhappily, the young Queen was not destined to enjoy a long life. Her first child died at birth on July 13, 1399 and Jadwiga died a few days later. She was only twenty-six years old. Although her life was short, she converted Lithuania to Christianity thereby uniting the two countries. This gave them their best chance to prevail against the Teutonic Knights. The resulting conflict had a great impact on Poland and Europe.

The marriage of Jadwiga and Jagiello began what was known as the Jagiellonian dynasty, which lasted 400 years. Jagiello remarried and had a son to succeed him, but it was said he never forgot his young Queen.

Even today, six hundred years later, many Polish people revere the memory of the young, sweet, pious Queen who sacrificed her own happiness for the sake of her people and country. These warm feelings can be contagious, and it's not difficult to reach out to her over the centuries and regret her early death.

Cracow, Poland's capital in Queen Jadwiga's time, is a beautiful old city that was spared being badly damaged during World War II. The churches and public buildings are original and were not greatly reconstructed, as in Warsaw. For this reason particularly, a visit to Cracow's Wavel Hill with its Castle and Cathedral on a hill overlooking the Vistula River, is memorable. One is able to walk in the rooms where Queen Jadwiga slept, ate, and conferred with her councilors. It was to this castle Queen Jadwiga traveled to be crowned ruler of Poland, where she spent her short adult life, and where she is entombed in the nearby cathedral.

Wavel Castle was the home of Poland's royalty for hundreds of years until the royal family moved its residence to Warsaw. Today, there are a number of exhibits of special interest to be seen. Unfortunately, one I particularly wanted to see, the opulent tents captured in front of Vienna in 1683, when the Polish Army lifted the siege of the Turks, was closed for renovations. However, the famous sixteenth century Flemish tapestries were on display.

The care of Queen Jadwiga's sarcophagus in the Wavel Cathedral is the responsibility of the Archbishop of Cracow. The Wavel Cathedral's most famous Archbishop, Cardinal Wojtyla, became Pope John Paul II, the first Polish Pope. As Pope, he presided over Queen Jadwiga's canonization in 1997 and, with this ceremony, bound together two persons who are dear to Polish hearts. In addition to royalty, many other famous Poles are buried in the Cathedral's crypt, including Tadeusz Kosciuszko, a hero of the American Revolution, and, later, the Polish resistance to the Russians.

After you visit Wavel Hill, it's a short stroll to the Main Market Square in the heart of the city. It is said be the largest square in Europe. It was here that I enjoyed sitting in a sidewalk café listening to strolling musicians and watching people walking past on a sunny October afternoon a few years ago. There is also an enclosed market hall here known as Cloth Hall. It is over 300 feet long with vendors selling souvenirs and folk art from their stalls.

Also in the square is the Church of the Virgin Mary, which keeps alive a famous tradition. Every hour a trumpet sounds from its tower to recall a similar warning sounded years ago to warn of approaching, hostile Tartars. The trumpet sound abruptly ceases, just as it did originally, when a Tartar arrow struck the trumpet player in the neck as he was playing.

The church has two steeples, which are of unequal height, and that also has a story. Two brothers were building the church and quarreled. One was killed and the murdered brother's steeple miraculously grew and overtook the other! The altarpiece inside the church is one of the most beautiful in Europe. This gilded and ornate masterpiece is huge, thirty by forty-two feet when fully extended, and was created by Wit Stwosz in the fifteenth century.

Battle of Grunwald

Large Field
Grunwald - Tannenburg
Poland
July 15, 1410

The camps of both the Teutonic Knights and the armies of Poland and its allies stirred early on the morning of July 15, 1410. The Order's troops had spent the night in the small village of Grunwald. The Teutonic Grand Master, Ulrich Von Jungingen, moved his army east even before the sun came up. He confronted the Polish army, which was camped in a forest area about three miles to the southeast, near the village of Tannenburg. The Teutonic troops took up their positions on a slight elevation and waited for the Polish Army to assemble on the plain below.

It promised to be a hot day, but fog and haze was still swirling around the ground between the two armies as the sun appeared. Grand Master Von Jungingen watched his troops form into companies, and, as he looked them over, he was well satisfied with what he commanded. There were over twenty thousand heavily armed knights mounted on large war-horses. Men and horses were both protected by expertly crafted armor.

These knights were not only from the Order but were fighting men recruited from all over Europe. Each foreign Knight - from Austria, Bavaria, Burgundy, Flanders and many more countries - had his own banner, and it made for a colorful assembly. These men had come for a variety of reasons: out of religious conviction, the promise of reward, for glory, or because they relished a good fight.

The mounted Knights were supported by about six thousand infantry equipped with swords, axes, or spears, many supplied by the craft shops of the Order. There were, in addition, five thousand armed and trained servants. Troops under the Order's banner totaled about thirty-one thousand. The Grand Master kept near him his finest men, the squadron of St. George, their banner a red cross on a white field. He also deployed about one hundred cannons that could hurl huge, iron balls.

As his field commanders, the Grand Master had with him this day the Order's most experienced leaders, Grand Marshal Frederick Von Wallenrode, Grand Commander Kuno Von Lichtenstein, and Commander of Supply, Albrecht Von Schwarzenberg. These men had taken part in numerous engagements and had commanded troops in many successful battles. The Knights of the Order each wore over his armor a white tunic with a huge black cross. They were brave, eager, and confident that God was on their side.

Across the field in the forest, King Jagiello, who had been converted to Christianity when he married Queen Jadwiga, had started his day with the celebration of mass in a special tent erected for this purpose. His subordinate commanders were with him. Most prominent among them was Grand Duke Witold, Jagiello's cousin, and commander of the Lithuanians.

To oppose the Order, Jagiello had eighteen thousand Polish knights, their twelve thousand retainers, and four thousand foot soldiers. There were also eleven thousand Lithuanians and just over a thousand Tartars, about forty-six thousand men in all. Although Jagiello had more troops, his troops were less heavily armed, except for some of the Polish Knights, and many of the foot soldiers had only clubs and wooden spears rather than superior metal weapons. Jagiello also had only sixteen cannons.

The Teutonic Knights sat on their horses as their foot soldiers stood in ranks. As the sun continued to rise, they waited for their enemies to emerge from the forest. Jagiello, who, at sixty years of age was older than any other commander on the field, was content to wait. He told his more impatient comrades to let the Order's knights and their horse's sweat in the July heat while they stayed cool under the trees of the forest.

After a couple of hours, the Grand Master and his commanders grew inpatient. They sent two heralds and a small entourage to the Polish King with two swords and a challenge to the King and Grand Duke

Witold for mortal combat. The first herald dismounted, bowed slightly, and laid the two swords at the feet of the King. He went on to say that the swords were sent in the event their courage had failed. The second herald also dismounted, bowed, and said that, if the field of combat seemed too small, the Grand Master would pull back somewhat so the Poles would have more room to come out from the trees.

Jagiello replied they had enough swords but would take these two as an omen of victory. As to the field of battle, he said that God would mark it out. The heralds rode back to their lines as the Order's troops "gave way" to make more room. As trumpets sounded, the Polish troops came out of the forest led by their most formidable knights and followed by the main group of mounted warriors and footmen. The Lithuanians and Tartars were on the Polish Army's right flank. One of the decisive battles of Europe, and one of the largest up to that time, was about to begin.

Von Jungingen had stationed his archers and crossbowmen in front of the left side of his formations and had them take positions behind shallow pits they had dug. He expected the heavy Polish cavalry to charge first, stumble into the pits while under attack from the arrows and cannons, and then be finished off by the heavy Teutonic cavalry.

Instead, Jagiello sent only the more lightly armed Lithuanian cavalry and the Tartars on their small, swift horses to meet the archers. Horns, bugles, trumpets, and whistles announced their galloping charge. They covered the ground quickly, jumped the pits, and were upon the archers, who were hard pressed to be fighting at close quarters. As soon as Grand Master saw what was happening, he ordered Frederick Von Wallenrode, who commanded the left flank, to charge the Lithuanians and Tartars.

Fourteen companies of Knights shouting, "Gott mit uns" started slowly forward, increased to a trot, and then to a gallop. The earth shook from the pounding of their horses' hoofs. When the Tartars saw the hard riding and heavily armed Knights charging toward them, they wheeled and fled southeast toward Lake Lubiecz. The Lithuanians light cavalry hesitated a little longer, but when their swords made little impact on the armor of their enemy, they too fled.

The Grand Master now commanded his main forces, lead by Von Lichtenstein, to attack from the center. The Polish Heavy Cavalry spearhead, singing their battle hymn, "Kyrie Eleison," rode forward to meet the attack supported by the less well-equipped Lithuanian Knights led by Duke Witold. The knights of both sides met in a violent collision. After their lances were broken in the initial charge, the knights on both sides took up swords, axes, maces, and huge iron balls on the end of chains. Blood soon flowed and coated weapons.

This was close quarter fighting, face to face, and the combatants glared at each other over their shields and through their visors. The advantage was with the better armed, and often more experienced, Teutonic Knights. Often, but not always, was the advantage with the Order. The Polish ranks had many warriors who were well trained in fighting as knights and didn't lack for courage. The Polish Knights had often competed and beaten the Order's Knights at tournaments and felt no fear in man-to-man combat.

When Von Lichtenstein rode back to confer with Von Jurgingen, he reported that the Order could expect a long, tough day. Their enemy was proving to be a skillful and courageous adversary. At one point, the Cracow Standard, sacred to the Poles, was captured by the Order and many Teutonic Knights thought this would dishearten their enemy and win the day.

The effect was just the opposite. The Polish Knights, seeing their sacred banner captured, made a savage attack and recaptured it. As the day progressed, the Germans still felt they would win, and it lifted their spirits to see the troops who had chased the Tartars, return. In the late afternoon, sensing this was the strategic moment, the Grand Master hurled his last reserves into the battle and led them himself in a final bid for victory.

Jagiello, who had been watching the battle from a small hill, now sent his foot soldiers and remaining reserves into battle. Some of these were small landowners on horseback without armor, and the footmen had only spears or merely scythes. Many had suffered at the hands of the order, but what they lacked in weapons, they made up for in ardor and spirit. As they ran toward the battlefield many had a prayer on their lips, "Hail Mary, full of grace, the Lord is with thee!" They swarmed over the sweating, heavily armed and mounted Knights.

Although a Knight swinging his heavy sword or axe could hold off several foot soldiers, he couldn't deal with a dozen or more. Many knights were unhorsed and beaten to death on the ground. The Order's Knights began to lose some of their usual confidence in the face of the determination and courage they had to confront on this long day. The less committed, foreign Knights seemed to be showing signs of having had enough fight for one day, as well.

Suddenly, at about 6 p.m., the Tartars and the light Lithuanian cavalry came charging back. The Tartars were in a rage because of how they had been humiliated in the morning. Less exhausted than those who had been fighting all day, they hacked and stabbed without concern for personal safety.

Von Jungingen had been engaged in the main battle but now broke free with a small group of Knights. He was soon surrounded by a large group of Polish foot soldiers. He was cut and slashed about the face before receiving a spear thrust into the neck. He fell dead off his horse.

The Order's Knights now began to form themselves into circles that became successively smaller under the onslaught of their completely aroused enemy. Swords, knives, broken lances, and clubs were pointed and thrust at the surrounded Knights in the gradually diminishing circles. Few Knights of the Order, even though the last survivor in a circle, asked to surrender, or were allowed to do so. Finally, the last Teutonic Knight was killed, unhorsed, badly wounded, or on the ground. If still able, he agreed to surrender and would be held for ransom.

Just before daylight ended, Jagiello rode onto the battlefield. He embraced his cousin, Duke Wihold. Together, with their captains, they rode through the battlefield identifying prominent enemies and arranging their proper burials. Enemy flags and standards were collected. Jagiello honored Poles who had fought particularly well and declared them battlefield knights.

The Teutonic Order lost more than half their forces, about eighteen thousand men, including fifty of their sixty leaders. Although the Order continued to function for a time, its power in the Baltic was now sharply reduced.

The Marienburg fortress avoided immediate capture after the Order's great defeat at Grunwald. The Order's Commander at Schwetz, Henrich von Plauen, who was responsible for the defense of Pomerania, immediately strengthened it. He was elected Grand Master and concluded a treaty with Jagiello, returning all territories captured by each side to each other. However, this was an uneasy peace and many of the Baltic subjects of the weakened Order now grew restless and felt able to rebel and cast off the Order's yoke.

The Treaty of Thorn was signed on October 19, 1466, between Poland and the weakened Order. It sharply reduced the Order's possessions. The Order's lost territories included Pomerania and with it Danzig and the Marienburg fortress. They continued to retain some sixty towns and castles, but the Grand Master became a vassal of the Polish King. The Teutonic Order's major role in the Baltic was over.

Aftermath

The Grunwald battle was such a pivotal part of Polish history, and the history of the Baltic, that it has often been described in books and film. America's foremost author of historical novels, James A. Michener, has described the battle of Grunwald in his book, *Poland*. It's an entertaining and gripping story about Poland's trials and tribulations stemming from its geographic position with aggressive neighboring nations surrounding it. In the book, the Teutonic Knights are described as the "threat from the west." The amber trade and its importance is also made clear.

Another well-known book that describes the Grunwald battle and the relationship of the Order to the Poles is a historic novel, *The Teutonic Knights* written by Henryk Sienkiewicz, Poland's 1905 Nobel Prize winner for Literature. The battle comes at the end of the novel after the reader has been entertained by a superb storyteller. You also become acquainted with many of the customs of medieval times, particularly those of knights.

In both of these novels, the Teutonic Knights are depicted, for the most part, as harsh bullies and worse. Friction between Polish and Lithuanian landowners and the Order are constant. The Order was ever encroaching on the land belonging to others, and the neighboring Polish and Lithuanian landowners were only protecting their homeland and families, which makes for a classic "good vs. evil" confrontation. A long Polish film called, "Krzyzacy," and also entitled, "Knights of the Teutonic Order," was produced from the Sienkiewicz book in 1960 and is available in Polish with English subtitles.

It's clear that the Order expanded its mandate by staying around too long and extending its territories too much. We should allow some skepticism about the origin of these unflattering tales about the Order, which are derived mostly from their enemies. In its defense, we would cite its effort in bringing Christianity to the Baltic's southern shore and developing the resources of the area, particularly in agriculture. Some historians also credit the Order, with their powerful castles and strongholds, with stopping the Mongol expansion west. The Teutonic Knights are now completely gone from the Baltic. The few members of the Order remaining today are mostly in Austria and are engaged in hospital work.

Marianburg Castle, near Gdansk, the former headquarters of the Teutonic Knights, is much restored and offers a good sense of the former power and position of the Order. It has both a military and amber museums. Imagine the Knights mustering their forces here and preparing for the confrontation at Grunwald with the Polish King Jagiello and his allies on July 15, 1410. The large courtyard would have been filled with mounted Knights clad in heavy armor and wearing, over this, a white mantle with a black cross. There would also be squires and foot soldiers. They would all be sharpening their weapons and practicing their fighting skills. Can you imagine the banging and clanging?

Baltic Sagas
Events and Personalities that Changed the World!

Holstentor Gate
Lubeck, Germany

III
Hanseatic League
Baltic Provides the Foundation for the World's First Commercial Empire!

Hanseatic League –
Alliance of City Merchants

Among the many problems merchants in north German cities confronted in the tenth century were robbers on the roads, tolls imposed by rulers of lands through which merchants and their goods passed, and pirates at sea. As an example, there were nine separate tolls imposed on the first fifteen miles leading out of Hamburg. Avoiding toll roads by using back roads could be even worse. A traveler might lose all his goods through confiscation and was in danger of bodily harm if caught by the territory's manor lord. Very often it was difficult to distinguish between the independent robbers and brigands who operated under the command of a manor lord.

Adding to the woes of the merchants was the restriction that provided only the upper classes with the right to bear arms. To improve their protection, merchants traveled in overland caravans or by sea in groups of ships. They sometimes hired guards. Merchants sharing in an enterprise, such as bringing a shipload of trade goods from overseas, also reduced risk. The captain and crew were often given a share in an enterprise to encourage them not to throw the cargo overboard in a storm and to strengthen their resolve when confronted by pirates.

Profitable trade motivated these merchants. Bringing raw materials from the far corners of Europe, or beyond, to their home cities, where they would be processed and traded or sold, was the business of the merchants. Timber for ships, hemp for rope, tallow for candles, furs for hats and coats, and fish were among the important trade goods. The church decreed that on feast days and Fridays fish had to be eaten. Outlying areas of the Baltic Sea were rich sources for herring. There was no refrigeration in those days so fish were dried or preserved with salt. Moving goods from where they could be found, adding value as appropriate (wool to cloth), and exchanging them for other goods or acceptable legal tender, at a profit, occupied the time and energy of the merchants.

Branch offices were sometimes established overseas to ensure quality, and to obtain local material for shipping over long distances in a timely manner. Firm representatives would stay in these places for periods of time until replaced by others. In these overseas branches, far removed from manor lords, merchants were much freer to develop their own rules for governing their activities.

Commercial instruments and procedures were developed - credit, contracts, shares, bonuses, and salvage rights, among others. North German merchants based overseas kept to themselves and were further united and separated from the local population by their German language and church.

By traveling together for mutual protection, sharing in trading enterprises, and working and living together in overseas branches, the merchants of a city gradually came together and formed an association. The association would then establish links with similar merchant associations in other cities.

These linked, city associations of merchants, bound by a common interest in profitable trade, is what gave rise to the Hanseatic League, or Hansa, as it is also called.

The merchants of hundreds of cities came to participate in activities of the Hanseatic League during the years of its activities and influence. The enterprising merchants of one city, Lubeck, Germany, were among the prime movers in establishing the Hanseatic League. Lubeck became a free city in 1159 and subject only to the Emperor, not local rulers. This date is a convenient starting point for telling the story of the Hanseatic League era. The Westphalia Peace Accord in 1648, following the Thirty Years War, generally marks an appropriate ending date for the final decline of the League.

The approximately five hundred years in between are an exciting story of pirates, peace treaties, new frontiers, trade disputes, greed, war, executions, and an introduction to many of today's business methods.

Hanseatic Cities

The Hanseatic League got its initial impetus from Lubeck merchants, who associated themselves with similarly organized Hamburg merchants. Hamburg provided the salt to preserve the Baltic herring brought to Lubeck from nearby fishing grounds.

Over the years other cities were brought into a loose confederation of merchant associations extending from Novgorod in the east and going west to Revel, Danzig, Visby, Lubeck, Hamburg, London and many cities in between. In the south, Cologne was a member and in the north the League extended to Bergen, Norway. This confederation was loose, flexible and focused on gaining trade advantages.

Political power, with a few exceptions, was still held by feudal lords or monarchs who had authority over the individual cities. This accounts for the difficulty in being clear, even today, about the power enjoyed by the Hanseatic League at any time. Situations varied depending upon the city, the trade goods involved, and the time period.

The importance of many of these cities stemmed from their location at or near the mouth of a river.
 Hamburg–Elba River
 Riga–Dangava River
 Gdansk–Vistula River
 Novgorod - Volkhova River
 London–Thames River
 Stettin–Oder River
These rivers provided a highway that brought raw materials from the surrounding countryside to the cities.
.

The Hanseatic League merchants needed a ship that could haul large quantities of goods from distant ports. The *Cog* design that was developed evolved from the Viking ships that had previously been used in the Baltic. The Viking ships were narrow, provided for rowing, had a shallow draft, clanker construction, and a single mast. They were curved at both ends, had a side rudder, and primarily provided rapid transportation for raiding parties. Some were modified to carry some cargo, but within this design.

The cog was broad beamed, had a raised platform on the stern, strong cross beams, and a centered rudder. It still retained clanker construction (overlapping planks) and a single mast. Quick turns and maneuverability gave way to load carrying capacity. The average modified Viking cargo ships could carry about two tons of cargo and the average cog about ten tons, or five times as much. It was also more rugged. As the ships continued to be made larger, more masts were added, and finally, the cog bore little resemblance to a Viking vessel.

Generally, the hinterlands provided raw materials and the cities provided finished goods. Skins were collected and sent on to cities, processed into leather, made into shoes and handbags, etc., and these were traded for more skins. A transaction profit was taken at each step.

For example, Danzig supplied inexpensive Polish wheat; Bergen collected fish from the surrounding Norwegian ocean and lakes; Novgorod sent timber and furs; London supplied wool; and Cologne sent wine from the Rhineland. Brugge, in Flanders, was one of the most prosperous cities in the Middle Ages, because it produced and exported highly desirable linen.

Groups of cities tended to focus on certain trade goods, organizing themselves to obtain the best marketing conditions for their commercial interests. The League came to have three sub-groups called thirds. There was the Prussian third based on grain, the Lubeck third based on the Baltic trade, and the Cologne third based on the Rhine trade.

These cities, bound by certain rules and traditions, prided themselves on being known as Hansa members, or Hanseatic League cities.

Major Hanseatic Trading Posts

The oldest, major, overseas Hansa trading post was in London, England. Here, German merchants engaged in trade even before the days of the League. The English had the Germans handle their trade, showing little interest in doing it themselves. Later on, of course, the English established a premier mercantile empire, with a fleet to match. However, during the early Middle Ages they fought in feudal wars among themselves and frequently were at war with France.

The Germans first set up shop in a building called, "The Guildhall of the Germans," later called "Easterlings Hall," and finally in a much larger complex called the "Steelyard." The Steelyard name probably derived from the Great Balance of the City of London, which was used to weight all imports and exports. The Steelyard was located at what was to become the Hansa site. There were also Hansa trading operations (on a more reduced scale) in other English cities.

The London Steelyard was of great importance to the merchants of the Hansa because England was a major source of wool, hides, and cheese. The wool was especially important and was sent to Flanders to be made into cloth. The merchants, in exchange, sent to England, yew wood (needed for archery bows), pepper, potash, Rhine wine, and many other goods not locally produced.

The Hansa's commercial complex on the left bank of the Thames River waterfront grew to encompass wharves, warehouses, living quarters, a kitchen, a garden, and an inn. This was close to an area called Dowgate, beyond London Bridge. It had the only city gate that commanded the water, and the Steelyard came to dominate the river and its commerce.

The German merchants usually enjoyed good relations with English rulers to whom they often supplied the funds needed in their wars. At one time, Cologne kept the British royal crown and jewels as collateral for loans to Edward III. Gifts were also given to local officials on appropriate occasions and further helped to smooth relations. Usually, relations between the Hansa people and their local commercial contacts were cordial, and business transactions were often concluded over a glass of Rhine wine in the Steelyard garden inn.

However, the local London population sometimes resented the German traders. This occasionally caused unrest and even riots. The Steelyard always had to be prepared to defend itself against local attacks. Each merchant was required to keep a suit of armor and weapons in readiness and, at night, watchmen and fierce dogs patroled the Steelyard.

The German representatives of the Hansa were sent to London for an extended period, urged to keep to themselves, and remain celibate. There were no women or families in the Steelyard. For the most part, the Hansa merchants were able to conduct their affairs independent of their English hosts. The Steelyard had its own internal government that maintained discipline by imposing heavy fines for infractions of its rules.

Unlike other overseas posts, the residents of the Steelyard didn't set up their own church. Since the local religion was similar to their own, they attended services at a local parish, All Hollows Church. They were generous in their support of the church—endowing stained windows, a chapel, carved stalls reserved for the Hansa, and an oak screen carved by a Hamburg craftsman. On feast days and holidays they were well represented in masses being sung and candles being lighted.

In contrast to many former Hanseatic cities, particularly those around the Baltic Sea, modern London makes little reference to its Hansa history. Its subsequent role as the capital of the British Empire and its position as a great financial center, undoubtedly, may have overshadowed the Hansa period's importance.

Far to the east of London, there was another Hanseatic trading post at Novgorod, Russia, on both banks of the Volkhova River. It was reached by first sailing east on the Baltic Sea to the Neva River delta, sailing east on the Neva to Lake Ladoga, and then south on the Volkhova River to Novgorod, just upriver from Lake Ilmen. This was many hundreds of years before St. Petersburg was built on the Neva's delta.

The trading center at Novgorod provided the Hanseatic League with raw materials drawn from the immense Russian hinterlands. Novgorod was the terminal to which came furs, hides, wax, and honey. The German merchants, in turn, provided finished goods such as cloth, shoes, and luxuries.

Russia was the eastern frontier of Europe and most of its inhabitants hadn't yet progressed much beyond growing, hunting, or collecting raw materials. They still didn't do much processing or trading, nor, not surprisingly, did the Hansa encourage it. The Hansa didn't allow any Russians to sail their own ships into the Baltic and trade. The Russian captain and crew caught doing this were harshly punished.

Their overbearing attitude and conduct made it clear to the Russians that the Hansa merchants considered themselves vastly superior to them. Quarrels and arguments over short measures and quality were frequent and often for good reason on both sides. Relations were based on mutual suspicions.

The Hanseatic League merchants conducted their activities on the east bank of the river, across from Novgorod's religious and administrative center. The merchants built and attended their own church, which they dedicated to St. Peter. They built the Hansa shops, warehouses, and guildhalls nearby and brewed their own beer. The complex became known as the Court of the Germans at Great Novgorod, or the Court of St. Peter. The enclave was built to be defended since the Russians sometimes would attempt to raid the Hansa warehouses and steal the goods of the German merchants. In the evening, it was closed and guarded.

Later, the individual trading houses built their own churches from which they conducted their business. This was done because the penalty for stealing from a church was more severe than stealing from an ordinary Hansa building. The threat of greater punishment was a way to discourage crime.

Winters were long and harsh in Russia, and there were few diversions. Social contact by Hansa men with the local population was forbidden. No wives or families could accompany them during their tour at Novgorod. Rules of conduct were strict and infractions severely punished. Novgorod was a hardship posting for a merchant representative, particularly when compared with London.

Almost half way up the Atlantic coast of Norway is the town of Bergen. It has a deep harbor, and, behind it, mountains rise steeply confining the town itself to a narrow coastal area. Its geographic location and good harbor made it a natural base for fishing vessels and as a stopping point when going farther north or returning. The Victual Brothers pirates had raided Bergen in 1393. Another pirate, Bartholauer Voet, raided it in 1428 and made a return visit the next year. These raids left the town shorn of its wealth and the manpower to protect itself.

Hansa merchants used the opportunity to move in and buy the prime waterfront property for themselves, and the inhabitants felt compelled to sell it to obtain the bare necessities for survival. The dispirited, local population relocated farther toward the mountains and a thoroughfare, called Shoemaker's Alley, separated the two parts of town. Shoemaker's Alley became a haven for the town's cruder inhabitants, and knifings and fights were frequent there. The pirate raids that had brought the Bergen residents to their knees were so advantageous to the Hanseatic League that it raised suspicions they may have been behind the pirates in some way.

All merchandise coming from Norway in ships was obliged to stop over in Bergen to insure the Hansa had right of first refusal. When ships arrived, the denizens of Shoemaker's Alley kept Bergen natives back until the Hansa traders had picked over the goods. The fish caught and brought to Bergen, particularly cod, made the Hansa trading post here a prime source of profits in an age when fish consumption was such an important staple.

At one time, there were about three thousand Hansa workers at Bergen. They held complete authority over the town. The Hansa employment rules for its members were very strict; a ten-year commitment was required: all members of the community were male and celibate; and all were to be within the Hansa complex at night, with the perimeter guarded by watchmen and dogs.

To add to the discomfort of restricted living conditions, there were a series of initiation ceremonies for newcomers, usually 14 and 15-year-old boys. They reached almost unspeakable levels of pain and cruelty.

New arrivals were made to climb up chimneys while burning, evil smelling waste produced smoke. Another rite was to take these new arrivals out to sea, throw them naked into the frigid water, half drown them, and then beat them. On another day, they were taken into the woods to collect birch branches and then were whipped with them until blood flowed. There were about thirteen rites, but these were the basics–fire, water, and whipping. Some sent their bloody shirts home to show they had survived. If the new apprentices lasted and served well during their tour, they could hope to rise in status to one of the ruling alderman of the Bergen Hansa. In the meantime, they could take their "fun" by initiating new arrivals.

Not all Hansa overseas branches were "hardship posts" in the style of Novgorod and Bergen. Brugge was a beautiful city, connected to the sea during the Hansa time, but whose waterway has since been allowed to silt up. It was the focal point for the most industrious and skilled people of the era, who fashioned beautiful linen and tapestries. Goods from the entire world found their way to Brugge. Silks and spices from Asia came through the Italian cities and then down the Rhine River. From England came wool to be made into cloth. From the Baltic came hemp used to make the rope so badly needed for ships.

In the middle of all this trading at Brugge were sixty merchant firms of the Hanseatic League. Their conduct here, however, was much less arrogant than in the other posts we have described. The local merchants here were well versed in the nuances of trade, and culturally gave no ground to the northern merchants. If anything, the Hansa representatives at Brugge learned from their local counterparts. Even so, the Hansa here had the important products from the Baltic region to trade, and the needs of the market gave them an important standing.

Envy of Outsiders

All this profitable Hansa trading aroused the interest and envy of outsiders, who felt they should have a larger share of trade revenues. The rulers in Scandinavia took particular notice. One of these monarchs was Waldemar IV, King of Denmark, an energetic and wily ruler who had united his country. Denmark was strategically located in the straits separating the North Sea from the Baltic.

During Waldemar's time, Denmark possessed Scania (today's southern Sweden), which was close to where the Hansa fishing fleets were catching much of their herring. These important fishing activities were centered at Visby, Gotland, a large island near the center of the Baltic. Gotland's strategic location made it of great concern to the Hansa, although the island belonged to Sweden.

Waldemar chose to make his resentment clear and attacked Visby, the center of the Hansa's herring business. In order to do this successfully, he decided to first visit Visby disguised as a merchant to find out its defensive strengths and determine where most of its treasures and valuables could be found. He put aside his crown and royal garments, and with only one companion, visited the city. He provided himself with appropriate credentials and passed himself off as a merchant.

While there, he met an important town official who was also a goldsmith. Waldemar immediately realized that this man would be the best possible source of information about the places and people who possessed the richest gold and silver necklaces, bracelets, rings, drinking vessels, and other precious goods.

During their discussions, the goldsmith revealed that he had a young, unmarried daughter. The goldsmith, like most fathers, was only too happy to introduce his daughter to this finely dressed and well-mannered visitor. Waldemar received permission to call on the young girl. Soon pride in her city and a growing affection for the deceitful suitor led her to disclose all that the King wanted to know concerning the whereabouts of the city's richest homes, the location of its treasures, and its defenses. Shortly thereafter, Waldemar left, promising to return. This was a promise he meant to keep.

When Waldemar returned to Denmark, he prepared his fleet and soldiers. In 1361, after a year had gone by, he returned with his fleet to Visby and savagely attacked it. The unprepared, peaceful inhabitants were no match for the Danish Army. Their defense was easily broken before the relentless onslaught of Waldemar's better-trained and armed soldiers. A reported eighteen hundred defenders died in the battle. The Danes entered the city and remorselessly plundered it. Although guided by the knowledge Waldemar had gained from the goldsmith's daughter, he gave her no further thought.

After Waldemar left with his fleet, there was a great outrage among the town's citizens. A number of them recognized the attackers' leader as the former visitor and realized he had been spying. They remembered his interest in the Goldsmith's daughter, the hospitality she had freely given, and her naiveté in supplying information. In their frustration and with no other outlet for their revenge, they seized the hapless girl and sealed her in one of the town's towers. The tower is still known today as the Virgin Tower.

However, King Waldemar wasn't able to fully enjoy his Visby booty. On his return voyage to Denmark, a great storm scattered his fleet, sank many of his ships, and carried their loot to the bottom of the sea. Waldemar barely survived the storm himself.

Visby's close ties to Lubeck, and the herring trade's importance to the Hansa, made its merchants thirst for revenge. They selected a former Lubeck mayor, Johann Wittenberg, to lead a punitive expedition of fifty-two ships each manned with about one hundred soldiers, plus a fleet of auxiliary vessels. The campaign succeeded at first and Copenhagen was sacked.

Wittenberg's next objective was to rendezvous with a Swedish army to attack the Danish fortress of Halsingberg. The Swedish army never appeared and Wittenberg took his soldiers off their ships and attacked the fort. A few days later, the Danish fleet arrived with Waldemar, and the virtually unmanned Hansa ships were attacked and sunk, or captured. Wittenberg and his Hanseatic army were in a hopeless position without his fleet to supply and support him. He sued for peace, went home to Lubeck in disgrace, and was publicly executed in the town's market square.

King Waldemar was so emboldened by his successes that he continued to attack other Hansa cities, which eventually spurred them into uniting against him and forcing him to sue for peace. An agreement was drawn up, the Treaty of Stralsund, which gave the Hanseatic League these important new rights:
* There was to be free passage of the straits between the Baltic and the North Sea.
* The League had the right to veto the choice of the Danish ruler for 15 years.
* Two-thirds of Scania revenues were to go to the League.
* The Danish strongholds were to be possessed by the League.

Margaret, the daughter of Waldemar, was the next royal leader to challenge the Hansa. Her aggressive reign underscored the adage that the apple doesn't fall far from the tree. Waldemar arranged to have Margaret married to Haakon VI, King of Norway, when she was a child. When Waldemar died, Margaret had her son, Olaf V, elected to the Danish throne and acted as his regent. When her husband, Haakon VI, died, she also secured the Norwegian throne for her son and added it to her duties as regent. In 1387, when Olaf died, Margaret was elected Head of State of both countries.

Margaret, however, feared opposition from the Hanseatic League and Albert, King of Sweden, although she enjoyed the support of many of the Swedish nobles. Eventually, she decided to declare war on Albert and succeeded in defeating and capturing him. Margaret then persuaded the legislature of all three countries - Denmark, Norway and Sweden–to declare Margaret's nephew, Eric of Pomerania, king of all three countries. He was crowned in 1397, although Margaret, as regent, was the actual ruler.

Combining all three crowns for the first time became known as the "Kalmar Union." All three crowns were elective, not hereditary. With respect to Sweden, the bond was not strong. Queen Margaret died in 1412.

After Margaret died, Eric had conflicts with the Hanseatic League. In addition, he was unable to hold the Union together. Finally, dethroned, he returned to Pomerania. Once there, he took to raiding commercial shipping as a pirate. If all three countries had maintained their combined strength, it might have created serious problems for the Hanseatic League.

Just twenty miles west of Copenhagen is the town of Roskilde, the site of the Roskilde Cathedral (Domkirke). This church was built on the site that became the spiritual center of Denmark when Harald Bluetooth, who brought Christianity to Denmark in 980, built an earlier church there. During her reign, Queen Margaret and her maids had sewn altar cloths for the cathedral and presented it with other expensive gifts. However, she wanted to be buried at the Abbey of Soro when she died, where her father, grandfather and son were already laid to rest.

A year after her death, however, her close confidant, the Bishop of Roskilde, Peder Jensen Lodehat, had her body moved and entombed at the Roskilde Cathedral. Her tomb is in the center of the church behind the altar and has an alabaster effigy. It is said to be a good likeness of her in her younger years. Her internment started the tradition of having the royals entombed at Roskilde. The art and architecture of their tombs and the stories associated with them are beautiful and fascinating.

The Roskilde Viking ship museum nearby makes visiting this city, and both of these sites, an interesting and informative experience.

Pirates

After the sack of Visby by Waldemar in 1361, the town had trouble recovering its former eminence. It became the lair of a band of pirates who called themselves the Victual Brothers. "Victual," because they pledged to keep the southern Swedish coast supplied with food and, "Brothers," because they pledged themselves to mutual support and to divide all loot between them.

They preyed on all merchant and fishing vessels that attempted to sail in the waters anywhere near Gotland. The pirates became so powerful that all fishing in the area became very dangerous and it stopped. Baltic fish became scarce and its trade sharply reduced. The pirates became so bold they would return a captured vessel to its owners, after emptying its cargo, and invite the owners to return with more cargo in the future!

Finally, the exploits of the pirates grew so disruptive that the Hansa organized a fleet of thirty-five ships and three thousand men. In 1394, after a fierce struggle, they sunk or scattered the pirate fleet, running them out of Visby. The pirates who survived the breakup of the Victual Brothers' stronghold at Visby now switched their activities to the North Sea.

During this time a young nobleman in Hamburg had been drinking up his modest inheritance. He was getting in trouble with the authorities for his general behavior and the debts incurred by his drinking habits. Finally, the authorities sold his armor to help pay his debts, and he ran off and joined the pirates. He met up with their leader, Godeke Michelson, who was very impressed with the young nobleman's physical strength and drinking prowess. He named him, "Stortebeker," meaning, "Pour down bumpers." A bumper is a large drinking vessel. Klaus Stortebeker had natural leadership ability, and, coupled with his physical strength and drinking feats, he was soon sharing command of the pirates.

When Visby was no longer hospitable, the two pirate chiefs made their base in Frisia, the area on the mainland European coast near the North Sea where they raided ships engaged in trade with England. Stortebeker met and successfully wooed the daughter of a local chief. She followed Stortebeker aboard his ship and added to his growing legend as a hard drinking, hard fighting, but amiable rascal. He would befriend his captives, and if they could match his drinking prowess, invite them to join his band. However, if they were old or weak, he didn't hesitate to throw them overboard.

Finally, the Hansa again felt it necessary to rid the seas of these remaining pirates, and Hamburg took the lead in organizing a fleet to accomplish this. A strong force was assembled and Simon of Utrecht, an alderman, who captained a large and powerful ship, The Bridled Cow, was put in command. After several weeks, the pirate fleet was detected near Heligoland, an island in the North Sea near Germany. Under the cover of darkness, a brave Hamburg fisherman in a small boat was able to disable the rudders of several pirate ships. The next day the Hamburg fleet arrived and engaged the pirate ships.

The fighting was ferocious. The pirates, if captured, knew their fate was the executioner's axe in Hamburg. Many of the men in the Hamburg fleet were mercenaries who had been promised a bounty for each pirate killed or captured. No mercy was expected or given on either side. Simon of Utrecht, on his ship, The Bridled Cow, was relentless. He pursued any pirate ship that tried to escape and forced it to fight. The battle lasted three days, when the pirates were finally beaten. Some of the pirates, under cover of darkness, escaped, but most were killed.

Only Stortebeker and the men with him aboard his flagship, The Mad Dog, were allowed to surrender and were taken back to Hamburg. After a short trial, they were condemned to death. Stortebeker attempted to save his life by offering to disclose where his loot was hidden. This offer was rejected, and he and his companions went under the axe in Hamburg's Market Square.

Now it only remained to capture the other pirate chief, Godeke Michelson, and his gang, who weren't among those taken at Heilgoland. Simon of Utrecht, in his flagship, The Bridled Cow, and his fleet set out again. The pirate chief was finally cornered, captured and, along with nearly a hundred of his men, taken back to Hamburg and beheaded. The threat to Hansa shipping from this most notorious band of pirates was ended.

The defeat of Waldermar IV, the breakup of the Kalmar Union, and the elimination of the pirates, TheVictual Brothers, marked the peak of the Hanseatic League's power and influence.

Hanseatic League Decline

By the fifteenth century, events were taking place in Europe that would adversely affect the Hanseatic League.

1. The Teutonic Knights decisive defeat by a coalition headed by Poland at Grunwald in 1410 weakened support for the League on the Baltic coast from Danzig to Tallinn.
2. Martin Luther and his reform movement in the church caused divisions within German communities.
3. Columbus sailed to the Americas and directed European attention to a major new source of raw materials and trade.
4. Tsar Ivan III, in 1494, closed Novgorod to the Hansa and cut them off from one of the cornerstones of their trading empire.

However, during this time, the League demonstrated that it still had enough power and influence to intervene successfully in the selection of monarchs in Scandinavia.

Christian II ascended to the Danish crown in 1513 after serving as governor of Norway. At the beginning of his reign, he renewed Denmark's commercial treaties with the Hansa in large part because he wanted its support in a war he was having with Sweden. However, it wasn't long before Christian voiced his true feelings about the Hansa and the power they exerted over passage through the Straits and in the Danish markets. His disdainful ways of expressing these feelings and his abusive manner made his remarks particularly offensive and troublesome. The Hansa became very alarmed.

After Christian defeated Sweden, he insisted on keeping Gustave Ericson, a young member of the Swedish house of Vasa, as a hostage. He was imprisoned at Kalo in Jutland and not fed or treated in a manner befitting his station. After enduring this for a while, he escaped and made his way to Lubeck, where he was warmly welcomed. When Christian found out where Gustave had fled, he immediately insisted on his return. He even threatened to search each house in Lubeck for Gustave. This enraged the Lubeck officials who gave voice to their feelings in haughty terms and assured Gustave he would never be given over to Christian. Relations between the two sides deteriorated further, and Christian vented his fury by executing ninety Swedish nobles and repeatedly sacking Hansa property whenever the opportunity presented itself.

Gustave secretly returned to Sweden and began to organize an uprising against the Danish King among the peasants. When Christian heard of this, he sent a Danish army to suppress this threat. The Danes enjoyed a great superiority in cavalry and artillery over the peasant army in this battle, which was to be fought near Upsala. The day of the battle there was a heavy snowfall, which nullified the Danish advantage. The Danish army was defeated. This success brought new recruits to Gustave. When Christian sent more men and ships against him, Gustave appealed to Lubeck for help. They sent him ten ships.

Lubeck also began negotiations with Christian's uncle, Duke Frederick of Schleswig, to determine his interest in taking the Danish crown. Frederick and Christian had never enjoyed good relations, so Frederick's reaction was very positive. Lubeck began forming a plan to topple Christian and replace him with Frederick.

When Christian learned of this, he planned a new campaign against the nobles. However, when the nobles learned of this, it had the effect of uniting them against Christian. General mistrust of Christian, an uprising by his own nobles and clergy, and active opposition to Christian by the Hansa, drove him to flee, thus putting Frederick on the Danish throne in January 1523. Gustave, as Gustavus I, ascended the Swedish throne in June 1523.

Two years later, a dispute arose between Frederick and Gustavus, which the city of Lubeck mediated. The resulting treaty not only brought peace, but also gave important treaty concessions to the Hansa in acknowledgement of their help.

In 1530 a new personality, a man from Hamburg, Jurgen Wullenweber, appeared for the first time in Lubeck's records, when he was named a member of its Burgher council. He was destined to be an influential and controversial figure in Lubeck's history. In 1533, when King Frederick of Denmark died, Wellenweber proposed that the Hansa take this opportunity to take possession of the strategic Danish Sound, and deny its use to the Netherlands, with whom Lubeck had gone to war. His energy and oratory were persuasive, and, in spite of the size and ambition of the undertaking, he convinced the councilors of Lubeck to his plan of seizing the Danish Strait. Treasures of silver and gold, taken from the churches as a result of the Reformation, provided the funds for the undertaking. There was also at hand a man to lead the expedition, Max Meyer, another man originally from Hamburg, but now in Lubeck.

Max Meyer was one of those swashbuckling, North German personalities the likes of whom we have met before. He was tall and strong and his first line of work was as a blacksmith. However, his thirst for adventure soon led him to military service, first under King Christian II of Denmark. Later, he was engaged by Lubeck to command eight hundred men it was sending to the German Emperor for his war with the Turks.

Meyer was so successful in this enterprise that, when he returned, he was loaded down with booty and outfitted in handsome armor and helmet. He looked so attractive riding into Lubeck accompanied by trumpeters, forty men in armor and two wagons of booty, that the rich widow of a burgomaster (mayor) immediately lost her heart to him. They married and Meyer's new connections and status brought him into contact with Wullenweber. They soon became close allies.

Max Meyer was put in command of a Lubeck fleet and, while pursuing some Dutch merchant ships, instead captured some Spanish ships loaded with English goods. After he captured these ships, he sailed into an English harbor and went to the English court, where King Henry VIII warmly received him. Henry greeted him as a fellow Protestant and potential ally in his quarrels with the German Emperor and the Dutch. English justice, however, required that Max Meyer be punished for piracy in capturing the Spanish ships, and so he was imprisoned for a short time. When he was released he returned to King Henry VIII's court. Henry demonstrated his favor by knighting Meyer, giving him a gold chain and promising him a yearly income.

The generous treatment by Henry VIII toward Meyer encouraged Lubeck to tighten their Baltic control. Lubeck's plans for attacking Denmark while continuing the war with the Netherlands, however, alarmed the other Hansa cities. A meeting was called in Hamburg, in

March 1534, to discuss these matters. Wellenweber and Meyer represented Lubeck and entered the city of Hamburg for the meeting in grand style–full armor, trumpeters and drummers, and sixty armed riders.

The Burgomaster of Hamburg spoke forcefully opposing Lubeck's war against the Netherlands and for peace. An Imperial Councilor expressed the same sentiments even more strongly. Wellenweber replied that his plans in Scandinavia were for the good of the entire Hansa. No agreement was possible. Wellenweber became annoyed, and he and Meyer left Hamburg in the same grand style as that they entered. Their return to Lubeck engulfed them in a cauldron of opposing viewpoints pitting the old establishment against the newer leaders represented by Wellenweber and Meyer. After an energetic defense of his strategy, Wellenweber carried the day. Lubeck was now firmly behind him, and he returned to Hamburg. The congress was reopened, and Wellenweber agreed to a four-year truce with the Netherlands allowing him to concentrate on the Baltic.

Wellenweber immediately mobilized, sending emissaries to the Hansa cities to explain his plans and enlist support. In May 1534, war was declared on Denmark. Sweden was also threatened. Sweden's King Gustavus appealed for help from his fellow rulers. Wellenweber soon captured most of the Danish kingdom. However, with success came greater difficulties in achieving unity, both in the Hansa and in Lubeck itself - party factions, religions quarrels, and personal jealousies all intervened.

Troops and ships from many power centers poured into Danish waters. Large numbers of mercenaries, with a variety of customs and languages, were recruited. During the fighting, Max Meyer was captured and imprisoned. Christian III was proclaimed King of Denmark. Intrigues abounded on all sides - between Catholics and Protestants, rival Princes and Kings, old establishment leaders and their new rivals, and between Hansa cities.

Meyer escaped from his confinement, and to replace Christian III, desperately and unsuccessfully offered the Danish crown to Francis I of France. Meyer also received some help from his old friend, Henry VIII. Henry VIII was also offered all of Denmark by Lubeck in return for substantial aid.

As the war progressed, the growing weakness of the Hansa became clear. The Hansa army no longer consisted of the merchants themselves, as in earlier times, but many more mercenaries. The merchants who had grown rich were satisfied with hiring others to go and fight. They were content with doing their own fighting close to home guarding the city's gate. The zeal was gone.

At a long battle at Assens, victory eluded the Hansa. In a sea battle shortly thereafter, some of the Hansa ships ignomiously fled before the enemy or surrendered. Wallenweber's enemies also employed bribes to undermine his less committed allies. Christian III's supporters soon recaptured most Danish territories. Max Meyer retreated to a strong position at a castle at Vardberg, where he was able to hold out.

In July 1535, a Hanseatic Diet was summoned to discuss the deteriorating situation. Lubeck became the target of complaints from other Hansa cities, many of which had harbored jealousies based on its long held leadership position in the Hansa. Cologne led the criticism. Its censure revolved around Lubeck meddling in the appointment and toppling of kings and princes. Wellenweber, who usually spoke for Lubeck, replied that an interest in who ruled in Scandinavia had always been of legitimate concern to the Hansa. He added that this concern had served the Hansa's interests very well in the past.

Cologne's representatives then shifted their argument to religion, and attacked Lubeck for its embrace of the Reformation. A former conservative burgomaster, Nickolas Bromse of Lubeck, who had lost out to the new forces led by Wellenweber, now saw his chance for a comeback. He had fled to Brussels and the Imperial Court, where he now persuaded the Emperor to issue a decree to Lubeck abolishing all democratic innovations and reinstating Nickolas Bromse and his supporters. At this time, with their fortunes ebbing, Lubeck felt it had to obey the Decree, and Wellenweber and his backers resigned.

This marked the end of Wellenweber's ambitious plan to again establish the Hansa's predominance in the Baltic. It also started him on the road to horrible suffering and death. He decided to journey to Max Meyer in his castle at Vardberg. However, his enemies resolved that this energetic and capable enemy should not be free to thwart them again. His trip to Vardberg led him through the territory of the Archbishop of Bremen, a notorious anti-Reformation zealot.

Wellenweber was captured and imprisoned in spite of a safe conduct document. Appeals to his former allies, including Henry VIII of England, were to no avail. He was tortured repeatedly, kept in damp and dark cells for a number of years and finally brutally executed.

Max Meyer was also persuaded to surrender, by the promise of a safe conduct, but this promise was broken. He was given over to his enemy, Christian III, who had him beheaded and his body quartered.

Events around the world continued to conspire against the Hansa in the sixteenth century. The herring catch, which had been the foundation of Hansa trade, shifted to the North Sea, making it more readily accessible to the growing Dutch maritime power. The English found a northern passage at Archangel for trading with Russia, allowing them to avoid the Hansa controlled Baltic Sea. The Livonia ports of Riga and Revel, both of which were under Hansa control and had assumed greater commercial importance with the close of Novgorod in Russia, were now threatened by Russia, Poland and Sweden. Sweden was emerging as an important new power in the Baltic. The Hansa's power in Bergen was lost as the Danish King, Frederick II, asserted himself as the ruler of both Norway and Denmark. Brugge's importance as a trading center was lost to Amsterdam and Antwerp.

A final blow came from England. Henry VIII had always been favorably disposed to the Hansa, but under his successors, Edward VI, Queen Mary, and finally Elizabeth, the Virgin Queen, relations eroded. The Hansa, supplying Spain with grain while it was at war with England, infuriated Queen Elizabeth. Finally, in 1598, the Queen ordered the Hansa merchants in the Steelyard to depart in fourteen days.

The religious differences between contending Protestant Reformation adherents and Catholic factions continued to divide the countries of Europe during this period. The antagonisms were particularly severe in Germany and were helping to further tear apart the former cooperation between Hansa cities. When war finally broke out in 1618, it gradually drew in other countries, such as France and Sweden, although most of the fighting was in Germany.

When the fighting finally concluded with the signing of the Peace of Westphalia in October 24, 1648, it was estimated that Germany's populations had been decreased by at least twenty percent. Economic activity in Germany was sharply reduced. Except for a proud memory by many former cities of the League, the Hansa was no more.

In the nearly 500 years between when Lubeck becoming a free city in 1159 and the signing of the Westphalia Peace Accord in 1648, the Hanseatic League linked the needs of far flung customers and suppliers, making an important contribution to the European economy, particularly in northern Europe. It was a flexible mechanism, having no standing Army or Navy, no chief executive, and no formal constitution or parliament. Instead, it organized itself to provide what was needed to meet a particular challenge at any given time. The various merchants within a city or the cities themselves didn't always agree, reflecting their own self-interest. But yet, the institution in its fluid form survived for nearly 500 years. Few other institutions can say as much.

Today's Hanseatic Cities

Many of the former Hanseatic Cities have been transformed to meet changing conditions over the years but still have an important role in today's world. Here is an update on some of them starting in the east with Novgorod.

Novgorod, Russia

Novgorod is one of the most historically important cities in Russia, stemming from its crossroads position between Western Europe and the exotic oriental world that lay to the east and south. As a trading center between these two areas and by gathering the riches of the tremendous landmass of the entire northern part of Russia, it became known as "Novgorod the Great." It's rich history as a cultural, political and religious center is still obvious from the many buildings, churches, and monuments standing today.

In 989 AD, the people of Novgorod were forcefully baptized and the city became an important center of Christianity, as well as a trading center. St. Sophia Cathedral, one of Russia's oldest churches, was built in 1045–1050 and its frescos and murals have recently been restored. Its famous Magdeburg Gate, made in that German City, can be seen today.

Also, on the market side of the city, divided by the Volkhova River, many of the churches there are undergoing restoration from the damage of World War II and Soviet neglect. St. Nicholas, one of the best known and famous for its murals, is undergoing restoration. Outside the construction site in 1997, there was a sign stating, " The restoration is financed by the cities of the reactivated Hanseatic Union."

Novgorod was situated as far east as the German Army advanced during World War II in this sector of Russia. Its front line position meant frequent attacks and counter-attacks with resulting damage.

As the city's territory enlarged during its early history, it set up the Novgorod Republic. For 400 years there was a General Assembly of Novgorod, called "Veche," which limited the power of princes and enabled a large part of the population to participate in ruling. The Veche elected the leading town officials and the commander of the town regiment. Representatives from the Sophia side and the market side sometimes met in the center of the connecting bridge across the Volkhova River to discuss civic matters and settle disputes.

The city attracted many enemies who sought its riches. The Tartars came and had to be mollified. However, under the command of Novgorod's Prince Alexander Nevsky, the Swedes were successfully fought off in 1240, the Teutonic Knights in 1242, and the Lithuanians at various other times. After failing earlier to conquer it, the Germans later came back as traders, and it became an important Hanseatic outpost.

It wasn't until Ivan III from Moscow conquered it in 1478, threw out the Hanseatic League, eliminated the Veche Republic, and sent archbishops from Moscow, that the city's fortunes were reduced. Ivan IV, the Terrible, also massacred many of its citizens in 1570, when he suspected them of disloyalty. Sweden came in 1611 and conquered Novgorod, holding it for nine years. The population was reduced to less than two thousand during this time. When Peter the Great later built St. Petersburg, Novgorod's position as northern Russia's leading city was permanently lost.

The city is a district capital now with a population of about 130,000 and reduced in prominence from its early days. A visit there today still gives you a remarkable insight into its former status and its important contributions to Russian history: the first ruling dynasty, extensive trading contact with western Europe, and religious and self-rule leadership. Its museum and churches display a rich collection of the religious art that made the city famous.

Tallinn, Estonia

Many former Hanseatic cities recall some of their past glories by preserving buildings and sections of their town erected in Medieval times. Tallinn has gone further than any other former Hanseatic city by preserving its entire historic central city to what it has been for hundreds of years. The locals say this was done not out of pride, but poverty. After the prosperous Medieval times, Tallinn couldn't afford to replace the old buildings with new ones. The result is one of the largest and most charming of old towns in Europe.

Estonia is independent today but has been ruled by Danes, Germans, Swedes, and Russians in the past, plus Livonia and the Teutonic Knights. All have left their mark on the buildings and fortifications of the old town.

The Upper town, Toompea, where the first fortress was built, was where the hierarchy lived, and which, today, is where the parliament is located. In its square is the beautiful Russian Orthodox Church, the Alexander Nevsky Cathedral, which was recently restored.

The lower town is where the commercial activity took place, is comprised of the merchant's homes, churches, warehouses, and the market square.

Much of the old town is still surrounded by a thick, high wall, which once completely encircled it. It includes many fortified towers, which were built by the different rulers at various times. Most have an interesting story behind them. I'll tell you about one.

"Peep into the Kitchen" tower got its name because the soldiers, when looking out from the top windows could often see the housewives working in their kitchens. It was a formidable stronghold judging from the six cannon balls still embedded in its walls.

In addition to fortifications, needed in the prosperous Hanseatic days for protection, many churches were also built to get God's protection. These churches included St. Olaf first noted in the town's records in 1267. Its tower, at one time, was considered the highest structure in the world, and still dominates the Tallinn skyline.

Estonians enjoy drinking their local beer, which I sampled at an out door café at the market square. At one end of the square is the Town Hall built in 1402–1404. Old Thomas, a weathervane in the form of a medieval warrior and the symbol of Tallinn, tops the tall tower at one end. Legend says he keeps watch to warn of approaching enemies.

I invited our local guide to join us in tasting the local beer, Sakie. She was a cheerful, outgoing college student who learned her English attending high school for a year in Minnesota. This is what she wrote in my guidebook.

"Well - don't you just love SAKIE? Hmm... Too bad you can't have it every day"! Helen Raudi (She reported taking a lot of kidding because her name is pronounced "rowdy" in America.)

Estonians take pride in their old town, their beer, and their singing. There is a massive national music festival every five years, which attracts a third of the Estonian population. It takes place in the Song Festival Amphitheater at Kadriorg. Tens of thousands of Estonians come together and blend their voices in one huge choir.

Among the three Baltic States, Estonia is making the best strides toward a successful free market economy, helped in great part by its close proximity to Finland, located just across the Gulf of Finland. The small population of about 1,500,000 is around twenty percent Russian, and how to assimilate them is a cause of some concern.

Lubeck, Germany

Lubeck is still a busy seaport even if it isn't as dominant as it was when it was known as the "Queen of the Baltic." To appreciate the life style in one of Lubeck's merchant families, I recommend reading, *Buddenbrooks,* a highly popular and realistic novel by Thomas Mann. Thomas Mann was born in Lubeck, and his family had been merchants there for many generations. He was awarded the Nobel Prize for literature in 1929.

Lubeck's best-known local products today include Rotwein (Red Wine) and Marzipan (an almond flavored, sugar candy). Lubeck is proud of its red wine, which actually comes from France in barrels aboard ships but is bottled locally. When French troops occupied the city during the Napoleonic Wars, they said it was better than the wine at home in France. Maybe it was, but saying it probably helped keep the natives serving it. The Lubeckers conjectured that perhaps the wine's quality was improved by the sea voyage. The wine is a little fruity for my taste but pleasant and refreshing.

Although Lubeck was badly damaged from air attacks in World War II, it is largely restored. I enjoyed visiting the famous landmarks: the Holstentor Gate, the Rathaus (city hall) and its square, and the churches. The large bells of one church, Marienkirche, crashed to the ground after an air raid and have been left there as a memorial. The food in Lubeck is particularly good, and I had a couple of good dinners in its restaurants and a fine breakfast each morning at the hotel.

Hamburg, Germany

Hamburg has been one of the world's great seaports for a long time, and it is still so today. It survived a devastating fire in 1812 and suffered a firestorm air raid in World War II that destroyed large sections of the city. But the city's will to survive and prosper always reasserts itself.

Its geographic location has always given its seaport a commanding position in both the North Sea and the Baltic Sea. The return of the eastern Baltic Sea to a free market economy, and the unification of Germany, with the tearing down of the Berlin Wall, have also added to the economic opportunities for Hamburg. The Museum of Hamburg History is a fine way to learn about the growth of this great port and city.

Hamburg's population today is about two million, and it is both a city and a state of the German Republic. The administrative center for both is at the Rathaus, a huge building with over six hundred rooms. Some are ornate public rooms befitting the city's prosperity.

In contrast to its formal and very stately city hall, Hamburg is also famed for its "Reeperbarn." This is a street of clubs, discos theatres and bright lights that offers all the attractions sought by sailors everywhere, and with some special attractions found only in Hamburg, I'm told. The waterfront greets a new ship every forty minutes and the sailors have always found a warm welcome at the Reeperbarn.

A Personal Connection With Hamburg

A few years after World War I, the German ship, SS Oliver, was tied up at a pier in Hamburg. It was the largest ship Germany had been allowed to keep, after paying reparations, following the war. In his kitchen, Chef Johann, had just finished the supervision of lunch service abroad the ship. Now Chef Johann turned his attention from lunch to his son Paul, who was scheduled to visit him in a few minutes. It was Sunday, an easier time for visitors to see their friends and relatives who worked aboard the ship.

Max Augener, the sous chef, the second man in charge of the kitchen, was also expecting visitors, his girlfriend Martha and her sister, Margaret. All three visitors arrived at the same time and introductions were made all around. Chef Johann and the four young people sat down for lunch at the table set aside for the senior kitchen staff. As usual on Sunday afternoon, all other kitchen staff had gone ashore. Paul and Margaret chatted and got to know each other. Paul had to leave at 4 o'clock to go to work. Paul and Margaret agreed to see each other again.

Johann was my grandfather. Paul became my father, and Margaret my mother.

After a couple of years, my father got a job offer in one of Berlin's top restaurants. He and my mother went to Berlin and married. My father's sister, Anna, lived in Berlin and prepared the wedding dinner.

Berlin, after the first World War, was an exciting place. The political climate was in turmoil as the Weimar Republic struggled to survive. Inflation was rampant. Dad told me you spent money you made as fast as possible since it's value decreased in mere hours. People had their life's savings rendered worthless as the value of money declined. Dad and Mom didn't have much, so they were less affected than many others.

At the same time, the creative energy in the city was pulsating. The cabarets were all in high gear, and artists filled the art galleries everywhere. There were thirty theatres in Berlin at this time. The film industry was at its peak with Marlene Dietrich, Peter Lorre, Emil Jennings, Billie Wilder, and Max Steinberg all working there. Classical music was centered in Berlin. It was a heady time to be young, newlywed, and in Berlin.

As alluring as Berlin was in those days, there was also a siren call from another direction. My father's brother, Fred, had gone to the United States and he urged my father and mother to join him in the "Land of Opportunity." Being young, they decided to go. They arrived in

America with $125.00. The Hamburg Museum records the names of the many other millions who went to America pursuing a dream.

Five months after they left Germany, I was born in Jersey City, New Jersey, USA.

Many years later, I was visiting Berlin. This was after President Kennedy made his famous speech in Berlin in which he said, " Ich bin ein Berliner." I also told the people I met in Berlin, "Ich bin ein Berliner." When they asked me what I meant, I explained I was born five months after my parents left Berlin, which means I was conceived here. This brought smiles of pleasure all around.

When I got back to America, I told my father how well I was accepted in Berlin when I told them, "Ich bin ein Berliner." My father asked me what I meant, and I explained I was conceived in Berlin, although born in America. My Dad shook his head. He told me he and mom lived during their last year in Germany in Hamburg. This means, "Ich bin ein Hamburger."

Doesn't have the same ring, does it?

Baltic Sagas
Events and Personalities
that Changed the World!

Peter the Great
Decembrists' Square
St. Petersburg, Russia

IV
Peter the Great

Mayhem, Chaos and Murder

Terem Palace
Kremlin
Moscow, Russia
May 15, 1682

Ten year old Peter watched in horror as the out-of-control soldiers roughly pushed aside his mother Natalya, the widow of Tsar Alexis. They seized her aging, white-haired, former guardian, Matveev. He had recently returned from exile, but he had once been chief Minister to Tsar Alexis. This morning, however, he was the victim of a rampaging mob of Streltsy soldiers. They were reacting to inflammatory rumors that the recently deceased, Tsar Feodor, and his brother Ivan may have been murdered. Their anger was also fueled by disputes over pay and promotions.

The Streltsy was Russia's first standing army and was organized by Ivan the Terrible. There were about 22,000 of them; a few were stationed on the western and southern borders, and the rest quartered near the Kremlin. When there was no war, they provided sentries for the Kremlin, guards for the city gates, and escorted the Tsar, lining his route on trips around Moscow.

They believed in the Orthodox Church, the Tsar, and their own well-being. In peacetime, they had little to do, and they often engaged in trade but paid no taxes. They lived with their families in log houses with clothing, food and pay all provided by the Tsar. It was a comfortable life, and they were sensitive to any threat to it.

Streltsy were armed with a sword at the belt, a musket in one hand, and an axe or halberd (long handled weapon with a battle-axe at the end) in the other. They were not well trained in the kind of drills or battlefield maneuvering then taking place in Europe. They did not receive much schooling but remained simple by tradition.

These soldiers dragged the frail Matveev to the banister at the head of the Grand Staircase and dropped him down onto raised spears. The soldiers below hacked him to pieces. Then the soldiers ran through the halls of the Kremlin Palace searching out officials for quick execution and dragged the bodies through the Kremlin gates and into Red Square.

Young Peter, although newly crowned Tsar, watched helpless and huddled in a corner with his mother and his half- brother, Ivan. The bloodletting went on all day as the soldiers settled scores with officials for past grievances. Sometimes these grievances were real, but, mostly, they were based on nothing but rumors designed to stir them up.

The family of Peter's mother, the Naryshkins, and their allies were the particular targets of the soldiers and were hunted down over the next few days. Their blood ran red and caked on steps and furniture throughout the palace. Finally, after days of the haphazard selection of victims, the mob's fury centered on finding Peter's young uncle, the twenty-three year old Ivan Naryshkin. Peter's mother, Natalya, had hidden her brother in a dark, basement storeroom.

The soldiers threatened to kill all the remaining officials if Ivan Naryshkin were not surrendered to them. Reluctantly, Peter's mother, who had seen her beloved former guardian, Matveev, slaughtered and was under no illusions as to what fate awaited her brother, agreed. She escorted him to the palace chapel where he received the last rites and then was turned over to the Streltsy. Their treatment of him was particularly savage.

He was pulled by his feet down the Grand Staircase into a basement chamber. Here he was whipped and tortured with hot irons. His wrists and ankles were snapped. His hands and feet dangled from his body. After a few hours, he was brought out into Red Square. He was barely conscious. The crowd cheered as his body was raised on spear points and held aloft. After the body was lowered, the hands and feet were cut off. The remains were hacked into pieces. Finally, all the body parts were trampled into the mud.

This final, savage killing finally brought an end to the slaughter. The Streltsy calmed down and presented their demands for restoring order. They included:

1. Back pay –this was to be provided by selling off the assets of the dead officials, melting down Kremlin silver plate, and a general tax.
2. Amnesty for the Streltsy.
3. Sharing of the Russian throne of Peter by his half-brother, Ivan, the sixteen-year-old who was feeble-minded.
4. Finally, Sophia, the oldest living child of Peter's dead father, Tsar Alexis, although a woman, was to become Regent and be the real ruler of Russia.

How did ten years old Peter survive this mayhem? He was now required to share his throne with a feeble-minded sixteen-year-old half-brother, but have the real power wielded by his twenty- five-year-old half sister, Sophia. In spite of all this, he finally emerged as Peter the Great – the Baltic's outstanding personality. How did he accomplish this?

Peter Grows Up and Seizes Power

Peter's father, Tsar Alexis, was the son of the second Romanov Tsar, Mikhail, and ruled from the Kremlin's Terem Palace in Moscow, the capital of Russia. Tsar Alexis shared the walled Kremlin citadel. The citadel included housing for ministry officials, military barracks, high Orthodox Church officials (including the Patriarch), and thirty-nine cathedrals. Tsar Alexis had married the daughter of a high-ranking family, the Mikoslavskys, and had fourteen children with her.

However, when Maria Mikoslavsky died in 1669, only three children had survived infancy: Fedor 9, Ivan 3, and the oldest, Sophia, 12. Alexis was forty years old when he became a widower, and after about a year he spotted Natalya Naryshkin, who was nineteen years old and living as a ward in the home of his chief minister, Matveev.

In spite of the difference in ages, they were married. This union produced a robust young son, Peter, and a daughter, Natalya. These were happy times for Tsar Alexis, his beautiful young bride, and his young son, Peter. During this time the relatives of the Tsar's first wife, the Mikoslavskys, were gradually replaced in the government by family members of his second, the Naryshkins.

When Tsar Alexis died, this happy life ended for Peter, who was just over three years old. Alexis's son from his first wife, Fedor, now 13, was crowned Tsar, although he was sickly and ruled mostly from his bed.

Natalya's former guardian, Matveev, was demoted to Governor of Verkoture in Siberia, and everything settled down until Tsar Fedor died after only a six-year reign. Fedor's younger brother Ivan was now next in line, but he was half- witted, nearly blind, and frail. He didn't have the imposing physical presence of Peter, who was now ten years old and on his way to the six-foot-plus height he would eventually reach. Moreover, Peter was in good health. After consultations between the boyars and church officials, Peter was announced as the new Tsar. In recognition of his youth, his mother, Natalya, was appointed Regent. She immediately sent for her experienced former guardian Matveev, and waited for his arrival.

During the days that followed, the Mikoslavskys used the time to upset this succession plan in order to preserve their position. Their chief instruments were the Streltsy; the soldiers living near the Kremlin. Their agitation among the Streltsy resulted in the cruel murder of Matveev, Ivan Naryshkin, and other Naryshkin supporters, as we have described. The agreement for Peter and Ivan to be co-Tsars was negotiated to obtain peace. Sophia, Tsar Alexis's daughter, was to be Regent. Peter's mother, who had been Regent only a few days, was too distraught by the killings and the fears for her son to object.

Sophia became Regent when she was twenty- five years old. Unlike most highborn women in Russia, Sophia had not allowed herself to be hidden away in the terem, quarters where the women sewed and gossiped all day. During her brother Fedor III's reign, she had attended sessions of the Boyer Council and discussed political situations with government officials. She came to realize she had the intellectual resources to rule. She felt only her sex and tradition barred her from power. She became the first in a line of future Russian female rulers - Catherine I (1725-1727), Anne (1730-1740), Elizabeth (1741-1762), and Catherine the Great (1762-1796).

Sophia appointed her own family members to high offices, as was customary, but Prince Vasily Vasilievich Golitsyn became her most important official. Prince Golitsyn was an educated man from an old aristocratic family who liked to live well, and who admired and socialized with foreigners. He wanted to expand Russia and bring the country into a new era of strengthened relations with the west. He also favored greater political and religious freedom. His ideas, in many ways, anticipated Peter's own vision for Russia.

Although Prince Golitsyn was fifteen years older than Sophia and married, she fell in love with him. She eventually named him "Keeper of the Great Seal," which made him her chief minister. Although Sophia had the power, rather than the young co-Tsars, this power was exercised behind the scenes.

At public ceremonies, Tsars Ivan V and Peter I presided and shared the throne. There was a removable panel and a seat behind the throne, through which Sophia could whisper instructions to the young co-Tsars. The throne is on display today in the Armory of the Kremlin in Moscow.

In their relations with the European nations, Sophia and Golitsyn affirmed all previous treaties. One agreement with Poland was awkward, because of the city of Kiev. Russia now occupied Kiev, but Tsar Alexis, by treaty, had promised to return it to Poland. The Russians found it difficult to return Orthodox Kiev to Catholic Poland.

A plan was developed, and Poland agreed that Russia could keep Kiev if Russia would campaign against their common enemy, the Ottoman Empire to the south. Russia agreed to this and in the summer of 1687, a huge Russian Army of one hundred thousand, led by Prince Golitsyn, marched south. The campaign failed and forty five thousand men were lost. Sophia glossed over this, and Prince Golitsyn was hailed as a hero upon his return. However, Russian's allies in Austria and Poland knew the truth.

In 1689, another campaign was mounted and an even larger Russian Army marched south. Although they got farther, it too was unsuccessful. As before, however, when its commander, Prince Golitsyn, returned to Sophia and the Kremlin, he was again received as a conquering hero and lavishly rewarded.

During these times, Peter's mother had become uncomfortable living in the Kremlin and feared for the safety of her family. She spent more and more time at a former Royal hunting lodge, Preobrazhenskoe, some miles out in the country northeast of Moscow. The hunting lodge had been used by Tsar Alexis, primarily to house his hunting falcons. There were hundreds of servants who had formerly attended them. Out here in the country, Peter was growing up and spending little time in formal classrooms. Instead, he engaged in military games. Peter used the younger servants and the sons of the older ones in his games. He drilled them, put them in uniforms, and engaged them in mock battles.

As the numbers grew, he formed them into two Regiments, the Preobrazhensky and Semyonovsky, named after two villages in which he housed them. He ordered the equipment he needed, drums, uniforms, and muskets from the Armory in Moscow and his requests were quickly filled. Peter most enjoyed beating a drum and firing a cannon, the activities that made the most noise. Peter took his place in the ranks and left command to experienced soldiers and foreigners who were employed in Russia. These military activities didn't disturb Sophia. The numbers engaged were too small.

Sometime during this period, Peter met a young man, probably a stable boy, Alexander Menshikov. Peter liked him immediately and promoted him to "Friend of the Tsar." For the rest of Peter's life, Menshikov was seldom very far from Peter's side. Menshikov was uneducated, but bright; corrupt, but loyal; and willing to try anything Peter ordered. He eventually became a military commander, a high government official, and a Prince of the Holy Roman Empire.

One day, when Peter was roaming around the countryside surrounding Preobrazhenskoe he came upon an abandoned boat in poor condition. Unlike the flat-bottomed barges found in Russian rivers, this vessel had a keel and shape suitable for sailing. In the nearby German suburb, a community where the foreigners lived who had been employed and brought to Russia for their special skills, Peter found a Dutch craftsman who helped him restore the boat and add a new mast and sail. Peter's interest in boats and shipbuilding, never flagged after this, but became a lifetime occupation.

He also enjoyed working with his hands and had a curiosity about how things worked. This curiosity brought him more and more frequently to the German suburb.

The German suburb was located between Preobrazhenskoe and Moscow. Here there were Germans, Dutch, English, Scots and others, but they were all referred to as "Germans." They were merchants, artists, doctors, engineers, mercenaries, and many others, who had come to Russia with their crafts and skills. They had their own churches and schools, wore western dress, drank and ate their native dishes, and socialized as they did in their home country.

The young Peter enjoyed visiting the German suburb, where he found not only interesting and learned men but also good companions for drinking and carousing into the late evening. Here he first met General Patrick Gordon, a Scottish mercenary. He had been brought to Russia (by Peter's father) and had also served Tsar Fedor III and Sophia. He also met Francis Lefort, a Swiss, whose personality, charm, gaiety, drinking capacity, and ability to organize a good time Peter found irresistible. Eventually, Peter's friends, both foreign and Russian, organized themselves into a "Jolly Company" that began their parties at noon and often went into the dawn.

When Peter was sixteen, his mother decided that he was to marry to make clear his maturity and fitness to actively rule. Peter agreed, and his mother organized a search. She selected a shy, young Russian girl, Eudoxia, from a noble family, the Loypukhinas, and they were married January 27, 1689. A year later, a son, Alexis, was born. The marriage, however, was not a success. Eudoxia came from a traditional background. She was religious and raised to stay in the background, away from the society of men. She didn't share any of the interests of the more outgoing, exuberant Peter.

Peter's growing up, his robust good health and vigor, and now his marriage were making clear his readiness to rule. Besides, the failure of Sophia's Tartar campaigns had reduced confidence in her. In August 1689, rumor of an attempt on Peter's life led him to flee farther from Moscow, to the Troitsky Monastery. Although a monastery, it was also a strong fortress with thick walls and round towers. At one time, it withstood a siege by thirty thousand Poles.

From this safe haven, the sixteen-year-old Peter used his authority as Tsar to summon the colonels of the Streltsy regiments to present themselves to him. Sophia intercepted this request, and instead sent the church patriarch to Peter to improve relations between them. Patriarch Joachim went to Troitsky and, once there, decided to support Peter's right as Tsar to rule. This opened the door to officials, other leading citizens, and finally the foreign officers in the German suburb to rally to Peter's side.

As the stream of officials traveling to Troitsky grew, those of Sophia's supporters, who had been responsible for violence against Peter's family, were handed over to Peter. Torture and killing were their faith. Prince Vasily Golitsyn's life was spared, but he lost his properties and was exiled to Siberia. Sophia was sent to the Novodevichy Convent. Peter proposed to Ivan that they continue to rule jointly, but without Sophia as Regent. Peter also proposed to Ivan that Peter not require Ivan's formal consent for appointment of new officials. Ivan, as the older, would still be the senior Tsar, and Peter said he would honor the ailing monarch as he would his father.

Peter now ruled Russia.

However, for the next few years, Peter left the day to day running of the government to his mother and his supporters who had helped overthrow Sophia. He continued drilling his regiments and engaging in mock battles, carousing at the German suburb, and building and sailing boats on Lake Plesclev.

His interest in furthering his nautical experience finally led him, in 1693, to Archangel, Russia's only ocean port far off in the north. This port opened out to the White Ocean and beyond that to the Arctic Ocean. Archangel could be navigated only during the warm spring /summer season. Foreign vessels, usually from England and Holland, used the good weather, when the ocean wasn't blocked by ice, to bring finished goods from Europe to trade for Russian timber, furs, and other raw material. Peter went aboard these ships and met their crews. He came back again to Archangel the next year and helped build a ship there.

In the fall of 1694, the largest Army maneuvers ever held, in which thirty thousand troops were deployed, were held near Moscow. Frustration with an ocean port that was open only in warm weather, the availability now of a trained Army, the failure of Sophia's two campaigns against the Tartars, and the continued marauding by the Tartars in the south, were the topics of conversation at the German suburb that winter. The resulting plan was for a new military thrust in the South. The objective was to be the Turkish southern stronghold of Azov, which blocked Russian access to the Black Sea. It was on the bank of the Don River, fifteen miles from the Sea of Azov.

Peter's Azov Army was to travel south using the Don River. Another, larger army, led by Boris Seremetev, was to come by land. Seremetev's objective was to capture enemy forts on the Dnieper River to the east and draw Tartar attention from the Azov army. The Azov army was in three divisions and each had a separate commander.

Although two supporting forts at Azov were captured, the campaign failed due to the divided command, supply problems, and the Streltsy not wanting to take orders from Peter's foreign officers. There was also a costly betrayal by a Dutch seaman who had been close to Peter and knew the disposition and habits of the Russian Army. Finally, in

October, Peter gave up his siege of Azov. However, he kept a strong garrison in the two captured forts, signaling he would be back. Seremetev's efforts in the east had been more successful. He captured all the enemy forts on the Dnieper River.

Peter set to work to make preparations for a new attempt on Azov the next year. In the winter too, Peter's co-Tsar, Ivan V died, leaving Peter to reign alone.

Peter's war efforts for 1697 were extensive. He built a supporting fleet at Voronezh on the Don River above Azov, appointed Alexis Shein, a boyer from a distinguished Russian family as supreme commander, and imported siege experts from Austria. It also helped that the Turks, following Peter's failure the year before, did little to improve their defenses during the winter.

In 1697, the assault on Azov succeeded, and Peter won his first Turkish stronghold, which had blocked Russia's way to the Black Sea.

After the capture of Azov, Peter announced a great shipbuilding program that would give Russia a fleet that could challenge the Turks in the Black Sea. To bring the necessary skills to Russia to build such a fleet, he sent young Russian men to Europe to learn the necessary crafts. They were to return with certificates attesting to their newly acquired skills.

In addition, Peter, responding to his own inclination, let himself be persuaded by Lefort and others of his foreign advisors that he himself travel to Europe. Holland and England were of special importance since they had the reputation for being the best ship builders. An interest in developing allies against the Turks also played a part in this decision. Except to go to war, it was very unusual for a reigning monarch of a major nation to voluntarily absent himself from his kingdom for a long period of time.

In order to avoid formalities, Peter decided to travel incognito. He would be just another member of the Grand Embassy.

Misunderstanding at Riga

City Fortifications
Riga
Livonia (now Latvia)
April, 1697

Peter's wish to travel incognito (to facilitate his freedom of movement and reduce time spent on formalities) often clashed with his expectation that his rank entitled him to his usual deference. This happened at his first stop, the strongly fortified Swedish city of Riga.

It had been hazy and raining in the morning, but now, in the afternoon, there was a drizzle and a slight chill in the air as Peter stood on top of a rampart. He was measuring and sketching the defenses protecting Riga's fortress. The twenty-four year old Tsar, for the first time, was seeing a fortress designed on the principles developed by Vaudon, the great, French fortress designer.

This fortress was unlike the straight walls between towers used to protect Russian cities. Here the bastions were constructed with angles so that firing from inside overlapped, and attackers could be subjected to firing from more than one side. The whole complex of moats, ramparts, and bastions was carefully designed. Attackers would incur the maximum number of casualties before the citadel could be breached and captured.

Peter moved about the fortification and moats taking measurements of everything and drawing details to develop an understanding for future reference. Suddenly, he was confronted by a Swedish soldier who told this tall stranger to stop what he was doing and move along. Peter treated him as he would any common soldier, he ignored him and continued making entries in his notebook. The soldier raised his musket and warned Peter to stop and move on or he would be shot.

Peter became upset, believing it was an insult and a breach of hospitality. The incident was reported to the Governor of Riga, Eric Dahlberg. The Governor apologized and explained that since Peter insisted on traveling incognito, the soldier was only carrying out his orders. No slight was intended since the sentry didn't know Peter was the Tsar of Russia.

There were further consultations between senior members of the Grand Embassy and the Swedish authorities. Adding to Peter's frustration, the Swedish Governor had not been informed in advance of the Grand Embassy's size. Things were finally smoothed over, but Peter sulked over his treatment.

Entertainment for the Grand Embassy was also limited because the harvest had been poor. In addition, Peter had missed the official greeting ceremony. Finally, ice in the River Dvina trapped Peter there longer than he intended. It all made for Tsar Peter becoming impatient, frustrated, and unhappy. Forever after, Riga was a sore spot for him.

The fortifications of Riga are nearly all gone now, but there is still a beautiful area of the city that Peter saw where the old buildings and churches still stand. There are also wonderful architectural details that are worth seeing.

Agreement at Sea-Koningsburg

Elector Frederick's Yacht
Konigsberg Harbor
Brandenburg
Spring, 1697

Peter was meeting with Elector Frederick of Brandenburg while sailing aboard the Elector's yacht on a warm and breezy afternoon in the harbor of Konigsberg. Frederick had traveled to Konigsberg from Berlin, his capital, expressly to convince Tsar Peter of their common interests. Peter had gone to Konigsberg in advance of the other members of his Grand Embassy.

Frederick had used the private time with Peter to discuss the important issue of a new treaty of alliance with him. However, Peter had demurred on a new treaty, and it was this afternoon that Frederick planned to take up the subject again.

Peter had not felt warmly welcomed in Riga. The next stop at Mitau, in the Duchy of Courland, had been better. The Duke of Courland had done his utmost to entertain the Tsar and his Embassy. Frederick proved to be even a warmer and more generous host. Frederick had provided a handsomely furnished house and took Peter hunting.

At Peter's request, he had put his artillery expert, Colonel Streltner Von Sternfeld, at Peter's disposal to teach him ballistics. Peter spent days firing cannons of various sizes while Von Strenfeld made corrections. When the full Russian Embassy arrived, Frederick greeted them with a lavish dinner and fireworks and granted them a generous expense allowance.

However, Frederick had not been successful in persuading the Embassy's ambassadors to sign the alliance he wanted. Now, he had invited Peter to a private afternoon sail aboard his yacht and to press again for an alliance treaty with Russia. Frederick knew Peter enjoyed being out on the water and hoped the sail would make him more agreeable. Frederick told him that Peter's efforts in the Black Sea won't do much for Russia's trade, and Baltic ports, now under Swedish control, would do substantially more. "Sweden is the common enemy of Russia and Brandenburg. Poland is beholden to Sweden and can't be counted on to be of help to Russia. Brandenburg is Russia's natural ally." He also said that helping Frederick strengthen himself by achieving recognition as" King," rather than "Elector," from Leopold, the Holy Roman Emperor in Vienna, would work to Russia's advantage.

Peter was reluctant to antagonize Sweden while he was still at war with the Turks. He did agree to treat Frederick's ambassadors at the same level of protocol as Russia's were in Brandenburg. This was helpful for Frederick in dealing with Emperor Leopold. Finally, Peter yielded somewhat, and an agreement to help each other against their common enemies was decided upon. The afternoon had been a success!

Peter stayed on in Konigsberg longer than expected because of an unsettled matter in Poland. The throne of Poland had been empty since last year, and France was promoting a French Prince for King. Austria, the German States, and Russia didn't want this French influence in Eastern Europe. For Peter it would end Polish help against the Turks. Peter moved Russian troops to the Polish border to make his point.

After spending seven weeks in Konigsberg, word went out that Elector Augustus of Saxony had been chosen King of Poland. Peter left immediately for Holland by coach. He would like to have traveled by ship, but French warships in the Baltic made this hazardous.

Grand Embassy

In August 1697, Peter arrived in Holland and stayed with the Dutch for almost five months. During this time, he and some of his companions helped build a ship, starting with assembling the material and ending with sailing the completed vessel. Peter's main purpose in coming to Holland was to learn shipbuilding and, perhaps, enlist Dutch help in fighting the Turks. He also learned a great deal about government and religious freedom, and what these disciplines contribute to a prosperous and vigorous society.

Holland had a population of only two million people when Peter arrived but enjoyed great prosperity. Thousands of Dutch ships brought in raw material from all parts of the world and sent back finished goods. Not only the oceans but also the rivers of Europe led to Holland. Wool from Spain and Ireland was woven; tin from England and iron from Sweden was processed; timber from Russia and Norway became lumber; and much more. Insurance, credit, bills of lading, and public financing supported this commercial activity.

The skilled manpower for these enterprises was available, in part, because Dutch farm production was so bountiful, only one in three people was needed for agriculture. The Dutch worked hard and fought hard to produce and protect their wealth. A strong standing army and the second largest navy in the world provided a powerful defense.

Holland was a constant source of wonder and knowledge for Peter. When not working in the shipyard, he met with architects, engravers, engineers, merchants, and others. He visited sawmills, paper mills, laboratories and museums, always wanting to know, "how does it work, what does it do?" He watched surgeons and dentists at work. He became so interested that thereafter he always carried around a kit of surgical tools and offered to help if someone complained of a toothache or required minor surgery. His associates learned not to mention their ailments if they didn't want their Tsar peering down their throats.

An extraordinary man whom Peter met in Holland was William of Orange, the Stadholder (elected leader) of Holland and, at the same time, King of England. He had come to power in Holland when Louis XIV, the French Catholic "Sun King," set out, in 1672, with an army of one hundred and ten thousand to conquer small, Protestant Holland. The Dutch commercial preeminence was an affront and created jealousy in larger France, which had Europe's biggest population of seventeen million people.

The French army advanced steadily across Holland, capturing its cities, destroying its fortresses, and advancing within twenty-five miles of Amsterdam. At this critical time, William was selected to defend the country, and made the tough decision to open the dikes and flood the countryside. Many Dutch farms and animals were destroyed, but the French Army was stopped. Young William had won. From then on, William's overriding concern was to enlist support from other countries against any future threat from France.

Later, due to internal squabbles in England between Protestants and Catholics, William's wife, Mary, came to the throne of England. William came along as King, when she refused to rule alone as Queen. Peter knew the history of William and had great respect for him.

The two monarchs got along in spite of their differences in age. By this time, William was twenty years older than Peter. Unfortunately, the Dutch weren't willing to support the Russians against the Turks, which was Peter's main objective in foreign policy. The Dutch weren't willing to spread their resources, which they needed against France.

Although Peter admired Dutch ships, his concern was that they relied on the skill of the individual shipwright. He wanted plans and drawings that could be taken back to Russia and copied. This was how England built ships. Accordingly, Peter asked William if he might visit England, and William readily agreed.

Peter went to England in January 1698. His journey across the channel was on the H.M.S Yorke, the largest warship on which he had ever sailed. It's handling was of great interest to him, and he even climbed into the rigging during the crossing constantly asking questions. Vice Admiral Sir David Mitchell commanded during the voyage. When they arrived in England, Peter asked William for Mitchell to be his escort and translator while there.

London, where Peter spent most of his time while in England, was very crowded, dirty, and boisterous. The streets were narrow. Garbage was often thrown from the windows. Traffic on the narrow streets could become very difficult and when carriages met, going in opposite directions, there was much shouting and bellowing. It could also be a dangerous place. Public hangings and floggings were regular occurrences, attracting crowds and people who paid for windows and places with the best views. Cockfights and bloody battles between dogs and other beasts attracted gambling.

Religion divided the nation between Catholics and the Church of England. Protestants further divided themselves into various factions. England's safety as an island and its growing fleet, were helping it emerge as a world power. It had recovered from its political crises that saw Charles I beheaded. It had an increasingly powerful legislative body, its Parliament. The emerging freedom of expression contributed to great strides in industrial progress. English craftsmanship was developing a reputation.

As in Holland, Peter spent his time not only in the Deptford shipyard but looked into all sides of English life. Peter observed closely two particular aspects of life in England, government and religion. King William took Tsar Peter to Parliament where he observed William surrounded by members debating the issues of the day. He was impressed with the open discussion between Parliament members and their monarch, but said that he couldn't tolerate the limits placed on a King's power.

The practice of religion also drew Peter's interest, and he attended services of different denominations. The Church of England hoped to persuade him to their beliefs, but, although Peter had misgivings about the Russian Orthodox Church, his interests in other religious practices didn't go that far. Peter's rule as an autocrat stemmed from his "selection by God" through God's instrument, the Russian Orthodox Church. He wasn't likely to jeopardize how he had been selected as Tsar. Accordingly, while the practice of government and religion in England was interesting to him, a fundamental change in Russian Orthodoxy or government wasn't going to happen.

Peter also made a new friend in England, Peregrine Osborner, Marquis of Camarthen. Osbourne contributed much to Peter's visit to England by being not only useful but also fun. He was young and a fine seaman. He was the designer for the yacht being built for Peter, The Royal Transport. In addition, he was a great drinker and carouser. He introduced Peter to brandy with pepper, which he learned to love. Peter also enjoyed being with a prominent actress, who moved in with him. Peter seems to have had more fun in England than with the more serious Dutch.

He signed a trade agreement for English tobacco importation into Russia, which yielded the immediate revenue that the Grand Embassy's coffers sorely needed. Unfortunately, Peter and his companions, whom he had frequently reminded to be on their best behavior during the European tour, forgot themselves in the beautiful home given them for lodging in London, Sayes Court. When they finally left, the place was in shambles.

Peter learned and received much from his stay in England, but he was disappointed not to get support for his campaign against the Turks. In fact, King William helped to promote peace between the Turks and Austria. This was in line with his objective to concentrate against the French. Although this annoyed Peter, he still gave William a new, large, uncut diamond upon leaving.

Peter stopped briefly in Amsterdam to collect his Grand Embassy. Starting east, he made important stops in Dresden, capital of Saxony; Rawa, Poland where Augustus, the new King of Poland, was staying; Vienna, to see the Holy Roman Emperor Leopold I, and finally Venice. He left Amsterdam May 1698.

The new King of Poland, Augustus, was also the Elector of Saxony and had his capital in Dresden. He was not present but had left instructions for his representative, Prince Furstenberg, to receive Tsar Peter. Augustus was the newly crowned King of Poland, in part because of Peter's support, and wanted Peter made welcome in his absence.

Saxony was a wealthy state due to the metals, particularly silver, which were mined there. One of the manifestations of this wealth was the collection of valuable and extraordinary objects that had been accumulated in the "Green Vault." The name came from the color of the walls in the rooms that housed this treasury. During WW II, it was taken by the Soviets as a war prize but was later returned to their ally of the time, East Germany. When I viewed it, it was in temporary quarters before being returned to its traditional rooms. The collection is stunning, and it must have dazzled Peter as it does every viewer, not only with the precious stones, gold and silver, but also the craftsmanship of how they are mounted. Rare books, precious clocks, and all kinds of swords, vases and many other valuable items are included.

Peter's next stop was Vienna, Austria, the Capital of the Holy Roman Empire. The current Emperor, Leopold I, was very sensitive to his position. The Holy Roman Empire traced its history back to Charlemagne. The Hapsburg dynasty had worn its crown for three hundred years. It made all other rulers seem to be latecomers. Although the power of the Empire was diminished from its heyday, it still had great prestige and lingering influence.

Austrians were eager to make peace with the Turks in order to concentrate their efforts on the growing power of France. Peter could not get them to agree to support his Black Sea campaign and settled for being advised in advance about any Austrian and Turkish treaty.

While in Vienna, Peter was also told that there had been a revolt of the Streltsy near Moscow. Just as he was planning to change his travel plans and speed up his return to Russia, he received the news that the revolt had been crushed. Peter decided to maintain his plans to meet with Augustus.

Augustus, the man Peter met in Rawa, was as physically imposing as Peter. Augustus was referred to as "Augustus the Strong" due to his powerful physique, which enabled him to perform such feats of strength as bending horseshoes. Augustus enjoyed women and practical jokes. He was twenty-eight when he and Peter met. They were contemporaries, Peter now being twenty-five. Augustus and Peter drank together in the evening and got along well on a personal level, immediately.

The country, Poland, to which Augustus had been elected King, was an anomaly. It was a large country and its population of eight million was about equal to that of Russia. It was one of the largest in Europe. However, it was a country deeply fragmented by religion and ethnic backgrounds. Germans, Lithuanians, Russians, and Jews made up half the population. Each had their own religion, and vied with the Polish half of the population, which was Catholic.

The political situation was equally chaotic. The noblemen, who owned the land, had a legislative body, the Diet, which elected the King, subject to their terms for ruling. Tax collection, foreign policies, raising and maintaining an army were all subject to unanimous approval of this Diet. In battle the Polish army was brave, and their cavalry superb, but it was subject to becoming quickly larger or smaller depending upon an individual nobleman deciding whether to fight or not. As a result, Poland's influence in Europe didn't reflect its size or population, and its fragmented state frequently made it the battleground for its neighbors. The unreliability of the Polish Army made it fortunate that Augustus could call on his Saxon troops for support when necessary. Although these troops were limited in size, at least they obeyed without prolonged negotiation or discussion.

In future years, Augustus was not always a dependable ally even though Peter had supported Augustus in getting Poland's crown. Augustus developed a growing reputation in Europe for being unreliable, but the fluid situation in Poland and his tenuous hold on the crown may have contributed to his maneuvering.

Augustus used Peter's four days in Rawa to forge a strong friendship and to promote the idea of attacking Sweden in order to wrest away their Baltic possessions. Sweden's hold on these ports blocked both Poland and Russia from direct trade with the rest of Europe.

This was the same idea proposed by Frederick in Konigsberg, over a year ago. Now, however, Peter's visits with William of Orange and Emperor Leopold convinced him there would be no support of further action against the Turks. The fact that the Baltic ports had once belonged to Russia further whetted Peter's appetite to get them back. Finally, the new Swedish King, Charles XII, was only fifteen years old. For all these reasons (and the new friendship between Peter and Augustus), the direction of Peter's policy for a warm water port shifted from the Black to the Baltic Sea.

This momentous decision was one of the results of the Grand Embassy. Many others were important to the future of Russia. Peter was convinced now, more than ever, after seeing the style of life in the West, that Russia was far behind Europe and needed help in many areas. He brought hundreds of skilled workers back to Russia to speed up closing the gap. He recognized that the greater freedom in politics and religion in the west had helped release men's minds to achieve its progress. However, Peter was not prepared to reduce his power as an autocrat but instead would force change by his will and decree.

He immediately signaled that Russia was entering a dramatic new era. As the dignitaries and officials flocked to greet him, Peter suddenly produced a sharp barber razor and personally began shaving their beards. Although banning beards started in a light-hearted, jovial way, it soon became the law of the land. The clergy and peasants were exempted and government officials enforced the ban. Only the payment of an annual tax allowed the keeping of beards. A bronze medallion was worn around the neck to proclaim the wearer had paid to keep his beard.

The next Russian custom to receive his attention was clothing. At first, Peter encouraged those around him to get rid of the long caftans, with their wide sleeves. Instead, they wore waistcoats, breeches, and hats in the western style. After a time, fines, decrees and guards enforcing the new dress at the city gates made change in dress compulsory.

Peter also changed the calendar in line with the rest of Europe and minted new copper, silver and gold coins to give Russia a new national monetary system. These replaced the German and Dutch coins, which had made up much of Russia's previous currency.

His time in Europe, particularly when he was being entertained, gave Peter a greater awareness of the contributions women could make in a more open society. On his way from Konigsberg to Holland, he had been persuaded to have dinner near Hanover with two of Europe's most highborn women. This dinner gave Peter his first experience with aristocratic, western ladies. Sophia of Hanover, one of the women, was than sixty-seven and an energetic ruler of that important German state. Her son, George Louis, went on to succeed her and also became King George I of England.

The other woman, her daughter, Sophia-Charlotte was married to Peter's recent host, Frederick of Brandenburg. When Peter was introduced to these two intelligent, confident and dazzling ladies he was at first a little shy. However, they placed him between them at dinner and used their very considerable social skills to put him at ease.

The dinner lasted four hours and was followed by dancing. Although Peter came to Europe to learn about practical skills and crafts, this evening also opened his eyes to other lessons on a social level. The role of women blossomed when Peter returned to Russia. Also, many future royal Russian marriages were made with German royalty.

This made him particularly dissatisfied with his shy, introverted wife. He tried through others to convince her to take vows and enter a convent. However, she resisted and, in a face-to-face meeting with Peter, she declared that duty to her son required her not to abandon her role as wife or mother. Peter responded by taking the eight and half year old boy, Alexis, from her at the Kremlin and gave him to his sister, Natalya, to raise at Preobrazhenskoe. Shortly thereafter, Eudoxia was sent to Pokvovsky Monastery in Suzdal. Ten months later, she became a nun, her head was shaved, and she was given a new name, Helen.

Before Peter's return to Russia there had been a battle between the Streltsy and the Guards outside the New Jerusalem Monastery. The Streltsy surrendered after coming under heavy cannon fire. One hundred and thirty Streltsy were executed on the spot. Nearly two thousand were brought back to Moscow in chains. After the welcoming home celebrations, Peter turned his attention to dealing with these rebels.

First and foremost, Peter wanted to know, who was behind their action? Who was the person or persons likely to benefit from their revolt and might have motivated it? In particular, was it the old enemies of the Naryshkins, the Miloslavskys, and their most prominent member, Peter's half sister Sophia? To find out, Peter had the prisoners tortured and questioned. They were whipped, burned with a hot iron, and often their heads were chopped off. Peter watched from horseback.

One execution was unusual. As one of the Streltsy was led to an execution block, already stained with the blood of several men who had gone before, he kicked aside a head in his way saying, "Out of the way, I have need for this space myself." Peter seeing and hearing this asked the man his name and the reason he could be so calm. He replied, "My name is Orlov and if my death this way is what my Tsar wants, I am glad to die." Peter was so impressed with the man's courage, he spared his life and placed him in a Guard Regiment. Sixty years later, five grandsons of Orlov would be serving in various Guard Regiments.

They were the leading conspirators in deposing Peter's grandson, Peter III, and putting his grandson's wife, Catherine, on the throne.

One person whose interrogation was handled by Peter personally was Sophia. He went to the Novodevichy Monastery and threatened her with death to reveal what she had done or what she knew about the Streltsy uprising. She revealed nothing. Peter wouldn't kill her and certainly wouldn't torture her. He did force her to shave her head and take religious vows as Sister Susanna. She was permitted no visitors. He hung three of the Streltsy ringleaders outside her window where the bodies remained all winter. She died six years later, in 1704, at age forty-seven.

Ilya Repin, Russia's great realistic painter, painted a picture of Sophia many years later. It depicts her at the Novodevivhi Monastery standing next to a barred window, through which can be seen one of the three Streltsy hanged there. It shows a stout, middle-aged woman, beautifully dressed with a fierce stare and the expression of anger that reveals her hatred for Peter. It can be seen today at the National Tretyakov Gallery in Moscow.

After the winter, Peter turned his attention briefly south again to the Black Sea. He had built a fleet at Voronezh to battle the Turks, and sail out to the waters of the Black Sea. But now Europe had made peace with the Turks in order to deal with the threat of the French "Sun King." Finally, Peter agreed to the,"Treaty of Constantinople" which allowed Russia to keep Azov but didn't give it Kerch or access to the Black Sea. Russia no longer paid tribute to the Tartar Khan, and the Russian ambassador to Constantinople was placed on an equal footing to those of England, Holland, France and Austria.

It was the best Peter could do here and freed his attention to face north and the Baltic.

Alliance against Sweden

A Livonian nobleman, Johann Reinhold von Patkul, did much of the work developing a plan to topple Sweden from its position in the Baltic Sea. He resented that the Swedish crown had reduced the land governed by the local aristocracy in order to increase the Swedish monarchy's revenues. This "reduction" began in 1680 and was applied to not only Sweden, but also Swedish-held Livonia. Patkul was sent by Livonia's aristocracy to plead their case but was unsuccessful. Thereafter, he dedicated himself to bringing about Livonia's freedom from Sweden. Even if not independent, he felt Livonia should at least be part of a kingdom of a more liberal monarchy. He was realistic enough to know that, small as it was, Livonia couldn't become independent of Sweden without help.

Poland, now ruled by Augustus, himself a German, seemed a likely ally. Frederick IV of Denmark, whose former Duchy of Holstein-Gottrop had been taken by Sweden, was another possibility. Finally Russia, which he knew had once had the Baltic ports now held by Sweden, could be expected to join in a war to get them back. The alliance Patkul put together lined up this way.

Frederick IV of Denmark, in the west, was persuaded to attack south to recapture the Duchy of Holstein-Gottrop and then cross the sound and attack Sweden's southern providence of Scania. Augustus, Elector of Saxony and King of Poland, was to use his Saxon Army to capture the city of Riga, Livonia. Augustus planned to add Livonia to his Polish kingdom and hoped the grateful Polish nobleman would make his Polish title hereditary. Peter would attack in Ingria, in the southeast area of the Gulf of Finland, seize the Baltic port of Narva, and clear the eastern Baltic of Swedish troops. What further encouraged the members of this alliance was that the Swedish King was now an eighteen-year-old boy, untried and untested. These monarchs had great respect for the Swedish Army, but felt it would lack leadership.

Three separate theatres of war against formidable enemies, and Sweden had to contend with them at the same time while being led by a young boy. It appeared to be a good plan to the alliance.

Charles, the young King, was raised by his father to be the King of Sweden and to be the head of its Army. His early childhood took into account his destiny. As a boy, he rode by his father at military reviews. He hunted and killed his first bear when he was eleven years old. His young mother died the same year, and his education and upbringing in hardy, military pursuits intensified.

After the death of his mother, the future King's father took a keener interest in his surviving children, Charles and his two daughters. Charles was the major recipient of this attention. He became a student of the military pursuits, a fine horseman, and an avid hunter. His tutors also found him intelligent, but as he matured, he liked to get his way and could be obstinate.

Charles was only fourteen when his father died. He was expected to receive the crown, when he was eighteen, as Charles XII. In the meantime, Regency Council was appointed to rule. This divided authority didn't work out, and, at the age of fifteen, Charles became King.

His thirst for adventure and his daring nature revealed itself early. He would test himself by riding off alone and sometimes getting into trouble. On one occasion his horse fell in the snow, pinning him down. When he was finally found, he was half frozen. He attacked bears with only a pitchfork. He also led military games and trained with Sweden's elite Royal Cavalry Guards, the Drabats. His madcap pursuits often were in company with another officer, Count Arvid Horn, whom we shall meet again.

The kingdom Charles inherited possessed most of the major eastern Baltic ports, the surrounding territories, and Finland. These ports controlled much of the trade in the Baltic Sea. The taxes and revenues collected made the Swedish kingdom and its merchants exceedingly prosperous.

He also inherited one of Europe's finest armies. Although only a nation of two million, the Swedish army was esteemed throughout Europe. It was highly trained, and, along with Charles, believed that death only came at your appointed hour. Training, discipline, and this belief gave them the courage to steadily advance in a deployed line, fire their muskets when in close range, and then charge with cold steel into the enemy lines. Most enemies reeled before this relentless attack, panicked, and ran. The King was expected to use this superb weapon to protect his nation's prosperity and defend its territories.

Young Charles was hunting in the forest when he was advised that King Augustus of Poland had invaded Swedish Livonia, without a declaration of war. This offended his sense of honor, and he made a promise to his council never to start an unjust war and also not to end one until his enemy was overcome. A few weeks later, he heard Frederick IV of Denmark had marched south and threatened Sweden's possessions there.

Charles decided to invade Denmark first, threaten the Danish capital of Copenhagen, and then deal with Augustus. Frederick had expected to prevent this with his superior Danish fleet, which would prevent Swedish troops from crossing over the channel separating the two countries.

However, William of Orange sent a combined Dutch and English fleet to aid Charles in order to prevent a prolonged war, which would divert resources from the effort against France. Charles trained his army tenaciously and refitted them with new muskets and bayonets. In July, protected by the Dutch and English fleets, the Swedish army crossed over to Denmark and besieged Copenhagen. The Danish King Frederick, with his fleet checkmated, his capital besieged, and his army away in the south, capitulated and signed the Peace of Travendal on August 18, 1700.

The Swedish Army withdrew back to Sweden, and Charles turned his attention to Augustus. About this time, Charles also learned that Russia had declared war on Sweden and was threatening Narva.

On October 1, Charles embarked for Livonia to deal with Augustus, who during the summer had threatened the major Swedish stronghold of Riga. Storms and bad weather hindered ship movement in the Baltic Sea at this time of year. Charles had difficulty moving his Army to the port of Pernau, near Riga, which he was using as his staging area.

However, by this time, Augustus had heard of the withdrawal of his Danish ally from the conflict. He lifted the siege of Riga, withdrawing his Army into winter quarters and deciding to wait out developments. Two of the three enemies that had challenged Sweden and its young King were now no longer a threat.

Augustus' disinterest in fighting frustrated Charles. He had hoped to win additional laurels for his fighting skills and decided this was not to be denied. Since Pernau was about the same distance from Narva as Riga, Charles decided to launch a winter campaign against the Russians. Charles hurriedly pulled together the soldiers arriving from Sweden, along with troops from the no longer besieged Riga. On November 13, he set off on the one hundred and fifty mile march to the endangered city of Narva. He had just over ten thousand troops.

In the meantime, Tsar Peter surrounded Narva with a large army and built a wall and trench four miles long, facing out from Narva, for protection. Peter started an artillery bombardment in early November. It did not go well. The gun carriages fell apart, ammunition ran out, and the guns became silent. The muddy roads and the poor condition of the horses slowed the arrival of new supplies.

When Peter heard that Augustus had given up his campaign against Riga, and that Charles was now free to march against him, he dispatched Sheremetev, with five thousand cavalry, west for reconnaissance of any Swedish relieving force. Although Sheremetev's cavalry force was sizable, he avoided engaging the Swedes, or even harassing them, in the three passes through which they had to travel. Peter's orders had been to observe only and return to the main camp at Narva to keep the Russian army intact.

As the Swedish Army got close, Peter unexpectedly announced he was going to Novgorod and taking the Russian commander, Fedor Golovin. Golovin was also his foreign minister. Peter appointed a foreigner, Duc du Croy, as commander. Croy was an experienced soldier and aristocrat from the Spanish Netherlands. He was sent by Augustus as an observer. The explanation Peter gave for leaving was that he wanted to speed up reinforcements and that no one expected an immediate Swedish attack.

Croy was not eager to assume command. He spoke no Russian and was not happy with how the Russian army was so thinly deployed around the four-mile perimeter of the camp. However, Peter insisted he take command, and he finally agreed. Peter left. The next day, November 19, the Swedish Army reached the village of Laguna, seven miles west of Narva. The Swedish troops were wet from the cold, soaking rain and splattered with mud. It didn't matter. The following day they appeared at Navra and the battle began almost immediately.

First Battle of Narva

Swedish Fortress/City
West Bank of Narva River
Eight-Miles Inland From Baltic Sea
November 20, 1700

At 2 p.m., Charles XII, King of Sweden, ordered his Army of ten thousand men to attack the forty thousand Russian soldiers besieging the Swedish garrison of Narva.

The Swedes had arrived on the battlefield after marching east seven miles in a cold rain from their overnight camp at Lagena. The Russian commanders hadn't expected an attack so soon. The audacious, swift attack would become the hallmark of the young Swedish King.

The Russians were spread out over a four-mile, half circle around the Narva fortress. The other half of the circle was the Narva River, already icy cold this time of year. Charles ordered his Swedish infantry to concentrate and storm into the center of the spread out Russian force. Once inside, they were to divide: half would swing north and half south, rolling up the Russian forces in the ensuing chaos.

Just as the attack started, a blizzard rose from behind the Swedes straight into the face of the Russians. Blinded by the storm, the Russians, behind their earthworks, were surprised by the suddenness of the attack. At thirty paces, the Swedes raised their muskets and fired at the Russians who were up on their earthworks. The fast moving Swedes then dropped branches into the ditches and climbed over them to get at the Russians with bayonets and swords. As the Swedes pressed forward, a breach developed in the Russian line. Fresh Swedish troops poured into this breach, and then, as planned, the Swedes divided themselves, with half swinging north and the other half swinging south.

The Streltsy regiments were concentrated in the south and were quickly routed. Sheremetev's cavalry, which was stationed behind the Streltsy infantry, panicked at the suddenness and fury of the Swedish attack. They retreated into the river where thousands of men and horses drowned.

The Swedes, advancing north also caused panic among the Russians who didn't expect to be fighting inside their own camp. Thousands of Russians fled across the river and over the single bridge, which soon collapsed. Within the camp, the terrified Russians began blaming the foreign officers and, with the bickering, discipline collapsed among most of the troops in the camp.

Only at the northern end had a Russian stronghold been quickly established by troops of the elite Preobrazhensky and Semyonovsky Guard regiments. To subdue them, Swedish cannons were brought up. This proved unnecessary. Negotiations allowed the Russians to surrender and leave with their small arms.

Actually, Charles was glad to put an end to the fight, since he realized he was still heavily outnumbered. Had any disciplined group of Russians with leadership started to attack the tired Swedes, things might have gone differently. However, leadership and discipline were absent among the Russians that day.

The wet, cold, and tired Swedish soldiers were also glad to see an end to the day's fighting. They quickly found the large supply of vodka the fleeing Russians left behind and celebrated their victory. Charles was exulted. His reputation soared in Europe with his victories over three major opponents in a few months!

How did it happen?

The Swedish infantry was the best in Europe. They got themselves organized and their attack started before the Russians knew what hit them. The Russians were commanded by a general appointed the day before–he couldn't speak or understand Russian. Russian troops were inexperienced; the unexpected appearance of the Swedish soldiers inside their camp panicked them; and Russian rifle fire into the swirling snow was ineffective. Also, leadership by their own King inspired the Swedish troops.

The Great Northern War

Both monarchs learned from the Russian debacle at Narva, which shaped their decisive conflict at Paltova nine years later. Peter was leery of depending on allies in the future, reflecting his disappointment in the efforts of King Frederick of Denmark and King Augustus of Poland. Also, the swift, successful attack of the Swedish Army against an entrenched force outnumbering them about five to one, and in appalling weather conditions, was a stunning shock. Peter's new respect for Charles XII and the Swedish Army was responsible for his heavy demands in developing a modern Russian Army. This meant great sacrifices by all classes of society in the nation.

The lessons Charles XII took from his first campaigns were: reliance on the swift attack, under almost any circumstances; confidence in his own military leadership; and disdain for Peter and the Russians as soldiers. The three adversaries of Charles XII had badly misjudged him. He turned out to be a daring and courageous soldier whose troops admired him, following his commands without hesitation.

The only good news for Peter, upon emerging from the first battle for Narva, was that the surrendering Russian soldiers were so numerous that the small Swedish force could only disarm them and send them off to nearby Russia. After a few weeks, twenty three thousand men of the vanquished Russian army were mustered in Novgorod. However, they lacked any equipment - tents, cannons, powder- and had only a limited number of small arms. A force of nearly eleven thousand men had been mustered from the Volga region but hadn't arrived in time for the battle. The arrival of Cossacks and the raising of new regiments quickly gave Peter the manpower for a new army of over fifty thousand.

The biggest problem was artillery. It had all been lost, causing Peter to issue a controversial order. He ordered churches and monasteries to provide a portion of their bells in order to immediately get the metal for new cannons. This dismayed many Russians, for whom their religion was important. Peter realized this would cause great unrest, but his determination to rebuild the army quickly was so strong that he went ahead anyway. Peter appointed Sheremetev to become head of the Russian army, while Peter concentrated his time on its training and equipment.

Meantime, Charles turned his attention and his army toward Poland. This allowed Peter's commander, Sheremetev, to institute military operations against the small force of Swedish field troops that Charles left behind to defend Livonia. Sheremetev was so successful that after a number of Russian victories, only the Swedish garrison cities of Riga, Pernau and Dorpat remained securely in Swedish hands. They were now unsupported by a field army. The Swedish ships in Lake Ladoga were also chased off.

There is a fortress taking up most of the land on an island where the Neva River starts down the channel from Lake Ladoga. The river empties into the delta at the Gulf of Finland, the eastern end of the Baltic Sea. The Neva River is only forty-five miles long, but it is a link to other rivers and lakes and allows passage to the vast northern territories of Russia, with its riches of metal, timber, furs, precious stones, and hemp. To protect this vital trade link, Novgorod had built a fortress on the island hundreds of years before and called it Oreshka. Sweden had captured it, securing its strategic location for itself. They renamed it Noteborg.

Having defeated the nearby Livonia Swedish Army, and with Charles and the main Swedish Army occupied in Poland, Peter attacked the small garrison defending the fortress at Noteborg. After ten days of bombardment with new siege guns, the fort surrendered and this strategic backdoor to the Gulf of Finland was captured. Peter was so thrilled by this victory that he renamed the city "Schlusselburg." Schlussel means "key" in German and Peter considered the control of the Neva River the key to access of the Baltic Sea, and thereby access to the West.

The island fortress of Schlusselburg was later used as a prison. Peter's half sister, Tsarevna Maria was held there. Later Empress Elizabeth imprisoned Ivan VI there. He was killed in 1764 during Catherine the Great's reign. Lenin's brother was hanged in the courtyard in 1887 for plotting to kill the Tsar. One cellblock remains today and a nice, older lady has made a cozy home in the corner cell. She offered me breakfast when I visited. There was fierce fighting around here during World War II and there is now a monument to Russia's defenders in the courtyard.

To secure the delta of the Neva River on the Gulf of Finland from attack, Peter immediately began construction of a fort on one of its many islands. He named it, "The Fortress of St. Peter and St. Paul." It was the first building in this desolate marsh area. "Neva" means swamp in Finnish, and, previously, only some Finnish fishermen lived here. However, in spite of its inhospitable nature as a building site, Peter's plans for the area grew as a result of Russia's need for a Baltic Sea port. Only an autocrat could command the enormous effort and resources building a city here required. Captured enemy soldiers and Russia serfs drove piles to provide a foundation for buildings, carved out canals, and hauled in the building materials needed. Thousands died in the construction effort. Sometimes strong winds and rain flooded the low land. Disease killed many.

Peter's ambitions for the city, however, continued to grow. He defended it against Swedish attacks, which came by land and sea, and had ships built, sailing them into the Gulf of Finland. Finally, he invited the nobles and members of his own royal family to build homes and live there.

During his military campaigns, Sheremetev captured a clergyman, Ernst Gluck, and his family. Included in their household was an attractive seventeen-year old girl who the pastor had brought into his family when she lost both her parents. Sheremetev took the girl into his own household, but, about six months later, Peter's close associate, Menshikov, noticed her. By now she had accepted the Orthodox faith and changed her name to Catherine. Soon her physical attributes began blossoming. Menshikov persuaded Sheremetev to let him "have" Catherine and she went home with him. Since Peter was often in Menshikov's home, Catherine came to Tsar Peter's notice. The same qualities that made her attractive to a Field Marshal and a future Prince also captivated a Tsar.

Catherine and Peter entered into a congenial relationship. She was his loving companion the rest of his life. He married her, and she was declared Empress upon his death. They had twelve children, one of whom became Empress Elizabeth.

During these early years of the eighteen-century, Peter was occupied with rebuilding his army; taking away pieces of the Swedish Empire in the eastern Baltic; improving his personal life; and finding ways to raise new taxes and manpower. He also wanted to broaden education among his subjects and to change social and cultural customs. In addition, he had to deal with rebellions, which occurred in the south, from time to time.

In the summer of 1704, Russia assaulted and captured both Narva and Dorpet. Peter was particularly happy to capture Narva. It revenged his earlier defeat and also confirmed that his efforts at rebuilding the Russian army were succeeding. This time the guns were fired without mishap, there was plenty of ammunition, the troops were disciplined, and there was no relieving Swedish Army. There is still a cross at Narva today erected to commemorate this Russian victory.

While Peter was busy in Russia and the eastern Baltic, what was Charles XII doing?

After his victory at Narva in 1700, Charles turned west toward Poland to defeat and humble Augustus. Here he won victory after victory and his military reputation continued to grow. However, Augustus and his Saxon Army always managed to slip away from a battlefield on which they were losing to fight another day. These battles were on Polish soil, so the country and its people suffered as the warring armies seized much of their food, ravaging the countryside.

Charles was told of the disasters befalling Swedish possessions and their people in the east at the hands of the Russians. He assured the messengers that he would soon set things right again after Augustus had been defeated and his Polish crown taken away. Finally, his mission to depose Augustus was accomplished. In 1704, the Polish Diet was persuaded to depose Augustus and select Stanislaus Leszezynk to replace him.

In December 1705, Charles was sufficiently satisfied with the situation in Poland to suddenly decide on a winter campaign in Russia. Nearly two hundred miles to the east, the Russian Army was settled in at Grodno where Charles planned to meet and defeat them. He set up camp within striking distance and awaited developments. Peter was in Moscow so the Russian command structure was not entirely clear. A European Field Marshal, Ogilvie, was to be in charge. But Menshikov was also present, and he and other Russian generals confused the situation. Augustus also arrived, and, as a King, Peter put him in overall command. Augustus promised that a Saxon Army would come to reinforce the Russians.

Supplies ran low, the Saxon Army didn't arrive, and Augustus left. News then reached Grodno that a small Swedish force of eight thousand troops, led by the Swedish General Rehnskjold (left behind by Charles in Poland), defeated a combined force of thirty thousand Saxon, Polish and Russian troops at Fraustadt, Poland. Peter got nervous when he learned this news and ordered his Grodno army to sink their cannons in the nearby river and retreat. Charles soon captured Grodno.

However, the participation of Augustus at Grodno made Charles resolve to return west to Poland and invade and capture Saxony, Augustus' homeland. He meant to firmly secure the area behind him before starting a major invasion of Russia.

He accomplished this at the cost of making Europe nervous about a Swedish Army thrusting into Saxony, far into the center of the continent. The Swedish Army camped in Saxony for a year, after which the Treaty of Altronstadt was signed. Augustus agreed to give up his Polish crown. The coordinator of the alliance against Sweden, the Livonian nobleman, Johann Reinhold Von Patkul, was shamefully given over to the Swedes for torture and execution. Charles now began serious preparations for a major invasion of Russia.

On August 27, 1707, seven years after his victory at Narva, Charles XII rode out of Alronstadt at the head of forty two thousand soldiers to invade Russia and capture Moscow. He decided to travel directly into the heart of his enemy's country rather than take the northern route near the Baltic Sea where he could receive supplies and be supported by the Swedish held ports. These areas had been the scenes of recent fighting, and he wanted to spare them the further devastation of a new conflict.

At first, when traveling through Poland and Lithuania, events developed as they had in the past. Peter wanted to avoid a major battle and not risk his Army outside Russia, so he moved them east. The

Russians tried to slow or stop the Swedes at river crossings, but Charles outflanked them and moved briskly ahead.

In July, after spending the winter encamped near Minsk, Charles and the Russians fought the battle of Golovchin at the River Bovisov. Charles led the Swedish attack personally and won. Europe noted the news of another victory by Charles over the Russians.

However, this battle revealed the fruits of Peter's hard labor in building a new Russian Army. They had stood their ground and retreated in orderly fashion. Most important, Russian casualties could be replaced, while the Swedish Army was far from home and manpower losses and equipment couldn't be replaced. Furthermore, the countryside was scorched, and the Swedes couldn't live off the land. As Charles advanced, the lack of replacements and supplies wore down his Army.

Charles planned to solve these problems by being reinforced from Riga by twelve and a half thousand Swedish troops led by General Lewenhaupt. Lewenhaupt's orders were to collect food and ammunition in wagons for his own needs and to replenish the main Swedish Army. Lewenhaupt was to make this journey of about four hundred miles in two months, leaving in June and arriving in August. Instead, the column moved sluggishly south with its heavy wagons, and in late September was engaged by the Russians. This engagement, the Battle of Lesnaya, was a disaster for the Swedes. The supplies were lost and only half of Lewenhaupt's command, six thousand men, finally reached Charles. These extra men now added to his supply problems.

A northern Swedish Army of fourteen thousand in Finland, under Swedish General Lybecker, was ordered to attack St. Petersburg to divert the Russian Army. This also failed due to the Russian's scorched earth policies and hesitancy when facing the defenses of a fortified city. The Swedes returned to Finland by ship, having lost three thousand men and six thousand horses.

Charles now gave up his plans to strike directly at Moscow, and turned south to the Ukraine where he hoped to replenish his supplies. He had missed the best summer campaigning months. A Cossack Hetman, Mazeppa, defected to Charles, and he now looked for other allies in the South, particularly among the Tartars. A severe winter and some inconclusive minor battles finally brought Charles and his hungry, depleted army to the outskirts of the town of Poltava. It was sited on two bluffs overlooking the Vorskla River, a tributary of the Dnieper River. Charles besieged the city hoping to lure the main Russian Army to battle.

Peter did arrive with the Russian Army and established a strong entrenched camp near the town of Yakovtsy, four miles north of Poltava and the Swedish Army. There were thirty two thousand Russian infantry in the camp and ten thousand cavalry nearby.

An event then occurred that was to have a major influence on the coming battle. King Charles was shot in the heel of his foot while on his horse reconnoitering the Russian troops. The bullet went through his foot, but Charles delayed returning to his camp and getting treatment. The delay caused the wound to become infected, and there was serious doubt if Charles would live. He recovered but couldn't mount his horse.

The total strength of the Swedish Army by now had been reduced to twenty five thousand men. They were hungry, tired, and much of their powder was wet. King Charles decided to give battle and stake everything on a quick victory over his enemy, as he had always done before. Due to his inability to mount his horse, Charles had to give command of his army to his senior commander, Field Marshall Rehnskjold. Instead of commanding only the cavalry, Rehnskjold now had to control the entire army, issuing orders to generals accustomed to receiving them from their King. Charles and Rehnskjold decided on a swift march north and a surprise attack. Unfortunately, Rehnskjold didn't inform his subordinate commanders of this plan.

The men that had to be left behind to guard the baggage train and continue the siege of Poltava also reduced the attacking army. King Charles would be carried on a litter to the battle, accompanied by a small escort.

Victory at Poltava

Russian Entrenched Camp
Near Village of Yakovtsy
Poltava, Russia
June 28, 1709

During the night before the battle, Peter had ten, small, earthen redoubts (small forts) constructed so that the attacking Swedes would need to march past them to reach Peter's main camp. A few hundred Russians, and one or two cannons, manned each of these small forts. They were designed to provide early warning of the Swedes coming and serve as a distraction that would occupy the Swedes for a time. Behind these forts, Peter stationed some of his cavalry who attacked and harassed the advancing Swedes.

The small forts made the attacking Swedes split their forces. However, instead of bypassing them, the Swedes lost time and men by seriously assaulting them. One substantial Swedish force never made it to the main battlefield and was both isolated and almost annihilated. Another large group of the Swedish infantry only rejoined the main force after veering off to the east and beginning a premature attack on the southern rampart of the main Russian camp. The lack of coordination by the Swedes reflected a lack of communication between Rehnskjold and his subordinates. The Russian cavalry, under the command of an aggressive Menshikov, also succeeded in delaying the Swedish attack.

When Marshall Rehnskjold finally formed up for his main attack, it no longer was a surprise. Moreover, he now had only about five thousand infantry.

Rehnskjold, at this point, decided that he had too few troops to attack Peter's soldiers (about thirty thousand entrenched behind earth ramparts in their main camp). Rehnskjold planned to put off battle until he could reinforce his main army. He planned to muster nearby

Swedish troops from the trenches facing Poltava, and those guarding the baggage train with others scattered elsewhere. The main body of the Swedish army formed into marching columns and prepared to withdraw southward away from Peter's camp.

Peter, seeing this Swedish maneuver, decided to lure the Swedes into immediate attack by attacking them while they were strung out in marching formation. Peter ordered the camp entrances opened up, bridges over the defensive trenches put down, and his troops formed into a battle line in front of the camp. This was quickly and efficiently done, reflecting the enormous effort Peter had put into his army and their training since Narva. Artillery was interspersed among the infantry and some kept behind on the ramparts to fire at the Swedes over the Russian heads.

The Swedes, seeing this Russian deployment and not wanting to be attacked while they were in marching formation, quickly regrouped back into battle line and prepared to attack the Russians. The five thousand Swedish infantry, now facing the Russians, was a thin line supported by fourteen regiments of cavalry with no cannons. In front of them, in two rows, were twenty-four thousand Russians with seventy cannons and cavalry support on both flanks. Tsar Peter was mounted on a horse behind the left side of the Russian lines. King Charles was on a litter behind the Swedish lines. It was as close as the two monarchs ever came to meeting. On the right, the Swedish infantry commander, Lewenhaupt, hoped to break through the Russian line at some point, create confusion, and scatter the larger force. Swedish courage and cold steel had done this successfully many times in the past.

The Swedish infantry started forward just after 10 a.m. and were greeted by Russian cannonballs and musket fire. Still, the Swedes came forward, ignoring their thinning ranks. The right side reached the Russian front rank and began stabbing and thrusting with bayonets and swords. Lewenhaupt looked around for cavalry support while checking on how the left side of the attacking Swedish line was doing. The Swedish cavalry failed to appear at this critical moment, reflecting the lack of Swedish battlefield communication. The left side of the attacking Swedish infantry was being shot to pieces by the Russian artillery that had been more concentrated on that side.

The uneven pace of the Swedish attack now created a gap between the faster moving right and the lagging left. The right side became separated from the left, and Russians from the second defensive line flowed through the gap to surround the Swedes and systematically cut them down. Only a small detachment of Swedish cavalry finally arrived, and it, too, was cut down.

The Russian soldiers in the past had often faced Swedish bayonets and swords and seen their comrades cut down. Peter had placed a Russian soldier in each regiment who had been captured by the Swedes in the past and had two fingers cut off by them. Now the Russians were the victors and not inclined to show much mercy. The slaughter of the outnumbered and overwhelmed Swedish soldiers went on until their bodies piled up in heaps.

Charles and his escort had been knocked about by Russian cannon fire, but he finally mounted a horse with his bleeding foot. Swedish soldiers, who were still able to do so, joined their disabled King in fleeing south. He sought temporary refuge at the Swedish camp at Pushkarinka.

Peter had won an immense victory over Charles, his great adversary!

The losses to the Swedish Army from the main battle and the skirmishes leading up to it were nearly ten thousand men dead, wounded, and captured, including five hundred and sixty officers. The captured included Field Marshal Rehnskjold, four generals, five colonels, and Charles's political advisor and Prime Minister, Count Piper.

After retreating to the Swedish camp at Pushkarinka, Charles organized the remnants of his shattered Army. It amounted to nearly fifteen thousand men, able and wounded, infantry and cavalry, plus six thousand allied Cossacks. The next day he led them south. After two, days they arrived at the juncture of the Vorskla and Dnieper River. Only a few small boats were available. The Swedish army was trapped. Charles was ferried across the Dnieper River with the wounded and a small escort. He sought refuge in Turkey and stayed there for five years.

The rest of the Army, now commanded by Count Lewenhaupt, surrendered the next day. There were about fourteen thousand Swedish troops and thirty-four cannons. When added to the three thousand captured at Poltava, Peter now had nearly seventeen thousand Swedish prisoners.

On the battlefield, Charles XII was the supreme tactician. He moved fast and decisively and, until Poltava, had always been successful in battle. However, as a strategist, he was less successful. After Peter's defeat at Narva, Charles gave him almost nine years to prepare and rearm, while he pursued a mostly personal vendetta against Augustus. A northern invasion route, where he could be supported by sea from Sweden and then strike swiftly south toward Moscow, would seem to have made more military sense. He could have marched through Swedish lands, recaptured former important possessions and added reinforcements from Finland and Poland to his army. He could have made his thrust for Moscow with seventy thousand well-fed and equipped men.

Instead, at Poltava, he was about nine hundred miles from the Baltic and about five hundred miles south of Moscow. Two years after starting out from Poland, he was finally left, with a hungry, tired and depleted army for his decisive battle with Peter.

In contrast, Peter didn't enjoy unbroken success on the battlefield. His green troops and poor equipment in the early days accounted for much of this. Battlefield command also added to the confusion. When he was missing, as at Narva and Grodno, and someone else was placed in command, things didn't go well. At Azov, and particularly Poltava, when Peter's direct orders controlled affairs, things went better. Although in smaller engagements, when Sheremetev and Menshikov controlled events, they also did well.

After Poltava

The Russian crushing of the Swedish Army at Poltava; the surrender of what was left of it trapped between the rivers at Perevoluchna; and Charles being in Turkey, resulted in the complete victory of Peter's Baltic strategy. Russians commanded by Menshikov invaded Poland, and Augustus was restored as the Polish king. The remaining Swedish garrison cities of Vyborg, Riga, and Revel fell to Russian arms in rapid succession.

Vyborg is a city about 75 miles north of St. Petersburg and could be used as a staging area for a Swedish advance through Finland to threaten Peter's new city. The city fell to Peter in June 1710, a year after Poltava. The area between Vyborg and St. Petersburg, when Finland owned it, was called the "Finnish Riviera." It has a beautiful seacoast. Later one of Russia's great painters, Ilya Repin, made his home there in Kuokkala. The town is now called Repino, in his memory.

The siege of Riga and its surrender on July 10 was, unfortunately, bloodier than necessary. When a major Riga bastion was breached, Peter offered generous surrender to its commander, Arvid Horn, Charles's comrade in his youth. In those times, when a town's defenses were breached, surrender was an honorable conclusion to the battle. Horn refused to surrender. As a result of Horn's stubbornness, the battle raged on and more casualties on both sides resulted. This so infuriated the Russian soldiers that Peter had difficulty in restraining them when they finally surged through the city. It turned into a slaughter. Horn's wife was killed in the rampage. Just a few months later, Revel also fell to the Russians, and the eastern part of the southern shore of the Baltic Sea was now completely in Russian hands.

Today you can go by boat from St. Petersburg to Moscow and on to the Black Sea or Caspian Sea. Using Swedish prisoners of war, Peter began the work of connecting the waterways of Russia by building a system of canals and locks. One of the last such projects, connecting the Volga

River with the Moscow River, was built by Stalin after World War, II using German prisoners of war.

Things were going so well for Peter up north that he turned his attention to the south again. Until the Baltic had been secured, Peter wanted the Ottoman Empire to remain quiet, but now he encouraged its people and states to rise up against the Sultan.

Eventually, in 1711, Peter led a Russian army south in what became known as the Pruth campaign. Unfortunately for Peter, his army of 38,000 infantry found themselves surrounded by 120,000 infantry and 80,000 cavalry troops of the Turks. This encirclement was next to the Pruth River. The enclosing circle included three hundred cannons. Making matters worse, Peter's wife, Catherine, had accompanied Peter and was in the center of the camp (with other ladies) in a shallow pit that offered very little protection.

Surprisingly, the Sultan's Grand Vizier chose not to press ahead but agreed to terms that allowed Peter, Catherine, and the encircled army to march out of the trap. The terms cost Peter the surrender of the Dnieper forts and Azov, gained in the 1696 campaign. But Peter knew it could have been much worse and was relieved.

Peter's good health and a desire to try his own hand at diplomacy led him on a second journey to Europe. This journey was entirely different from the first. Nineteen years earlier, he was a young, relatively untested ruler (except for Azov), anxious to learn and willing to do manual work with his own hands. Now he was forty-four, confident, and the absolute ruler of a much larger nation that he had won by beating in battle, Charles XII, one of Europe's most acclaimed military leaders. However, his diplomacy in Europe didn't get the result Peter wanted. His plan had been to form an alliance to invade and subdue Sweden as Charles XII had tried to do in Russia.

Peter spent the winter in Amsterdam and visited Paris in the spring. The French visit was now possible because the Sun King, Louis XIV, had died. Peter was thinking about a new, French northern alliance. Substituting Russia for Sweden, this arrangement might even be sealed with a royal marriage. Peter enjoyed cosmopolitan Paris during his six-week visit and was well treated. However, nothing diplomatically important came of his visit.

Peter left Paris in June, traveling through Holland and Germany back to Russia to face the most important personal crisis of his reign.

Tsarevich Alexis Killed

Trubetskoy Bastion
Peter and Paul Fortress
St. Petersburg, Russia
June 26, 1718

Alexis, the twenty- eight-year-old son of Peter the Great, and, until recently, heir to the Russian throne, lay sprawled on his stomach on the floor of the Trubetskoy Bastion in the Peter and Paul Fortress. He had been subjected to forty lashes of the knout across his thin back, and his hold on life was ebbing. The knout was a hard leather whip, about three and a half feet long. A man skilled in this particular form of torture did the lashing.

Torture by lashes of the knout had been administered to him twice, twenty-five blows on June 19 followed by fifteen more on June 24. Alexis' arms had been tied to an overhead beam and the lashes applied across his back. Welts rose immediately and in many places the skin was broken and bleeding. As the whipping continued, the skin was torn off in many places and hung down. Repeated blows reached bone, and blood ran freely. Few strong men could survive more than twenty such blows. Alexis was frail and had received forty. He had difficulty remaining conscious the pain was so severe.

The evening after his second session of knouting, Alexis confessed to wishing his father's death. He also confessed to offering to hire troops from Austrian Emperor Leopold to seize the throne from his father. This was the confession of treason needed to justify his death. While the Tsar considered the next step, Alexis lay in his cell the whole day of the 26th in a pitiful state.

Earlier this day, as Alexis clung to life, he asked to see his father. Peter came with his entourage. The son asked his father to forgive him and to have prayers said for his soul. Peter said he would, and the father and son parted with overflowing tears and lamentations on both sides.

Thoughts of his mother, Eudoxia, known as Nun Helen now, and his lover, Afrosina, who had given birth to his child, and then betrayed him, ran through Alexis's head as life slowly slipped away.

By late afternoon, he was dead.

How did Peter's oldest son, his heir to the throne, come to be killed in such a cruel and barbarous manner by Peter's own orders?

Last Years

Being the son of Peter the Great and his potential heir, was bound to be difficult for Tsarevich Alexis. Peter expected his son would share his vision of a Russia focused on the West and would be eager to fight Russia's enemies as the head of the Army and Navy. Instead, Tsarevich Alexis grew up with a contemplative nature and resembled more his mother's withdrawn personality. Peter paid little attention to young Alexis nor to how his personality was being shaped.

Alexis was not interested in accompanying Peter on his second European journey. He also lacked interest in participating in Russia's battles and wars. He was more attracted to Russia's old style Orthodox religion. Dangerously, he served as a hope for the future among those resisting Peter's reforms. However, Alexis did enjoy strong drink, a trait he shared with his father.

Peter arranged to have Alexis marry a German Princess, Charlotte of Brunswick-Wolfenbuttel in October 1711, but the marriage didn't go well. Alexis drank too much, he was inattentive, and she felt isolated. They did have a son they named Peter, but Charlotte died less than two weeks after he was born.

However, Peter's wife Catherine, in 1715, also had a boy they named Peter. Tsar Peter began to focus on a successor for himself other than Alexis. At the same time, he was somewhat circumspect, since Russians who resisted Peter's ideas, particularly in the church, were fond of Alexis.

Finally, while Peter was still in Holland, during his second European journey, Alexis fled to Vienna, by way of Danzig, with his Finnish lover, Afrosina, and three servants. In Vienna, he told the Vice Chancellor of the Imperial Court that the Tsar planned to deprive him of the throne, place him in a monastery, and perhaps kill him. His arrival in Vienna was awkward for Emperor Charles VI. Peter was a powerful monarch and to come between him and his son could have serious repercussions. To provide time to sort things out, Alexis and Afrosina, were sent to the castle of Ehrenberg in the Austrian Tyrol. As it became clear the Tsarevich had fled, Peter, who was spending the winter in Amsterdam, was outraged, embarrassed, and concerned anew that Alexis would serve as a focal point for dissidents.

When Peter's agents learned that Alexis had moved to Naples from Ehrenberg, Peter sent his most trusted agent, Peter Tolstoy, to convince Alexis to return to Russia. An important concern now of Alexis was Afrosina, who was pregnant. Upon assurances of good treatment, Alexis agreed to return to Russia.

His return started a wave of torture and execution as Peter determined to rout out anyone who played a part in his fleeing, or hoped to benefit from Alexis's succession to the throne. The net thrown out was wide and included Eudoxia, Alexis's mother. Also arrested was the captain of her guard, who had become her lover, Major Stephen Glebov. His death was particularly brutal. He was beaten with the knout, burned with hot irons, his body stretched on a plank and held with spikes for three days, and finally impaled. Impaling involves thrusting a sharp pole into the rectum; standing the pole up and then letting the body weight slowly cause it to sink down the pole until a vital organ is struck. Peter approached him as this was happening, offering to kill him quickly if he would confess to treason. Globov spit in his face.

While this was going on, Afrosina had returned to Russia separately, having Alexis's child on the way. Nothing further is known about this grandson of Peter. Afrosina was repeatedly questioned alone and in Alexis's presence. Finally, she told the Tsar that what Alexis had spoken to her about included treason. That was what Peter needed to hear and his oldest son was tortured until he confessed and died.

From the time of Alexis's death in 1718 and until he died in 1725, Peter's major concern was signing a peace treaty with Sweden. This was aided by the death of Charles XII, which happened in a trench while besieging Kristiania (now Oslo, Norway) in November 1718.

The peace Treaty of Nystad was finally negotiated and received by Peter in September 1721. It confirmed Russia's ownership of the Baltic ports and Sweden's retention of Finland at a borderline above Vyborg. There is a border marker still standing at a spot just east of Kotka,

Finland. During the treaty celebrations, Peter was petitioned and agreed to accept the titles, " Father of the Fatherland, Peter the Great, Emperor of all Russians."

At about the time the Treaty of Nystad was freeing Peter of northern concerns, he appointed one of his younger able men, Artemius Volynsky, to assess the possibilities of new territories in the Caucasus area where the Persian Empire was crumbling. Peter campaigned there in 1722, but, finally, he and the Ottoman Sultan settled the matter peacefully by dividing up the Caucasian provinces of Persia.

Peter also continued to try improving the governing of his nation. He was determined to be remembered as a reformer, as well as for his military exploits. He reorganized the Senate and government ministries and continued to promote able people based on merit. To help promote the appeal of government service, he established a Table of Ranks for the Russian Empire. It divided the branches of state government, which a young man could enter, into three parts–military, civil, and court. Each branch had fourteen ranks of service, and promotion up from the bottom rank depended on length of service and merit. Although this Table of Ranks should have worked well to insure good government, corruption and favoritism often undermined it.

Peter continued to toil endlessly at establishing St. Petersburg as a commercial center. He relaxed by working at carpentry. In 1712, he moved the Senate to St. Petersburg. He married Catherine, and, in 1723, proclaimed her Empress. In 1724, he sent a Captain Bering, born in Denmark, to explore the waters between the Asian continent and the Americas. Captain Bering sailed from Kronstadt, finding and naming the Bering Straits.

Peter died in bed on January 28, 1725. A few months before, he had jumped into the cold waters of the Neva to save some sailors and never really recovered.

The succession went to Catherine and, after she died, ironically to Peter II, the son of Peter's son, Alexis. He had survived Peter's own son by Catherine, also named Peter. Menshikov brought young Peter to live in his St. Petersburg palace, the first stone building in the city. It still stands on the banks of the Neva River and is now an annex of the Hermitage Museum. Menshikov planned to marry young Peter off to one of his daughters. This didn't happen as Menshikov fell ill and his enemies forced him into exile. Peter II died at fourteen, prompting a series of mostly short-lived reigns until Empress Elizabeth.

What sort of Russia did Peter leave behind? On the Baltic, he left a string of major ports for Russian trade and commerce - historic Riga and Tallinn and the new capital, St. Petersburg. St. Petersburg was guarded in every direction. The new Russian Navy Peter established had its base at Kronstadt, on the island of Kotlin, guarding the approaches to St. Petersburg from the west.

What had been a society and culture primarily rooted in semi-oriental customs was abruptly yanked into a society of European manners. Women came out from their restricted quarters; fashions in dress and grooming were updated; education opportunities were broadened; and promotion was more often based on merit. Peter strove constantly to organize government to be more responsive to the nation's needs.

However, he would not cede or share any of his power; left the succession in a muddle; had his own son cruelly killed; didn't do much for most of the population; and spared no one in achieving his goals.

Truly, however, he was the father of today's Russia, and a claimant for the most outstanding personality of the Baltic.

Baltic Sagas
Events and Personalities
that Changed the World!

Peterhof Palace Estate
On the Gulf of Finland
Russia

V

Catherine the Great
It's Not Always a Man's World
If You're Patient and Clever.

The Day that Changed Russian History

Mon Plaisir Villa, Peterhof Palace Estate
On the Gulf of Finland
West of St. Petersburg
June 29, 1762

Alexis Orlov came through the open French windows of Catherine's bedroom at Mon Plaisir Villa on the Peterhof Estate. It was very early on the morning of June 29, at a time of year known as the "White Nights," when the sun doesn't set very long, and it doesn't get very dark at night. Orlov had come to warn her that immediate action was necessary. The plan to topple her husband, Tsar Peter III, was being jeopardized by the arrest of one of their confederates, Captain Passek, who might reveal their plans if tortured.

Alexis Orlov was the brother of Gregory Orlov, Catherine's lover, and one of five Orlov brothers who were officers in the Imperial Guard Regiments garrisoned in the capital to protect the Monarchy. He had evaded the Holstein soldiers who Tsar Peter III had ordered to guard her at the Villa. Catherine was restless all day and had been in an uneasy sleep.

Her husband, Tsar Peter III, was in residence at the nearby palace at Oronienbaum with his entourage and mistress, Elizabeth Worontsov. Since he had attained the throne six months before, Catherine had feared arrest and imprisonment due to their increasingly antagonistic relationship. Now Catherine quickly donned a simple black dress, used during the mourning period for Empress Elizabeth, and slipped out of the villa. She and Alexis Orlov headed for the headquarters of the nearest Guard Regiment, the Ismailovsky Regiment.

On the way, they met Gregory Orlov in another carriage, and Catherine transferred to it. Gregory had alerted the regiment commander, Count Kyril Razumovsky, and its chaplain, Father Alexis, that the takeover of the throne by Catherine would be today. Catherine and both Orlov brothers arrived at regimental headquarters just before eight o'clock in the morning. Gregory entered the building.

The drummer came out first and drummed roll-call. Officers and enlisted men tumbled out of the building. Catherine stepped from the carriage and approached them.

She exclaimed, " I come to you for protection. I fear arrest and execution by the Tsar." The soldiers rushed forward and kissed her hands and the hem of her dress. The Chaplain, Father Alexis, held a cross, giving an oath of loyalty to Catherine in which all the regiment joined. The regiment commander, Count Razumovsky, kneeled at her feet.

The entire throng proceeded to the headquarters of the Semenovsky regiment, and they also pledged their loyalty. The two regiments, with shouting and drum rolls, marched down St. Petersburg's main street, the Nevsky Prospect, to the main Cathedral. The Horse Guards and the Preobrazhensky Regiment joined them there. A frenzy of shouting, weeping, and general cheering ensued.

In the Cathedral, the Metropolitan, Head of the Orthodox Church in St. Petersburg, was waiting for Catherine. He held a gold crown over her head and blessed her as she took the oath as "Empress and Sole Autocrat of all the Russians." She was thirty-three years old.

Empress Elizabeth had sent for Catherine, then known as Princess Sophia, to come to Russia when she was not yet fifteen years old. She was summoned as a potential bride for Grand Duke Peter, Elizabeth's nephew and heir to the throne. She spoke German, not Russian. She was a Lutheran, not Russian Orthodox. She was regarded suspiciously at the Russian court, where she had no friends when she arrived. She had been a Princess of the minor German principality of Anhalt–Zerbt.

She toppled Tsar Peter III, a grandson of the venerated Peter the Great, and eighteen years after she arrived became Empress. She reigned for thirty-four years and is remembered as Catherine the Great.

How had she accomplished this?

Dinner with Frederick the Great

Dining Room, Opera House
Berlin, Germany
Mid-January, 1744

Before traveling to Russia, in answer to the summons of its ruler Empress Elizabeth, fourteen- year- old Princess Sophia of Anhalt-Zerbt and her mother, Princess Johanna, were received in Berlin by King Frederick II. The King invited them to dinner. He was the most renowned military figure of his day and is remembered as Frederick the Great. Sophia's mother was reluctant to share the stage with her young daughter and said she had no suitable court dress. The King declared that a suitable gown would be gotten from one of his sisters and insisted Sophia be present.

Princess Sophia was also received that day by the Prussian Queen and was advised by Prince Ferdinand of Brunswick upon leaving the Queen's chamber that, at dinner that night, he would accompany her at the King's table. Her mother sat unhappily at the Queen's table. Upon arrival, the Prince of Brunswick rushed over to greet Sophia and, offering his arm, led her to the head of the table to sit to the right of the King. During dinner, the King chatted with Sophia about her education, knowledge, and interests. She handled herself so well that the other guests were surprised that the cultivated, intelligent and sophisticated monarch was so captivated by his young guest.

After dinner, the King escorted Princess Sophia to a nearby divan where they couldn't be overheard and said to her, "This is one of your last nights as my subject, one of your last nights as a German and as a Lutheran. When you reach Russia, assuming everything goes as well as I expect, you will become a subject of Empress Elizabeth, you will become a Russian, and you will become a member of the Orthodox Church. I am confident you will please the Empress and that she will select you as the bride of her nephew, Grand Duke Peter. Russia is a very rich country with vast resources in land and population and forests teeming with timber, furs, ore, gems and more. The people you will meet at Elizabeth's court continuously seek her favor, hoping to improve their position in availing themselves of these riches. Some will see your marriage as benefiting their cause, and others, who have plans of their own for the Grand Duke, will try to discourage it. Be careful in selecting and making friends. The good will of Empress Elizabeth is your greatest asset."

"I'm not particularly well liked by many of the people at the Russian court or by Empress Elizabeth, for political and other reasons. Your intended husband, Peter, is one the few there who seems to admire me. Be careful not to speak too well of me yourself since you are to become Russian and a subject of Empress Elizabeth. As a grandson of Peter the Great, Peter has direct bloodlines to the Russian throne and can take more liberties than you. We will not meet again. If, as I expect, things work out and you remain in Russia, it probably would be best not to speak to anyone about our conversation."

Sophia remained silent and listened carefully to what the King said. What the fourteen year old Sophia and the powerful King left unsaid was their realization that if, indeed, "things work out," this very young girl would one day be sitting alongside the Tsar as Empress of one of Europe's most powerful nations. In this position, his former subject one-day could influence his affairs and her former Prussian homeland. What neither of them foresaw was that in nineteen years she would sit *alone* on Russia's throne.

She never spoke to anyone about this conversation, but she heard and heeded the King's advice, which gave her a good start in Russia. Later, she steered through the shoals of the Russian court using the good sense that the King had detected in her.

Princess Sophia Augusta Frederika of Anhalt-Zerbst

Princess Sophia was born April 21, 1729 in Stettin, Germany, which is now Poland. Her father was Prince Christian Augustus of Anhalt-Zerbst, a minor principality in fragmented Germany. He was a general in the Prussian Army, and he and his brother shared the rule of Anhalt-Zerbst. Prince Augustus had married Princess Johanna of Holstein-Gottrop, a much more important principality.

Johanna was resentful that her family had not arranged a more brilliant marriage than to this minor Prince with limited resources. Princess Johanna soon became bored with life in Stettin and spent a lot of time travelling to see relatives in Germany's larger and more cosmopolitan cities, Berlin and Hamburg.

Young Princess Sophia soon came to understand her mother's disappointment and the reasons for her travels. Sophia's interest in upgrading her own status was perhaps aroused during these times she and her mother traveled. She could then compare her lifestyle with her more prominent relatives.

Princess Sophia first met Charles-Peter, her future husband, in 1739. He was eleven, and she was ten. They met at the home of the Bishop of Lubeck, the guardian of Charles-Peter since his father died the year before. The Bishop was a cousin of Charles-Peter's father and was Sophia's uncle, making them distant relatives.

Charles-Peter at eleven was remembered by Sophia years later in her memoirs. She reported he was "good-looking, well mannered and courteous," and considered a prodigy. He was pale and delicate looking. The trouble was that his entourage tried to make this child behave as an adult, forcing him to a strict discipline, which developed in him deceitfulness and hypocrisy.

She reported that he already drank heavily and was hot-tempered and rebellious. She reported that one of his tutors, Marshall Brummer, was deliberately undermining his character. The relatives hovering over the young Princess and the Duke were already dropping hints of a possible, future liaison. He was, at this time, intending to become the King of Sweden. The thought of him as her destiny met with Sophia's approval. The title, Queen, "rang sweet to my ears."

However, until Sophia's summons to Russia, not much came of this for the next few years. When the summons to Russia did arrive, marrying Charles-Peter wasn't a completely new idea.

Bullying by Marshall Brummer

Study Room
Palace
Duchy of Holstein-Gottrop
Spring, 1740

The eleven-year-old Duke Charles-Peter was trying to follow Marshal Brummer's instructions as best he could. The lesson for this afternoon was the history of the siege of Narva by his grandfather, Peter the Great. Peter's adversary in this battle was Charles XII, the era's most brilliant soldier, the King of Sweden, and Charles-Peter's great uncle.

Narva was located on the Narva River near the Baltic Sea. A castle had been built first by the Danes and added to by the Swedes as the area became of greater strategic value. Across the river was the Ivanograd fortress built by the Russian Tsar Ivan IV, known as "Ivan the Terrible."

There had been two battles for Narva. The first was won by the Swedes with the timely arrival of Charles XII and his reinforcements. Peter the Great later captured the city and its garrison in a successful second siege. The two battles, the names of the various commanders, and the coming and going of the attackers and defenders, were confusing young Charles-Peter. The bullying by Marshal Brummer, who was standing over him, added to his anxiety as he tried to blurt out answers to his questions. Finally, the Marshal lost complete patience and had the eleven-year old kneel on his bare knees on hard dried peas ordered from the kitchen. He stayed in this painful position until it was time for supper.

Supper was no respite for the young boy. The Marshal's bullying continued during the meal. Young Charles-Peter couldn't choke down his food any longer and finally threw it up. He narrowly missed the

Marshal, getting some of the debris on his own clothes. He was immediately sent to bed.

As he lay in bed, the hapless youngster actually welcomed being alone and thought about the fate which made him Duke of Hollstein-Gottrop, heir to the Crown of Sweden, and even a possible claimant for the throne of Russia.

Against this, when he was only three years old, he had to balance the death of his mother, Anna, daughter of Peter the Great. He never remembered, couldn't even have known, a mother's love and care. In his mother's absence, he was given over to tutors and caretakers since his father, the Duke, had major governing responsibilities. After his father's death the previous year, his care became even more impersonal.

The death of his father meant it was likely he would inherit the Swedish crown sooner, and his new guardian, the Bishop of Lubeck, called for even more discipline. Marshal Brummer's approach was to treat the eleven-year-old as a battle to be won. Although there was no whine of bullets or exploding shells, he bellowed and bullied as he would at confused troops on a battlefield.

By the time little Charles-Peter became Grand Duke Peter of Russia, heir to the Russian throne, he turned the bullying and sadistic behavior he had learned from his teacher on his own subordinates.

Duke Charles Peter Ulrich
of Holstein-Gottrop

Few bloodlines in history could equal those that came together in Duke Charles Peter Ulrich of Holstein-Gottrop. His mother was Anna, the daughter of Peter the Great of Russia. His father was the Duke of Holstein-Gottrop, and the nephew of Charles XII, the brilliant soldier and King of Sweden, who was finally defeated by Peter the Great at Poltava. These bloodlines were reflected in his name "Charles Peter."

Unfortunately, these bloodlines converged in a receptacle that was ill prepared to receive them. His mother's death of tuberculosis when he was only three months old, and his father's death when he was ten, deprived him of a normal childhood. What his father left him were his claims to the Swedish crown. Accordingly, he was raised a Lutheran and became an admirer of Frederick II, King of Prussia, the most renowned military leader since his great uncle, Charles XII.

Descendants from Peter I's half brother, Ivan V, the half-wit side of the family, held the crown of Russia, during this time. When Elizabeth, Peter's other daughter, and the sister of Charles Peter's mother, became Empress, everything changed. Elizabeth wanted her side of the family to inherit the succession. Since she was childless, succession meant her sister's son, Charles Peter.

Russia's throne had become more important then Sweden's. Charles Peter's guardians decided to forego the claims to the Swedish crown in favor of Russia. Accordingly, at the age of thirteen, he left Holstein-Gottrop for the unfamiliar terrain of the Russian court and his aunt, Empress Elizabeth.

He was thirteen years old. He didn't speak Russian. He was raised as a Lutheran. He had been brought up in a German environment - strict and orderly. He thought he would inherit the throne of Sweden. He grew up admiring the most renowned living soldier, Frederick II, remembered as "Frederick the Great." He went from the familiar comfort of Europe to the more exotic eastern-influenced atmosphere of Russia.

He was a fish out of water. His assured inheritance made lavish fawning unavoidable. It was an intimidating challenge for even the most assured, self-reliant, and confident individual. Unfortunately, Charles Peter did not have these virtues. He had grown up to be suspicious, self-centered, arrogant, and belittling of his surroundings. He enjoyed the privileges but never accepted, or grew comfortable, with the providers – Russia, the Orthodox Religion, or the Russian military.

The only familiar face he saw was the horror Brummer, who accompanied him to Russia to manage his affairs. Peter imported soldiers from his old Duchy of Holstein-Gottrop and flaunted their uniforms and drill.

This was the man Princess Sophia had been summoned by his aunt, Empress Elizabeth, from Germany to meet. Although they had met before, he was now a prospective bridegroom and, if they wed, she would sit on the thrown of Russia with him.

Grand Ball at the Old Winter Palace

St. Petersburg, Russia
Winter, 1745

Empress Elizabeth, in 1745, was thirty-six years old and at the height of her physical charm and beauty. She had never married, and, instead of being surrounded by family, enjoyed the winter social season of St. Petersburg. There were concerts two nights a week, a French comedy performance another night, and balls on Thursday and Sunday.

For an imperial ball, the old Winter Palace (the current Winter Palace was built later) was brightly lit by thousands of candles, both inside and out. Hundreds of guests would alight from their carriages and go up the marble staircase past men standing at attention in dress uniforms of the Imperial Guard Regiments. Flowers and potted plants decorated the passageways. Large mirrors, lining the walls, permitted the ladies in stylish gowns (many imported from France) wearing tiaras, necklaces and other jewelry and accessories to inspect themselves as they sparkled and glittered in the galleries and halls.

The men wore formal dress often with sashes and ribbons across their chests denoting rank or honors. Other men were dressed in official court uniforms embellished with carefully woven gold braid. The more gold braid, the higher their position. The most colorfully dressed men wore military uniforms in a multitude of hues and set off with medals and decorations from many nations.

On some occasions, the Empress announced one of her famous transvestite balls, when the women wore male attire and the men wore frocks. Few of the guests showed themselves to best advantage in this cross-dressing, but one who did was the Empress. She looked splendid in masculine attire, as she was large, forceful, and tall.

At 8:30 in the evening, an Imperial Ball would begin when the Grand Master of Ceremonies tapped the floor three times with a staff that was topped by a gold, Romanov double eagle. An orchestra would play and men and women would take to the dance floor. Even when not dressed as a man, a ball showed Elizabeth off to her very best advantage. She never wore the same dress twice. Her gowns were sometimes set off with beautiful furs, ermine and sable, from the Russian forest. She selected her accessories from a large collection of diamonds, rubies, emeralds, and other precious stones. The Empress was a graceful dancer and her natural exuberance kept her whirling through a polonaise, a quadrille, minuet, a waltz, or mazurka.

She was the center of all eyes and not only because she was the Empress. She had been a beautiful child and the pride of her father, Peter the Great, and had grown into an exceptionally beautiful woman. One observer described her: "She is a beauty the like of which I have never seen …an amazing complexion, glowing eyes, a perfect mouth, a throat and bosom of rare whiteness. She is tall in stature, and her temperament is very lively. One senses in her a great deal of intelligence and affability, but also a certain ambition."

A supper was served in adjoining rooms at midnight. Tables groaned under the weight of shellfish, smoked and fresh fish, chicken in various styles, salads, potatoes, rice in many varieties, and roasted meats sliced to order. Caviar, there was lots of caviar. Deserts of pastry and whipped cream, ice cream, preserves, and imported fresh fruit followed. Punch and wine flowed copiously. There was ice-cold vodka.

The food was served on presentation platters that were often presents from other monarchs, including Meissen porcelain from Germany and Serves from France. Heavy silver service, gold candelabras, and ornate table decorations encrusted with jewels, reflecting the finest workmanship, contributed to a glittering table setting,

An army of servants in resplendent Romanov livery whisked fresh dishes to the tables, and removed platters no longer sufficiently full to be attractive. The presentation of the food itself reflected great care and style. Chefs from France supervised locally trained cooks. Manpower was never a problem for Russian rulers and their circle.

Conversation was in French, the language of the aristocracy. Gossip was the coin of the realm. Outside the snowdrifts whirled and through the frosted windows the solidly frozen Neva River could be seen. There would be fireworks in clear weather.

Later, when the Empress retired, Alexis Razumonsky, the lover with whom she enjoyed a long and close relationship, usually would join her. He has described as the most handsome man at the Russian Court. She made him a Field Marshal and a Prince, and to please Elizabeth, the Emperor of Austria made him a Count of the Holy Roman Empire. He was a Ukrainian peasant, a simple man, first brought to St. Petersburg because of his beautiful singing voice and referred to as, "the Emperor of the Night."

The other guests would disburse soon after the Empress left and might continue their merriment elsewhere or seek out their own liaisons.

Elizabeth, Empress of Russia

After Elizabeth's father, Peter the Great, died in 1725, the ruler of Russia changed four times in sixteen years.

1725-1727 – Catherine I, Peter the Great's wife.
1727-1730 – Peter II, Peter I's grandson from his son Alexis. He died young of smallpox.
1730-1740 – Anna Ivanova, Daughter of Ivan V, Peter I's half brother.
1740-1741 – Ivan VI – Came to throne as a two-month-old baby, grandson of Ivan V, and his mother, Anna Leopoldovna, acted as his Regent.

More important to Elizabeth, the succession after her mother went to branches of the family not directly related to her. By the time Anna Leopoldovna came to rule as Regent for her son, Ivan VI, another descendent of Peter I's half brother, Elizabeth decided the time was ripe to make her move for the crown.

When still a very young child her father, Peter the Great, wanted his beautiful daughter Elizabeth to marry the heir to the French crown, but the French demurred. Instead, at the age of sixteen, she had been betrothed to Prince Karl-Augustus of Holstein-Gottrop, but he died just days after the betrothal. After this disappointment, she did not allow herself to be married off to a distant European Duke or Prince but stayed in Russia.

During recent years she had cultivated the military, particularly the Preobrazhensky Regiment, established by her father. She played cards with the officers, flirted with them, flattered them, and reminded them of their days of glory when they conquered the Swedes. The power brokers had denied her the throne up to now because she reminded them too much of Peter the Great and his reforms and changes. Now, however, there was general disillusion with the German-leaning policies that had been in place since Catherine I's reign.

After one year's reign by Anna Leopoldvona, Elizabeth went to the Preobrazhensky barracks and donned their uniform. She declared the Regent planned to put her, Peter the Great's daughter, in a convent or exile her. She implored their help. They whispered an oath of allegiance to her and she led them to the Winter Palace. The guards there joined her cause. Elizabeth went into Regent Anna's bedroom and whispered in her ear, "Wake up sister." The coup was over in two hours without bloodshed. Anna was allowed to leave Russia with her family, except for the young boy, Ivan VI, who was imprisoned, and for whom Anna had acted as Regent. Elizabeth came to power at age thirty-one and ruled Russia for twenty-two years.

Elizabeth, as the beautiful daughter of Peter the Great, having lived in Russia without ever leaving, instilled in the Russian people a renewed sense of national identification. She spent a lot of time in Moscow, the heart and soul of the country, with its traditional link to past rulers. She had been brought up in the Russian Orthodox religion and frequently went on pilgrimages to churches, convents, and monasteries. She reigned long enough for people to think of her as the "Mother of all the Russians."

After Elizabeth had sent for her sister's son, and named him her heir, the next piece of business was to get him suitably married and assure the succession by the birth of a son. Thoughts of a bride for the now renamed Grand Duke Peter brought Elizabeth's mind back to Prince Karl-Augustus of Holstein-Gottrop, her great love who died just days after their betrothal. His sister, Princess Johanna, had kept in touch with her. She had a daughter, just a year younger than Grand Duke Peter. A severe illness of the Grand Duke hastened her decision to send for them. Princess Sophia and her mother arrived in Moscow in time for Peter's birthday. Princess Sophia and her mother had first gone to St. Petersburg from the dinner in Berlin and then traveled on to Moscow when told Empress Elizabeth had gone there.

The initial meetings of the three principals went well. Grand Duke Peter was happy to see fifteen-year-old Princess Sophia and her mother. They were German, Lutheran, and subjects of his idol, Frederick the Great, and distant relatives. However, it wasn't long before his childish nature revealed itself to the much more intelligent and shrewd Sophia. He prattled on about being in love with someone else and told her he only agreed to marry Sophia because the Empress desired it. Sophia kept her own counsel and concentrated on studying Russian and the Orthodox religion.

However, Sophia caught a chill and became very ill. Her mother, Princess Johanna, argued with the doctors about treatment for her daughter. Sophia went into a coma. Johanna wanted to call a Lutheran priest but Sophia, in a moment of consciousness, asked for her Orthodox instructor, Simon Theodorsky. This made a very good impression on the Russians attending her.

Elizabeth rushed back from a church pilgrimage and took charge of the young girl. Her mother was ordered from the sick room, and the Empress nursed her personally for over three weeks. These days of intimate contact forged a bond that sealed Elizabeth's selection of Sophia as Grand Duke Peter's wife.

Sophia was the name of Peter the Great's sister, who had tried to block him from power and had bad memories for Elizabeth. Catherine was her mother's name, so Sophia's name was changed to Catherine. Catherine became Orthodox and she and Peter became betrothed.

Just as everything was moving into place for the marriage, the Duke contracted measles. More seriously, shortly thereafter he contracted smallpox. This made him deeply pockmarked and he wore a wig over his shaved head. Catherine tried not to give any outward sign that his appearance bothered her and attempted to be cheerful when seeing him, but Peter sensed her dismay and his confidence took a further beating. However, the Duke's illness made Elizabeth even more resolved that the wedding should move ahead quickly.

The Empress made all the wedding arrangements and was determined it would be an occasion that made clear to the world Russia's wealth and position. The pre-wedding festivities were elaborate and the church ceremonies before the wedding particularly pious. Nothing was spared on the wedding dress nor on the gowns of all the participants. Every piece of jewelry in the empire saw service during the celebrations. The bride and groom were carried along by Empress Elizabeth's enthusiasm.

They had little voice and had little desire to have a voice in the wedding arrangements or festivities. The wedding itself deployed one hundred and twenty carriages all manned by exquisitely dressed coachmen. The Guards and churchmen were all in their finest raiments. There was a great wedding feast in the Winter Palace and the newlyweds sat on the dais with the Empress. The Empress gave the newlyweds expensive gifts as well as providing gifts for them to exchange.

Only one last piece of Elizabeth's plan now remained to be put in place - the birth of an heir. Peter was now only seventeen, immature and probably, at this time, not sexually capable. Catherine was sixteen, naïve, and a virgin. Nothing happened, and Elizabeth was getting frustrated. She assumed they were dallying with others in the beginning and she kept them under surveillance. Elizabeth blamed Catherine for the failure to produce an heir since Peter was her sister's son. It wasn't until some years passed that she allowed herself to contemplate that maybe the silly, awkward, and immature Peter was at fault rather than the intelligent, self-assured and respectful Catherine. In any event, Elizabeth meant to have an heir.

After seven years of marriage, the twenty-three-year-old Catherine was still a virgin. Now she was brought into contact with a handsome member of an old aristocratic Russian family, Serge Saltikov. After a time, in 1754, Catherine gave birth to a son who was named Paul. He was taken away by Empress Elizabeth and rarely seen by Catherine while Elizabeth lived. Although Saltikov was generally assumed to be the father, Peter had recently undergone an operation and for the first time had marital relations with Catherine. Peter accepted Paul as his son and Saltikov was sent away.

Elizabeth raised Paul, leaving Catherine bitter by not being able to mother and raise her own son. She devoted herself even more to reading and self-education.

England sent a very experienced and charming new Ambassador to Russia in 1755, Sir Charles Hanbury-Williams, who was accompanied by a handsome Polish nobleman, Count Stanislav Poniatowski. Count Poniatowski fell in love with Catherine and they started an affair that produced a baby girl in 1759. The girl was named Anna after the Empress's sister. However, the child died. The young count continued to love Catherine for the rest of his life. However, she backed off.

The English ambassador, Sir Hanbury-Williams in addition to befriending Catherine, advanced her funds. Their friendship lasted until the Seven Years War began in 1756. This led to his recall, since England was aligned with Russia's enemy, Prussia.

Peter's disfiguring illness, just before their marriage, was a further impediment to a harmonious relationship between him and Catherine. Although Catherine had successfully found sexual fulfillment, in spite of Peter's inability to perform until his minor operation, they gradually grew further apart. Usually they appeared together only at official functions. Although she was tolerant of his antics and at first accepted that her road to being Empress was only by being his wife, the birth of the heir, Paul, changed their relationship.

She now felt there were three dangerous avenues open to her: to share Peter's future wherever it led; to deal with whatever eventuality Peter decided for her; or to go a separate way.

The war with Prussia put Catherine in an awkward, even compromising, position. She had her own and family ties to Prussia; her husband, Grand Duke Peter was known to be fiercely pro-Prussian; and she had accepted loans from the English ambassador, Prussia's ally.

When military actions first favored Russia and then reversed, the Russian military commander, General Aproxin, was arrested along with the Grand Chancellor Bestuzhev, and others. There was also a movement to implicate Catherine in treason. Catherine was brought before Elizabeth to explain herself. In this confrontation, she handled herself brilliantly and came away with the Empress more inclined in her favor than she had been for some time.

In a second private meeting with only the two of them, matters improved even further and they probably became very frank in discussing Peter's general incompetence.

In 1758, there was a large and very bloody engagement between the Prussians and Russians, which became known as the Battle of Zarndorf. Thousands were killed in both armies, and it was not a real victory for either side. A Russian Guard's officer, Gregory Orlov, distinguished himself during the battle, and, in recognition, he was appointed escort officer for a captured Prussian soldier and aristocrat, Court Schwerin, Frederick's personal adjutant.

Protocol required Count Schwerin be taken to St. Petersburg and treated in accordance with his high station. At one of the social occasions the Count attended with his escort, Gregory Orlov, Catherine met Gregory. She quickly fell in love with this brave, handsome, twenty-five year old Guard's officer. Their torrid affair had major consequences for themselves, personally, and the nation.

The health of Empress Elizabeth had been deteriorating for a number of years. From time to time she had fainting spells and sometimes her speech was impaired. Her energy declined and she ruled the Empire more and more frequently from a sofa or armchair. Finally, on Christmas Day of 1761, she died.

Peter III's Short Reign

As soon as Elizabeth died, Catherine's supporters were ready immediately to enthrone her and overthrow Peter III. To the confusion of her supporters, Catherine ordered them absolutely not to attempt any coup. Unknown to most, she was pregnant with Gregory Orlov's child at this time and didn't want to draw attention to herself. This holding back by Catherine and her group allowed Peter to become Tsar Peter III.

He immediately ordered the cessation of all hostilities against Frederick the Great. In addition, all territory captured from Prussia was to be returned. Frederick, who had his back to the Baltic Sea and his Army besieged on three sides by Russia, Austria, and France, unexpectantly found himself extracted from a ruinous situation. When Russia changed sides, France and Austria negotiated peace. Frederick had avoided a calamity.

After Empress Elizabeth's body was laid out, Peter announced that a supper would be served only three rooms away from her corpse. Before the supper, an oath of loyalty was administered to Peter alone, and excluded the new Empress Catherine and the new heir, Grand Duke Paul.

Starting with Elizabeth's funeral, Peter's behavior became more and more outrageous. Elizabeth had been the daughter of Peter the Great and in her twenty-two year reign had come to occupy a sacred place in the hearts and minds of her subjects. During the solemn funeral procession, Peter lagged behind the hearse. When it got about thirty feet ahead, he ran to catch up with it. The older court members, who were carrying his black train, couldn't run fast enough to keep up and had to let the train go. It was caught by the wind. This amused Peter so much he repeated it several times. His behavior at the funeral and at other public occasions scandalized many of the court people, government ministers, and foreign officials who observed his antics.

On one occasion, four members of his entourage were flogged in front of the diplomatic court, and guests, because of his perceived notion that they were insufficiently respectful. The military, already angered that their military victories over Prussia and their sacrifices in dead and wounded were being ignored, were to be further insulted. The new Tsar decreed that they change their uniforms, formations, and tactics to conform to the Prussian model.

He also announced changes in the Orthodox Church. He wanted it brought more in line with the Lutheran Church, which had been his religion until coming to Russia. He decreed priests should not have beards and that sacred images, except for Christ and Mary, were to be removed from churches. A Lutheran Chapel was built in the palace. Protestants were given religious freedom and priests were to become civil servants. All church property was confiscated.

With these actions, Peter III cut himself off from the three pillars that supported the monarchy in Russia - the Aristocracy, the Church, and the Military. He was left with his Holstein Guards and his own circle of court attendants.

The magnificent new Winter Palace was finished in March. Peter III took apartments in the main wing, and his mistress, Elizabeth Worontsow, had adjoining rooms. Catherine was given an apartment at the other end of the palace.

In her new apartment, Catherine gave birth to a son on April 11. His father was Gregory Orlov. The baby was smuggled out of the palace and named Alexis Gregorevich Bobrinsky. The selection of Bobrinsky as a last name is interesting. It means "beaverskin," in which he was first swaddled. There is also a hint that a natural, wild animal recalls his virile, untamed father, Gregory Orlov.

Now Peter III and Catherine were on a collision course. Her last obstacle to organizing and staging a coup, her pregnancy, was removed. Peter III had decided to wed his mistress Elizabeth Worontsow, and to do this he had to remove Catherine. Catherine was aware of this.

What finally activated the events on June 29 was that Peter III planned to take military action against Denmark to take back the province of Schleswig, which his dukedom of Holstein had lost. He had assembled a Russian Army and fleet at Revel, Estonia for this purpose. He went with his entourage to the estate of Oranienbaum, west of St. Petersburg, which was on the way to Revel, and from where he planned to join his military expedition. Catherine was ordered to Mon Plaisir at Peterhof, which was nearby.

Catherine was sure he would deal with her (either imprisonment or execution) before he left. She and her supporters acted first, as we described at the beginning of our story.

Catherine Quickly Consolidates Her Power

After the crowning ceremony, Catherine went to the Winter Palace with a large throng that now included priests and the populace as well as the Guard Regiments. At the Winter Palace, the Senate and Synod had gathered to pledge their oath. Catherine took her son Paul to the balcony and lifted him up for all the wildly, cheering crowd to see.

She had clearly captured St. Petersburg, but, after the cheering and exhilaration had stopped, Catherine and her advisors realized that Peter III's status still needed to be resolved. He had the large force at Revel that had been assembled to fight Denmark, the fleet to transport them, and his own Holstein troops.

It would be best if he signed an act of abdication. Catherine had enough troops to deal with the Holstein force and she decided to march against them with herself dressed as a colonel in a Guard Regiment. She sent Admiral Talysin to Kronstadt to secure the loyalty of the base and fleet there.

Peter dithered most of this critical day. He went to Peterhof and was surprised not to find Catherine there. From a Holsteiner, who came from St. Petersburg, he learned of the revolt. His advisors couldn't agree on what to do. He sent orders with advisors to St. Petersburg, but the orders were ignored and the advisors captured and made to swear loyalty to Catherine. In the evening, he set off for nearby Kronstadt in his yacht but was driven off.

He was finished.

He returned to Oranienbaum and then went on to Peterhof where Catherine, through intermediaries, had him sign his abdication. He asked to be sent to Ropsha, a small estate nearby with his mistress, his dog, Mopsy, personal servant, Narcissus, and his violin. At this point, he would have been glad to settle for returning to Holstein. His mistress was denied him, and he was sent to Ropsha under a guard that included Alexis Orlov, Gregory's brother. Within a week, he was murdered.

Catherine II ruled for almost thirty-five years. She aligned herself closely to the memory of Peter the Great. Near the beginning of her reign she commissioned the famous equestrian statue that still stands in Senate Square and inscribed it, "Petro Primo, Catharina Secunda" (Peter One, Catherine Second). Peter the Great had concentrated on bringing to Russia the science and craftsmanship of the West and had imported skilled and experienced men to do this. He also established the Kunstkammer (Museum of Anthropology and Ethnography). Catherine set out to build on this.

Although Peter had also started collecting art, Catherine resolved to expand this activity. Her establishment of the Hermitage, which endures today, is in the forefront of the world's great museums and is one of her enduring legacies. One of her first large acquisitions was an art collection, which a dealer had assembled for Frederick the Great to be hung at his San Souci ("Without Worry") palace. The costs of The Seven Years War didn't allow him this expense, and she bought the collection instead. Events had come full circle from the dinner in Berlin.

She kept her ambassadors in important European capitals on the alert for art that could be acquired. She corresponded with Diderot, the French compiler of the Encyclopedie, and had him come to St. Petersburg. She purchased his library and also brought that to St. Petersburg. She corresponded with Voltaire, as well.

In addition to constructing the Hermitage to house her growing art collection, she built many of the palaces that adorn St. Petersburg today. She built two palaces for Gregory Orlov, a country estate known as Gatchina and the Marble Palace in the city. She also gifted him with 200 paintings and a Sevres porcelain service known today as the "Cameo Service."

Later, she built the Tauride Palace for Gregory Potemkin. For her favorite grandson, she built the Alexander Palace near the Catherine Palace in Tsarskoe Selo, now Pushkin Village. These buildings have enjoyed a rich history and served various functions, over the years, beyond their original purpose. Most can be visited and enjoyed today.

Many people figured in Catherine's long reign, but special mention must be made of Gregory Potemkin. He came to her attention about the time she first took power. He was only twenty-three years old at this time, ten years younger than Catherine. He was brought to one of her early parties by the Orlov brothers, where he imitated her speaking Russian with her German accent. She was first surprised and then laughed.

Potemkin's remarkable personal qualities made Catherine employ him in more, and increasingly important, tasks in political and foreign affairs. He was a remarkable man - intelligent, with a great lust for life, statesman, organizer, warrior, charmer, and he stood up to Catherine. They became lovers for a time and although their relationship was sometimes tumultuous, she relied on him because she could count on him. He was sometimes referred to as co-Tsar. There are even stories that they were secretly married. He defeated the Turks, extended her Empire in the Caucasian region, and colonized the area by bringing in people and building villages, churches, and docks.

In 1787, he arranged for Catherine, her court and foreign officials to take a six-month grand tour of her southern realm. For this majestic inspection, he had fresh paint put on the buildings and the inhabitants dressed in their best clothes. This effort came to be called by his enemies, "Potemkin Villages." This was unfair since, to the contrary, he established many of Russia's southern cities, including Odessa. Grand Duke Paul, heir to the crown, was not included in this tour. It was another sleight that made him increasingly bitter, and he came to hate Potemkin. Eventually, when their ardor for each other cooled, Potemkin helped select new "gentleman of the evening" for Catherine.

In the west, Catherine participated in the annexation of a large piece of Poland. Prussia and Austria joined in this annexation of Poland, taking large parts for themselves.

By the time she died on November 16, 1796 at age 67, she had outlived most of her closest associates, substantially enlarged Russia, added to its culture and art, and earned the title, "Catherine the Great."

Catherine's Funeral

Nevsky Prospect
St. Petersburg, Russia
Winter, 1796

The new Tsar, Paul I, decreed, that his mother, Catherine the Great, was to be entombed in the Cathedral of Saints Peter and Paul. She would rest, side by side with her former husband, Peter III.

First, however, he had his father exhumed from his crypt at the Alexander Nevsky Monastery where it had rested for thirty- four years. Peter III's skeletal remains were dressed in one of his military uniforms, robed in ermine, and then placed on the throne in the Winter Palace. The crown of Russia was placed on his skull and the scepter in his bony hand. Officials were required to come and pay homage to this macabre apparition. While this was going on, the body of Catherine the Great lay in state.

Finally came the double funeral down the Nevsky Prospect, St. Petersburg's main street. It proceeded with elaborate pomp in two royal corteges, one for each of the remains of the two former rulers. A bizarre touch: next to the cortege of Peter III walked Alex Orlov, now grown old. He was dressed in deepest mourning and carried Peter III's crown on a black velvet pillow.

At the end of the funeral procession, the coffins were placed side by side in identical white marble sarcophagi in the Cathedral of Saints Peter and Paul. They rest there to this day.

Aftermath

The throne a last! Catherine's son had waited a long time to be crowned Tsar Paul I. At the time of his father's death, Paul was eight years old. Some thought he should have been declared Tsar, with Catherine as Regent, when Paul's father of record was deposed. Catherine wasn't having any of that.

When he became older, Peter the Great seized power when he was seventeen. Paul might have expected to be crowned then with Catherine as Regent or Dowager Empress. Perhaps he could even have shared the crown as co-ruler. Catherine demurred.

As Paul grew older and Catherine's reign stretched out, he became ever more bitter about his lack of power and what he learned about the circumstances of Catherine's crowning. She had deposed Tsar Peter III, his father of record, who had then been murdered. There was gossip that Peter III was not really his father His mother, Catherine, had many lovers whose coming and goings was common knowledge.

His great aunt, Empress Elizabeth, had kept him away from Catherine, his actual mother, when he was young, so strong bonds were forged with her rather than Catherine. Ever since Elizabeth and his father died, Catherine had the power.

Her only concern had been that Paul and his second wife, Sophia of Wurttemberg, produce an heir. This they did and very successfully. They had six children, three boys and three girls. Catherine named the first, Alexander, and he was her favorite. As Paul grew older he came to hate Catherine and turned more to memories of his father, Peter III. He attributed to him virtues as a good, martyred man destroyed by his evil, ambitious mother.

As soon as Catherine died, Paul showed signs of willfulness and even paranoia. He had hated Potemkin, and in addition to the bizarre funeral for his mother, Catherine, he gave orders that Potemkin's burial place be covered by earth and all memorials destroyed. The beautiful and expensive palace Catherine had built for Potemkin, The Tauride Palace, he turned into a stable and barracks.

He immediately tried to turn upside down all his mother's work. He pardoned her foes and promoted her enemies. He issued directives one day and issued the opposite instructions soon thereafter. He issued orders that when passing the Winter Palace one had to stop and salute whether Paul was there or not. When he came by in his carriage, other riders had to stop, dismount, and salute. He followed in his father's footsteps by admiring Frederick the Great and wanting the Russian army to be more Prussian. His officials lived in fear of going to prison or being removed from office.

The atmosphere around Paul became sullen and suspicious. The mood permeated everyone and even affected Paul. He became concerned about treason. He tore down the beautiful Summer Palace built by Rastrelli for Empress Elizabeth, and, in its place, erected a fortress /castle called Michael's Castle. In there, he expected to be safe.

In March 1801, he moved into this stronghold. However, after four years of his rule, and with concerns about dangers posed by Napoleon, patience with Paul ran out. One night after just a week in his stronghold, a group of officers went into his bedroom. They demanded he sign an act of abdication. When he refused, he was strangled.

His son became Tsar Alexander I. Catherine the Great had the last word after all.

Baltic Sagas
Events and Personalities
That Changed the World!

Yusupov Palace
94 Moika Embankment
St. Petersburg, Russia

VI
Rasputin and the Prince
A Murder that Convulsed a Nation!

The Murder

Prince Yusupov's Basement Study/Dining Room
Yusupov Palace
94 Moika Embankment
St. Petersburg, Russia
Evening of December 16/17, 1916

Prince Felix Yusupov screamed, " Purishkevich shoot, shoot! He is alive! He is escaping!" Yusupov was bounding up the stairs from the dining room below where he had earlier shot Rasputin and left him for dead. He was scrambling up the steps in shock and ran off to his parent's apartments in another part of the huge palace.

Purishkevich hesitated only a second, then pulled his revolver from his coat and ran down the steps. He followed the fleeing figure of Rasputin through the side door. Rasputin left footsteps as he ran through the courtyard snow screaming,

"Felix… Felix…I will tell the Tsarina everything!"

There wasn't a moment to lose. In a few moments, Rasptutin would cross the courtyard, reaching the double iron gates and be out and free on the street. Purishkevich raised his pistol and fired. The noise at this quiet time in the middle of the cold, dark night shattered the silence.

Missed!

Purishkevich fired a second time and missed again. Rasputin was still running and would soon reach the gates. The next shot hit Rasputin in the back and stopped him. A fourth shot rang out. Rasputin was hit again; he fell and rolled over.

His face was in the snow, his arms stretched out in front of him. He no longer moved. Purishkevish ran up to him and kicked him in the head.

He stood over him long enough to convince himself he was dead. While firing at Rasptutin, he had noticed two men outside the gate in the street, but they had rushed off.

The shooting in the courtyard, and the body outside the palace near the courtyard gate, was not what had been planned. Purishkevich realized that he would have to deal with the situation as it had finally developed. Yusupov had originally lured Rasputin to this rendezvous with the promise of meeting his beautiful wife, Irina, and fed him poisoned cakes, without any effect. Then he shot him only to see him rise again.

Purishkevich first needed to move the body back into the palace. He went to the main entrance lobby where two soldiers were stationed. He told them what had happened, and that he had killed Rasputin. They were pleased about this, and he secured their agreement to remain silent. Purishkevich then asked them to drag the body from the courtyard through the side door to the small entrance hall.

Purishkevich next went to find Yusupov who he found spitting into a basin in a bathroom. He told him he had finished off Rasputin and led him to where the soldiers had dragged the body. At the sight of it, Yusupov broke away from Purishkevich's grasp, grabbed a two-pound rubber truncheon and began beating the body around the head in a fit of excitement.

When Purishkevich realized what was happening, he had soldiers pull Yusupov away. They seated him on a couch in his nearby study. The soldiers were sent to find some cloth with which to wrap the body. While one of them did so, the other reported that a policeman on duty had heard the shooting and had come to find out what was happening.

Purishkevich asked the soldier to bring the policeman to Yusupov's study. When the policeman, named Vlassiyev, was led in, Purishkevich asked the policeman if he could identify himself and the other man in the study. Vlassiyev said he could and did so. After questioning Vlassiyev, Purishkevich satisfied himself that the policeman loved the Tsar and Fatherland and that Rasputin hindered the war effort. He also had Vlassiyev assure him he would remain quiet. Purishkevich then revealed the killing of Rasputin. While Vlassiyev agreed to remain silent, he said that if put under oath he would have to tell what he knew. He then left.

After a short while, having been sent to burn some of Rasputin's clothes, a car containing the young Grand Duke Dimitri Pavlovich, Ivan Sukhotin, an army officer, and Dr. Stanislas Lazavert returned. They had driven off on their mission after Yusupov shot Rasputin, and the five conspirators thought he was dead.

Purishkevich, Dr. Lazavert, and Sukhotin, along with one of the palace soldiers, placed the body in the back seat of the car. Grand Duke Dimitri drove and the five men, with the body of Rasputin, headed for Petrovsky Bridge, which connected the two islands of Krestinsky and Petrovsky. It was now about 4 a.m. and the streets were quiet, dark, and cold. The Grand Duke drove slowly to avoid alerting anyone. At the far end of the bridge was a small watchman's shack, but the figure there was sleeping.

The Grand Duke shut off the car lights, and the scene plunged into darkness. While the Grand Duke kept watch, the other four men threw the body into a hole in the otherwise frozen tributary of the Neva River. The rapidly swirling current around one of the arches of the bridge evidently had created the hole in the ice.

They moved quickly but forgot to attach a chain they had brought to weigh down the body. When they realized this, they threw the chain and a Rasputin boot they found in the car, in after the body and sped off.

Who was Rasputin? Why were these important people representing the army, the political world, royalty, and the aristocracy so intent on killing him?

Winning the Confidence of the Tsar and Empress

Bedchamber of Tsarevich Alexis
Alexander Palace
Tsarskoe Selo, Russia

In the middle of the night, Rasputin had been summoned to the bedside of the Tsarevich Alexis, the young heir to the throne. Empress Alexandra had reached the end of her tether and didn't know where else to turn. The doctors had told her the hemophilia from which her young son suffered was beyond their power to help.

Hemophilia is a disorder that prevents blood from clotting. Hence, when bleeding does occur, with a hemophiliac it won't stop, as with most people. Instead, bleeding would continue and, in the case of internal injuries, the blood would seep into the nearby body cavities and organs causing dangerous swelling. The pressure from this would cause excruciating pain to the sufferer. Alexis would moan and cry out to his mother in his agony. Each cry was a stab in the heart to the helpless Empress.

The Tsarevich's illness had been hidden from all but those closest to the Royal Family, and great precautions were taken to prevent injuries to him. Two sailors took turns constantly caring for him in order to prevent injuries. However, a young boy is bound to stumble and fall, or bump into a piece of furniture. Even a minor bruise was often enough to start the blood flowing.

Finally, the piteous cries of the suffering young Tsarevich drove the Empress to send for the peasant mystic who had often visited with the Royal Family, impressing them with his simple piety. He had comforted Alexis before and was also credited with helping other close family associates. He even eased some of the anxieties of the Empress herself.

When Rasputin entered the Tsarevich's bedchamber, he went to the foot of the bed and examined the child. He prayed and smiled down at the boy. The boy relaxed and fell asleep. Rasputin told the Empress that Alexis would sleep and feel better in the morning. He told the Empress not to let the doctors bother the heir too much. She took the mystic's hand and wept.

Similar events happened time after time once Rasputin had met the Royal Family. The Tsarevich Alexis would cry and suffer. The doctors were off to the side muttering, "Nothing can be done." The Empress choked with anxiety. The Tsar would wring his hands and look grim. Rasputin would be contacted and come, or send a reassuring message. The Tsarevich would become calm, sleep, and recover. The Empress and Tsar would be relieved, faith in the mystic reinforced and his influence growing day-by-day, ending only with his murder.

Where did Rasputin come from? How far did he travel to get to a position where he eventually influenced the very workings of the government?

Grigory Efimovich Rasputin

Rasputin was born in a small Siberian village, Pokrovskoe, located on a bank above the Tura River. Siberia was the frontier, many miles from the secret police and the Russian capital of St. Petersburg. It was a backwater. It was a little wild. The people were rough and ready, always eager for a little horseplay and adventure. Very little of the cultural and political life of the Russian mainstream reached here, but people enjoyed more personal freedom.

In the absence of city entertainment and diversions, people amused themselves with drinking, dancing, and carousing. By the age of fifteen, young Rasputin was well initiated into strong drink and sex. Three events are often mentioned in descriptions of Rasputin's early life.

When he was eight years old, Grisha, as Rasputin was called then, and his ten-year-old brother Mischa, went swimming in the river shallows where the cattle were watered. Mischa drifted out and was caught by the current, dragging Rasputin along. A farmer rescued them from drowning, but the ten-year-old Mischa developed pneumonia and died.

In the small village, there were few other boys Rasputin's age. He stayed by himself more and more after his brother's death and grew more introspective.

A meeting was once convened in his father's house to discuss the theft of a horse in the village. Rasputin was ill with a fever. In the middle of the discussion, Rasputin pointed to one of the people present accusing him as the thief. Everyone else in the room was startled and expressed their disbelief. His father beat him.

Later, however, some villagers followed the alleged thief back to his barn and found the horse. Rasputin's first evidence of second sight was established. Had he seen the horse being stolen? Was it based on intuition? Was it luck? These questions would be asked in the future about his often, unexplainable insights.

As a young man, Rasputin drove his father's cart to the larger town of Tyumen. He made deliveries and picked up other articles to take back to Pokrovskoe. On one such trip, he saw an attractive young, blond woman in a carriage on Tyumen's main street. He followed her in his cart until she went through the gates of an estate. He sat there on the estate's wall for a time before departing.

On his next visit to Tyumen, he saw the woman's carriage again. This time her maid came over to him with a message. Her mistress invited him to return and sit on the same wall again. He drove out to the estate and, after sitting on the wall a short time, the woman appeared. She led him to a summerhouse. There she fondled his trouser front a couple of times before going into the next room, telling him to come along quickly. He stripped off his clothes and went into a darkened chamber where he found her stretched out on a sofa, fully clothed. As he stepped forward, she raised her arm and gave the command, *"Now!"*

Four maids stepped out from behind curtains to jeer and torment him in his aroused and naked state. A fifth maid cooled him off by throwing a bucket of cold water on him. After they had enough fun poking and laughing at him, they carried him out of the house and flung him on the ground. One of the maids felt sorry for him, however, and brought him his clothes.

The perpetrator of the cruel hoax was Madame Irina Kubasova, the attractive daughter of an artillery colonel in Moscow. To settle his gambling debts, this colonel gave his daughter in marriage to his commanding officer, General Kubasova. The general was forty years older than his wife and had resigned from his regiment in Moscow to enjoy his estate outside Tyumen with his new wife. His young wife had to use her ingenuity to find amusement away from Moscow, and her cruel joke at Rasputin's expense was one result.

When he was nineteen, Rasputin met a girl at a festival at the Abulatsky Monastery. Her name was Praskovia Fedorovia and she was from the nearby village of Dubrovnoye. They were first drawn to each other by their mutual enjoyment of dancing and singing. It was also about this time Rasputin's father began remarking that another pair of hands would be useful on the farm. Praskovia was a pretty girl with blond hair and dark eyes. She was three years older than Rasputin. Most importantly, she was willing and strong. They were married after a six-month courtship.

Rasputin was frequently absent, so she ran the family farm, doing it ably enough to employ two people. He was home enough to sire four children, Maria, Dimitry, Varya, and another who didn't live long. In spite of his continuous womanizing, Rasputin had no prolonged romantic attachment except for his wife. She was tolerant of his drinking and continued interest in bedding other women. When she was told of his infidelity, she remarked that, " He has enough for all." He always returned to Praskovia, and she was always glad to see him.

Rasputin's boisterous behavior and drinking finally got him into some trouble in the village. After some accusations of stealing and threats of exile, Rasputin and his wife decided he should leave for a while and stay at the nearby Monastery of Verkhoturye.

Here he lived in a stone cell and slept on a cot. He made daily pilgrimages to a staret living in a nearby hut. A staret is a self-proclaimed "holy man" who lives simply and alone. Rasputin visited this nearby staret, Makari, who was well known and was visited by many important men who found help in his counsel.

Makari and Rasputin prayed and talked together, and, from this time forward, Rasputin found his calling. To be a staret was to be respected in Russia. It was a way of life suitable to Rasputin's talents. He was self-confident, he spoke well, had a smattering of religious knowledge, and he was physically imposing. Without education or commercial leanings, being undisciplined and married, the opportunities for him in the formal church, army, or trade were out of reach. A career as staret was perfect. He returned to Pokrovskoye a changed man. He now had a mission.

He gave up drinking (for a time) and smoking. He no longer ate meat and sweets.

One day when working in the fields, Rasputin claims he saw a vision of the Virgin Mary dressed in sumptuous robes. She pointed toward the horizon. He understood this to mean he was to travel as a pilgrim.

Rasputin told his family of the visitations and his intentions to embark on a journey to find God. His father thought it was a way to avoid work.

During the spring and summer, he wandered to distant monasteries and churches. He sought food and lodging in the homes of peasants. He begged for money. He saw at first hand the sects and religious practices in the rural countryside. Two of these sects were the Skoptsy and Khlysty. These were old believers who resented some of the current practices of the Orthodox Church.

The Skoptsy practiced castration. This belief was based on a Bible passage referring to eunuchs, which they interpreted was a way to salvation.

The sect whose teachings appealed most to him seemed to be the Khlysty. They believed in purifying the soul and finding redemption by first mortifying the flesh. They held services in hidden places and engaged in mass sexual orgies during which women didn't limit themselves to their husbands but coupled with all the men present. Here at last was a belief Rasputin could embrace and, at which, he could excel. Since at these services women often outnumbered men, Rasputin worshipped by extending his fervor freely.

At least two incidents of his practicing this religion are recorded. The first incident occurred when he sought shelter and food with a peasant family whom he impressed enough to be invited to a service in the evening at a secret meeting place. The service went on for a while until the leader signaled it was time for the physical mortification to begin. The women and men fell upon each other. One of the first to clasp Rasputin was his hostess. Since he was one of only three men present, he was kept busy.

Another time, he came upon three nude women bathing in a pool of water in a glen. He took off his clothes and joined them. He ended up coupling with all three on the ground nearby. Although he seems to have enthusiastically accepted at least some of their practices, he always denied being a Khlysty.

His travels took him as far as Mount Athos, Greece, where he visited a monastery, but was not favorably impressed by the piety of the monks and some of the practices there.

On his wanderings, he listened and observed. From the priests he picked up a smattering of theology and Bible stories. To the peasants, he preached and prophesized.

He was a fast learner. He was also cunning and sly. He paid careful attention to how people responded, what they wanted to hear, and what was enthusiastically accepted. When he returned to Pokrovskoe, he developed a following. He was so successful that the church authorities investigated his teachings for heresy. However, he was exonerated and his reputation grew.

Finally, in 1903, he felt ready for a bigger stage and went to St. Petersburg. There Bishop Sergius, the rector of the Theological Seminary, cordially received him, and he lived for a time at the Alexander Nevsky Monastery.

The formal church was aware that there was a large gap between the sumptuously-robed bishops, who worshipped behind their icon screens in large, elegant cathedrals, and the simple peasants in far off villages and hamlets. A man of the people, in clothes soiled by wanderings on the road, would give them a link to the millions of peasants scattered over the vast lands of Russia.

Rasputin filled this gap. He was a novelty in the elegant salons, mingling with the bejeweled matrons of the capital. They thought at first they could use him; that he would divert them for a while. While they were contemplating him and his usefulness, he was doing the same thing with them. He took the measure of these elegant upper levels of society and church and decided he could be successful among them. After his first visit to St. Petersburg, he returned to his Pokrorskoe village. After 1905, he was mostly in St. Petersburg, but he continued to visit his family in Pokrorskoe, from time to time.

Two members of society, the Nikolaevna sisters, Milita and Anastasia, princesses from Montenegro, took a special interest in him. They wanted greater control over him, however, than he was prepared to yield.

At the end of 1905, he requested an audience with the Tsar in order to present him with an icon. It was granted, and it was the second fateful coming together for the Tsar since meeting his wife, Alexandra. The Tsar and Empress Alexandra were on the lookout for a new "friend" since their old friend Philip had just died.

Their new friend told them what they wanted to hear. He had wandered all over Russia visiting simple people in their homes and praying with them. Their subjects, he told the Tsar, loved "Mama and Papa," in contrast to St. Petersburg society who ridiculed them behind their backs.

He was good with the royal children, amused them, and led them in prayer. Most important, he was able to comfort the Tsarevich Alexis when he suffered from pain caused by his hemophilia.

Assassination of Alexander II

Winter Palace
St. Petersburg, Russia
March 1, 1881

Nicholas, heir to the Russian throne, was thirteen years old when he was summoned to the Winter Palace to see his grandfather, Tsar Alexander II. The Tsar was lying on a couch, mortally wounded and dying. A short while before, the Tsar was riding in a coach on a St. Petersburg street when a bomb was tossed at his coach, missing its target. When the Tsar got out of the coach to see what had happened, a second bomb was thrown at his feet. It went off and blew his legs away. He was still alive and murmured, "To the palace, to die there."

The members of the royal family were summoned to the side of the dying Tsar. Before long, the doctor announced that he was dead. It was a cruel and ominous introduction for the young Nicholas to the assassinations and the dark days that were to come for the Royal family and Russia. Nicholas's father, who was now the new Tsar, Alexander III, left the palace under heavy guard.

Alexander lll was a large, imposing figure and believed in autocracy. He had a " hands on" approach to government. His wife, Empress Marie Fedorovna, was the former Danish Princess, Dagmar. While he ruled Russia, she presided over St. Petersburg's social world.

The beautiful Church of the Resurrection of Christ was built in the old Orthodox style at the spot where Tsar Alexander II was attacked. It has been restored recently and can be visited.

Tsarevich Nicholas and Princess Alexandra

Tsarevich Nicholas, as a member of the Tsar's family, and as heir apparent, had his early life filled with ceremonial occasions and happy family times.

Near Kotka, Finland there is a salmon stream. On the shore there his Finnish subjects built for Alexander III a beautiful, rustic, wooden dacha, called Fisherman's Cottage. It could only hold the immediate family and a few guests and guards. The Imperial Family would cruise the Gulf of Finland in the royal yacht and stop off for day visits. They returned to the yacht at night for security reasons. The pots and pans, which the Empress herself sometimes used for cooking, still hang there.

Not much attention was paid to the training of Tsarevich Nicholas for his future duties as Tsar. His father was relatively young, so no one looked beyond his reign. The Tsar seemed to have reservations about giving responsibility to young Nicholas. The agreeable Nicholas enjoyed reviewing troops and saluting while mounted on a white horse and dressed in a splendid uniform.

He had an affair with an attractive ballerina, Mathilde Kschessinskaya. He served in the Horse Guards and enjoyed the social life of St. Petersburg, which offered balls, receptions, and theaters. He was always treated with great deference everywhere he went.

In 1884, at the wedding of his uncle, Grand Duke Serge, to a German princess, he saw the bride's sister, Princess Alix of Hesse-Darmstadt, for the first time. They saw each other from time to time thereafter, and Nicholas fell deeply in love. However, she had some reservations about marrying Nicholas, as it would require converting to the Russian Orthodox religion.

Alexandra (Alix), Princess of Hesse-Darmstadt, was the daughter of Princess Alice, who was the daughter of the English Queen, Victoria, making Alix one of Victoria's many grandchildren. The ties of Princess Alice to her mother and England were strong, and visits there were made annually.

Alix's father was Grand Duke Louis of Hesse, Germany. The Duke's Palace was in the center of the old German City of Darmstadt. Two years before Alix's birth, the Duchy lost its independence and had been incorporated into the German Empire.

Alix was growing up bright and merry, guided by an English nanny, until the age of six, when her mother died of diphtheria. It had a shattering effect on the young Alix's personality. She became aloof and shy. She was uncomfortable in unknown surroundings and only opened up with her family, avoiding unfamiliar people. She was a good student and was well educated. She played the piano with great skill, but was shy and only played reluctantly in front of people. She grew up to be very attractive with beautiful golden, red hair. She also developed an interest in politics and was conscious that her grandmother, Queen Victoria, a woman, was the dominant monarch in Europe.

As she grew older, marriage opportunities presented themselves, but the young Princess held off. Once she overcame her reluctance to embrace Orthodoxy, however, she agreed to the ardent proposal of Nicholas.

While Nicholas was trying to convince Alix to marry him, he was also trying to persuade his father and mother, the Tsar and Empress, to the idea of the marriage. There were reservations about Alix for reasons that were shared by many in St. Petersburg. During a six-week visit to St. Petersburg in 1889, she hadn't impressed the Empress or the other leaders of society as being chic or fashionable.

There was also an interest in having Nicholas take a suitable French bride to firm up relations with France. While these events were taking place, Tsar Alexander III became ill, and his physical condition began to rapidly deteriorate. After Nicholas convinced Alix to marry him, he made his first important decision by insisting on the marriage in spite of his parents' objections. It proved to be a fateful decision for the future Tsar.

When it became clear that Alexander III wasn't likely to live much longer, he and the Empress reluctantly agreed to the marriage of Nicholas and Alix. Tsar Alexander III hoped that by marrying, his son would be less distracted than as a single man, and be better able to reign.

Princess Alexandra of Hesse-Darmstadt was asked to come to the Crimea and to the Royal Palace at Livadia, where the Tsar was dying. The Tsar greeted her by making the effort, in spite of his illness, to appear before her in full dress uniform. She and Nicholas kneeled before him and were formally betrothed. On November 1, 1894, the Tsar died.

On November 26, one week after the funeral, Nicholas and Alix were married in the chapel of the St. Petersburg Winter Palace in an appropriately subdued ceremony. It was a very passionate bonding, and their correspondence makes clear that, for the rest of their lives, their love for each other remained strong and never wavered.

About six months after their marriage, Nicholas and Alexandra traveled to Moscow for elaborate and traditional coronation ceremonies. During the ceremonies in the Ouspensky Cathedral, Nicholas, following tradition, crowned himself and then Alix. Later there was a coronation banquet for seven thousand guests, followed by a grand ball.

The next day the people of Moscow had a traditional feast in an open field, where the newly crowned monarchs could greet their subjects. Arrangements were made to distribute a souvenir-enameled cup stamped with the imperial seal. Hundreds of barrels of beer were also ordered. Thousands of people were expected and began arriving the evening before. By morning an estimated half a million subjects were there.

A rumor started that there weren't enough souvenir cups and beer! A stampede occurred with too few guards to control the crowd. People were knocked down and trampled. Hundreds died and thousands were hurt and wounded.

The Tsar and Empress were shocked and shaken.

A ball to be given by the French was planned for that evening, and the new monarchs were urged to go, for diplomatic reasons, in spite of the disaster. Unwisely, they did so, and the people took notice. The first small descent into diminished veneration had begun of the "Tsar - leader of the Russian people, chosen by God to protect them."

Generally after marriage, the first duty of monarchs is to produce an heir. Nicholas and Alix did their best. Over the next eight years, Alexandra gave birth four times but always to daughters, and the realm required a male heir. Her reclusive personality and pregnancies kept her from assuming the leadership of society, which Empress Marie had always enjoyed. A distance developed between her and the society people, who should have been her staunchest supporters.

In 1902, a Minister of the Interior, D.S. Sipyagin, was assassinated. Two years later, in 1904, a second Minister of the Interior, V.L. Plehve, also was killed. If the men in charge of the police couldn't protect themselves, what protection was there for others?

The Tsar and his wife came to develop and share an interest in mysticism. They came to believe that the spirit of Christ could be best found among the simple people in the remote villages of Russia's vast lands and wilderness. This belief led to an ongoing search for "a man of God" from among the common people. In their search, the Nikolaevna sisters, Milita and Anastasia, the daughters of the King of Montenegro, aided the Royal Family. Milita had read extensively in the literature of the East and its exotic beliefs. Stories of other gods and Eastern mysteries captivated Empress Alexandra, who had not been exposed to this in her strict Victorian upbringing.

The earliest candidate, as a messenger of God brought by the sisters to the palace, was "Mitya." He wore his hair long, went barefoot, and wore a cassock. He was said to have the gift of prophecy. It was hoped that he would intercede with God to produce a male heir. When this didn't happen, his mumbling got tiresome.

Next came "Matryona the Barefoot," a woman who brought an icon. This made a good impression. She didn't last too long because Alexandra lost patience with her hard-to-follow murmuring. Next, the Nikolaevna sisters found a reputed miracle worker from France, Monsieur Philippe. He spoke well and made a good impression. The

Royal couple referred to him as "their friend." In spite of his intercession, Alexandra gave birth to a fourth daughter in 1901.

However, Philippe explained this happened because Alexandra's faith was weak. He told her she needed to ask for the aid of a Russian Saint. This saint, he said, was Serafim of Sarov. Alexandra and the Tsar made a pilgrimage to Sarov. The miracle came to pass. Tsarevich Alexis was born on August 12, 1904. Joy quickly turned to anguish when it became clear he was a hemophiliac. When he bled, it wouldn't stop. Alexandra suffered with the knowledge that this disorder was inherited from her side of the family. Philippe died in 1905, but he had given mystics a good name, preparing the way for another.

In addition to the mystics, someone else entered into the daily lives of the royal couple about the time Tsarevich Alexis was born. Anya Taneyev was the daughter of Alexander S. Taneyev, Director of the Imperial Chancellery. He also composed music, and Anya learned to sing and play the piano. As a young girl, she attended an exclusive dancing school and was occasionally partnered with Prince Felix Yusupov. She was plain and somewhat plump.

When she was seventeen, she was in the hospital and was visited by Empress Alexandra. This gesture ignited gratitude and warm feelings in Anya. She was later invited to the palace where the Empress was happy to discover Anya could sing and play the piano. The Empress now had someone with whom she could share her musical interests. In 1904, Anya was formally presented to the Empress and designated a maid of honor. She suited the Empress's need for someone close to her in whom she could confide. Anya became so devoted that Alix came to trust her. From that time forward, she was so close to the Royal family that she accompanied them on the royal yacht, Polar Star. She went with them almost everywhere, practically becoming a member of the family.

After a short unsuccessful marriage to a naval officer, Alexander Vyrubov, which was later revealed to have been unconsummated; Anya came to live at Tsarskoe Selo. She lived there in her own small house. Here Nicholas, Alix, and Anya, sometimes joined by Rasputin, would spend cozy evenings. Alix and Rasputin would discuss what actions Nicholas could best take for the good of Russia and the Monarchy. Anya would nod, murmur agreement, or withhold comment. All other people not included in these intimate tête-à-têtes speculated about them. Plain, unattractive Anya was at the center of the action. She also acted as go-between for the Royal Family and Rasputin.

Anya never asked for favors for herself or her relatives and never appeared at official functions.

The Monarchy Assailed

The trials of the Imperial Family and Russia were moving into their most crucial and challenging period - the events of 1905.

January 9, 1905–a group of peasants and workers led by a Father Gapon began a march to the Winter Palace to petition the Tsar, "Papa," for modest alleviation of some of their grievances. Troops were called out. Shots were fired and people were killed. The Tsar wasn't even at the Palace. It went down in history as "Bloody Sunday."

February 1905 - a terrorist bomb tore Grand Duke Serge (Governor of Moscow, the Tsar's uncle and husband of the Empress's sister, Elizabeth) to pieces shortly after he left his palace.

May 27, 1905–The Russian Fleet, which had traveled half way around the world, was engaged and defeated by the Japanese in the Battle of Tsushima. It was a severe blow for Russia's military reputation, particularly in the eyes of other European nations. It was also a personal humiliation for Nicholas, since many of the other concerned Royal families were his relatives.

October 30, 1905 - Finally, strikes by workers, mutiny aboard Navy ships, murders of policemen, riots, and more disorders (stemming from the above events) resulted in an important reduction of the Tsar's authority. He was forced for the first time to accept a legislative body, the Duma, and share power.

It is somewhat surprising that someone else wasn't put forward to replace Nicholas as Tsar. There was ample precedent in Russia's history for a change in the head of government.

1. Peter the Great - When Peter was seventeen years old, he summoned the leading military and civilian figures, generals and boyars, to rally around him and repudiate the Regent, his half sister, Sophia. Peter

called on them to recognize him as their ruler. They did so, and Sophia was sent to a convent.

2. Empress Elizabeth-For over sixteen years, Peter's daughter watched four Tsars, sometimes with Regents, rule the country after her father's death. When she decided it was her turn, she donned the uniform of the Preobrazhensky Regiment and led a takeover of the Winter Palace. She personally went into the bedroom of the Regent Anna, who was asleep, and whispered in her ear, "Wake up, sister." Elizabeth wore the crown for twenty-two years.

3. Catherine the Great–This German Princess was told that Tsar Peter III, the deceased Empress Elizabeth's nephew and Catherine's husband, was planning to have her killed or sent to a convent. For many years Catherine had cultivated the aristocracy, the Church, and most importantly, the Guard Regiments. When she felt her life threatened, she gathered the regiments behind her and had Peter deposed. Six months later Peter III was killed. Another potential rival, Ivan VI, was kept in prison at Schlusselberg. It was there that he was killed, when it appeared a rescue might be attempted that would threaten her crown. She kept her own son off the throne until she died.

4. Alexander 1 - This grandson of Catherine probably acquiesced in the murder of his own father, Tsar Paul I, when his bizarre behavior threatened Russia. The power brokers couldn't risk Paul I on the throne with Napoleon rampaging around Europe. He was strangled in the bed of his specially built stronghold, Michael Castle.

Sisters, husbands, fathers, and sons–none stood in the way of removing incompetent rulers. Why wasn't something more done after the disasters of 1905?

What did happen next, at the end of 1905, only served to further distance the Tsar from what should have been his closest supporters and the seat of his government.

The Tsar decided to get away from St. Petersburg, the primary location of his miseries. The Winter Palace was the scene of "Bloody Sunday," and where he watched his grandfather, Alexander II, bleed to death. On the other side of the city was the Tauride Palace, now home to the detested Duma. His mother, the Dowager Empress Marie, lived in the Anichkov Palace on the Nevsky Prospect. Around her clustered the other royals and the aristocracy, who were increasingly critical of the Royal Family and particularly, Empress Alexandra. Unfavorable comparisons were also made between the slight, shy, unassuming Nicholas and his large-than-life father.

The Royal Family decided to make the family's regular home the Alexander Palace at Tsarskoe Selo, fourteen miles from St. Petersburg. Here they circled the wagons.

This also put distance between Nicholas and his ministers and other advisors back in St. Petersburg. The influence of Empress Alexandra would increasingly fill the void of the St. Petersburg advisors.

There was also growing concern about the condition of Tsarevich Alexis, which was continuing to shape the actions of the Tsar. Concerns about Alexis's health and the desire to keep his condition secret kept the family closely bound together. They met Rasputin at this time, and his ability to comfort the heir strengthened his influence on Alexandra, and through her, the Tsar. Gradually, the Tsar and Alexandra permitted only their two close confidants to share their intimate circle - Rasputin and Anya Vyrubova.

Fanning the Flames of Anarchy

From 1906 to 1911, Russia's Prime Minister was Peter Stolypin. He was from the country and worked his way up gradually to the top government positions in St. Petersburg. Stolypin was an able man and struggled fairly successfully in balancing the interests of the Royal Family, the Duma, the government ministries, Rasputin's influence, and Russia's interests, as he saw them. However, through the Royal Family, Rasputin's influence continued to grow on government appointments and policies.

After a time, Rasputin's relations with the Royal Family became more widely known, and stories about it began appearing in the newspapers. Rasputin's drinking and womanizing cut a wide swath in the nightclubs and boudoirs of the city. Scandalous cartoons started appearing, suggesting the most intimate relations between the Empress and the mystic. The Tsar insisted that Stolypin stop the stories and cartoons from appearing in the newspapers. The publishers were fined but continued printing the stories because they sold newspapers.

Rasputin continued to turn the face of a holy man of God to the Royal Family. Away from them, however, he indulged in every available vice. Petitioners for favors visited him in his apartment. The men usually offered money. If the women were attractive, he would try to fondle them and would suggest cleansing themselves through sex with him. He wasn't insistent. There were always others in line who would be more accommodating if a particular woman wasn't agreeable.

The Tsar turned aside, or even broke relations, with anyone who tried to inform him of Rasputin's often-scandalous behavior.

In 1911, the Stolypin era closed when he was fatally shot in Kiev at an opera performance attended by the Tsar. His death opened the way to a revolving door of Prime Ministers. From 1911 until 1917, there were five different individuals. These Prime Ministers served such a short time that some didn't even bother to move into the official apartment provided since it wasn't likely to be their home very long.

While these local doings were happening in Russia, outside events that would reverberate in Russia were also moving forward in the rest of Europe. For a long time, Germany had been a fragmented collection of small principalities headed by Prussia. Led by Bismarck, Germany united and won the Franco-Prussian War of 1871. It now wanted overseas colonies with their commercial advantages just as the other major nations of Europe had been enjoying. Germany was flexing its muscles. France and Great Britain weren't eager to enhance a competitor's position in the world and feared Germany's growing dominance in Europe.

This came to a head in 1914 when Russia and the rest of Europe stumbled into war. Germany and Austria were on one side, and England, France, and Russia on the other. France urged the Russians to immediately invade westward toward Germany to take pressure off themselves, but Russia was ill prepared for war. The army lacked equipment, organization, and leadership. The size of Russia and the lack of suitable railroad transportation made organization difficult. Equipment took time to produce. In the initial engagements, the Germans, with superb organization and armaments, slaughtered the untrained, poorly armed, but courageous Russians.

The most depressing story told about the Russian army's lack of arms was the report that only the front ranks of charging infantry had rifles. The men who followed were told to pick up the rifles of their fallen comrades after they were cut down by German machine guns. In one engagement, the best troops, the Guard Regiments, were mowed down by strafing planes while they slogged through a marsh.

Tsar Nicholas decided to go to military headquarters, presumably to help solve the leadership problem. He also decided to take his son. The generals at headquarters now must include deferring to and consulting with the Tsar, in addition to entertaining a young boy, to their daily tasks. Both father and son enjoyed reviewing the troops and taking their salutes.

Back at Tsarskoe Selo, the Tsar had left the Empress, as Regent, in charge of the government. She was determined that her son would inherit the crown with maximum power. She divided government appointees into "those that are with us and those who aren't with us." Rasputin helped guide these decisions based on his own agenda. Competency didn't loom large in these discussions.

The Duma met and the members made speeches. It was organized into parties representing various interests that splintered into sub–groups and sometimes formed again into new factions. Anti-government forces assassinated officials and circulated propaganda opposing the government. The secret police executed, exiled, or imprisoned terrorists when they caught them.

The St. Petersburg population was going hungry because there was insufficient transportation to bring food in from the countryside, while also supplying the army. The population was increasingly desolate as their sons and fathers were reported dead or battlefield casualties. The relations of the Empress with Rasputin, real and perceived, plus her being born a German, fueled discontent. Discipline in the St. Petersburg garrisons was reduced, as the best troops were sent to the front.

In the midst of this growing upheaval in Russia, let's turn our attention to Prince Felix Yusupov. You'll recall that, at the beginning of our story, he was running up the steps of the basement dining room in his Palace on the Moika Embankment.

Broken Pearl Necklace

Bear Restaurant
St. Petersburg, Russia
About 1906

Prince Felix Yusupov was having a grand time this evening. He had outfitted himself in one of his mother's beautiful dresses and a wig, and had come with his friends to the Bear, one of St. Petersburg's most fashionable restaurants in pre-Revolutionary Russia. He was flirting, laughing and cavorting in high spirits.

To complete his masquerade, Felix had borrowed one of his mother's fabulous pearl necklaces, and, after wearing it, began waving it around and using it as a lasso. Suddenly, the necklace chain broke and expensive pearls fell to the floor, scattering all about. Immediately the Prince, his friends and many of the restaurant guests and waiters, were on their hands and knees attempting to gather as many of the pearls as they could find.

This commotion was too much for the restaurant manager and the Prince was asked to leave. However, Felix had been recognized, and the next day his father was sent the other pearls that had been recovered after he left. His father, who was Commandant of the Horse Guards and a stern soldier, was not amused and made Felix agree not to dress in woman's clothes again nor carry on in this fashion.

The pearl necklace escapade is only one of the many stories involving Prince Felix's enormous wealth, his good looks, and the title inherited from his illustrious forebears, that were gossiped about in St. Petersburg society. It gives a fair picture of the Prince as a young man - flamboyant, fun loving, careless about expensive baubles, ambivalent about his sexuality, and not too concerned about what people thought. He developed his reputation for high living in St. Petersburg society quite naturally, given his family background.

Prince Felix Yusupov

Prince Felix Yusupov was heir to one of the oldest and most illustrious names in Russia and one of its largest family fortunes. There are variations on the spelling of the family name, but we will use, "Yusupov." In one of his books, Yusupov traced his family and his Tartar ancestors to the sixth century, and he suggests even possible kinship with Prophet Ali, a nephew of Mahomet.

These very early ancestors had religious and political authority in large areas of what is today Egypt and Constantinople. The shores of the Caspian and Azov Seas also had large tracts of land ruled by his ancestors. The first recorded mention of a Yusupov is Khan Youssouf, who allied himself with Tsar Ivan IV, known as Ivan the Terrible. Tsar Ivan IV was the first ruler of Moscow to style himself Tsar, Ruler of all the Russians, not just Moscow.

From this time forward, the Yusupov family's activities and fortunes were intimately associated with Russia's ruling family. They served, entertained, and were richly rewarded by Peter the Great, Empress Anne, Empress Elizabeth, Catherine the Great, and the Russian rulers who followed.

Prince Yusupov's father married into the family and took their name when he married Princess Zenaide Yusupov, a great beauty and the last of her line. He himself had come to the marriage as Count Sumarokov-Elston, the title that had been granted to his father Felix Elston. The father received his title when he married Helen Sergeievna, Countess Sumarokov, and the last of her line. Felix's grandfather, Felix Elston, was said to be the son of a King of Prussia, Frederich William IV. It was said his birth resulted from a liaison between the King and a maid of honor to a Russian Empress, the King's sister, who was visiting him. This son, Felix Elston, later came from Germany, where he had lived until the age of sixteen. He was given command of the Don Cossacks.

This lineage of ancestors came together in Prince Felix Yusupov and reflected nobility, loyalty, honorable service, and even royalty. The long history and association with Russia's Royal Family provided the Yusupov family with possessions and wealth that is hard to grasp, even in today's world. The Yusupov family had homes and estates throughout the Russian Empire. Their main residence still stands in St. Petersburg and is a lavish palace located on the Moika Embankment. It is here where Prince Yusupov was born March 24, 1887.

Felix's mother, the beautiful Princess Zenaide Yusupov, had expected a baby girl and had bought pretty clothes with ribbons and bows. Actually, dressing a boy in frilly feminine baby clothes was not uncommon in the Yusupov's social circle. They often dressed their boys and girls that way until a certain age, keeping their hair long and curly. While the other boys grew older and resented the skirts and curly hair, young Felix seemed to relish it. On walks with his nanny, he would call out to a passerby, " Look, isn't baby pretty?"

When Felix was twelve years old, he accompanied his parents on a holiday to a European spa. While walking around one evening he peered into a hotel window and saw a man and a woman making love. Unlike most Russian boys at that time who were brought up on farms and came to know about these things at an early age, Felix was entranced, but reported he was puzzled by what they were doing. The next day, he met the man on the street, introduced himself, and told him what he had seen. The man, who was from Argentina, was amused and invited Felix to join them later in the day when he again planned to meet with the woman. Felix did so but did not reveal what happened.

The Yusupov family had a regular, annual schedule based upon the seasons. The Moika Palace in St. Petersburg was where winters were spent. There were balls and receptions at various palaces. They enjoyed the ballet and opera at the Marinsky Theatre. The Yusupovs were members of the most exclusive clubs. Felix particularly enjoyed the city's nightspots - Cubat's, the Bear, Villa Rode, and the Aquarium Club. He visited the gypsies on the outskirts of the city and caroused until dawn. The Yusupovs had other homes in St. Petersburg and in many other parts of Russia.

In the spring the family moved to their villa at Tsarskoe Selo. The Imperial Court entertained in the magnificent Catherine's Palace. The

Yusupovs next went for a brief stay at their dacha at Krasnoe Selo, where they watched army maneuvers during July.

Summers were spent in Moscow, where one of their homes formerly belonged to Tsar Ivan IV, the Terrible. Near Moscow, the Yusupovs had their great country estate, Arkhangelskoye.

In the early fall, the Yusupovs went to their rural estate in central Russia, Rakitnoe, for the hunt. In the late fall, it was off to the Crimea on the Black Sea and its warm climate. Here the family had three estates.

Each of these properties employed hundreds of servants–field workers, dairymaids, veterinarians, carpenters, and other craftsmen. The villas and palaces had cooks, scullery maids, kitchen boys, butlers, ladies maids, valets, and drivers. There were also tailors, shoemakers, and others trained to perform as singers and musicians. The estates were used to entertain both informally and as part of official functions.

Felix had a brother, five years older, who was first in line to inherit the Yusupov fortune. Felix and his older brother, Nikolai, were spoiled. Their mother denied them very little. Their father, who was a soldier, occasionally stepped in to discipline them, but he was away a lot and didn't have much influence. The boys ran around the palace doing pretty much as they liked and had a full coterie of servants and tutors to do their bidding.

Nikolai grew up to be a handsome man and a rake, who enjoyed seducing the young beauties of the day. Felix and his older brother started making the rounds in St. Petersburg together once Felix grew into his teens. Felix was growing up to be very attractive. He had fine features and long eyebrows. For fun and diversion, Nikolai and his friends would often help dress a willing Felix in feminine attire, makeup, and wig, and parade around St. Petersburg's streets and nightclubs. Attired this way, Felix always attracted male interest and attention.

After the pearl necklace episode at the Bear Restaurant, Felix stopped doing this in St. Petersburg. One night in Paris, however, on one of these escapades, he attracted the attention of a well-dressed gentleman with a gray beard, who turned out to be Edward Vll, the British King.

Finally, Nikolai, found a beautiful woman, Countess Marina Heiden, with whom he fell in love. Unfortunately, she was engaged to an officer in the Horse Guards, Baron Arwid Manteifel. However, he couldn't compete with the Yusupov wealth and Nikolai's charms. She and Nikolai became lovers keeping their affair secret while they tried to convince his parents that they should be allowed to marry.

The Yusupovs wouldn't agree to this, and finally Manteifel, who was getting suspicious, got Marina to agree to a marriage date. A date was set, and she went off to Paris for her trousseau. Nikolai followed her and the affair continued in the French capital. She returned to St. Petersburg and the marriage to Manteifel took place.

The newly married couple went to Paris for their honeymoon, and, again, Nikolai followed. The husband finally learned of his new wife's infidelity and challenged Nikolai to a duel. However, Manteifel, after meeting with Nikolai's parents, declared the duel was off; he would divorce his wife. His fellow officers, however, convinced him that honor required a duel. After some further bobbing and weaving about whether a duel was necessary, the cuckolded husband finally insisted upon it and the duel was arranged.

Nikolai was killed. The Yusupov family was distraught, but Manteifel was momentarily satisfied. Society, and even his regiment, later ostracized the husband. The officer and the woman were soon divorced. Felix was now sole heir to the Yusupov fortune. With his teen-age years behind him and the death of his brother, Felix had complete responsibility for the future of the family's heritage. It was time to do something constructive. Felix decided to attend Oxford.

He traveled to England with appropriate letters of introduction and was admitted to University College on the High. He took rooms on the ground floor. Because of their location, they were referred to as the Club, since, traditionally students had the habit of "hanging out" there. This was fine to the ultimately social Felix who often hosted parties in the rooms. He also provided an entrance to the building through his window when the door was locked after hours. The students would knock, and he would pull them up with a sheet through his window. This went on until one night when he pulled in a policeman. Most other students would have been thrown out of the school then and there, but, being who he was, they settled for campus confinement, which he, of course, ignored by sneaking out. His rooms at Oxford are still known as the Yusupov Rooms.

At the end of the first year at Oxford, students were allowed to live off campus. Felix rented a small house nearby with two friends, where he could expand his lifestyle into something more appropriate to his station in life. A staff was engaged to cook, drive, care for his clothes, clean, and groom his horses, a hunter and two polo ponies. This was how he lived for two years until he earned his degree in 1912.

Felix was well connected and enjoyed his stay in England. He decided to stay on after graduation and rented two adjoining apartments in Curzon Street in London. Here his taste for enjoying life expanded further with a maroon car and a steam launch for cruising on the Thames River. At a costume party at the Albert Hall, he "wowed" everyone by appearing in a Russian boyar outfit, styled to an earlier time, and featuring a jeweled sword. Shortly after this flourish, he returned to Russia.

Finally, it was time to settle down. Pressure came from all sides–his parents, the Royal Family, and family friends. It was time for marriage and a family. Grand Duchess Olga, the Tsar's oldest daughter, was a possibility, but this was quickly ruled out as Felix was not of royal blood. Also, there were the stories the Empress heard about his various notorious escapades. However, another Grand Duchess, Irina, daughter of the Tsar's sister, was twenty-two and eminently suitable.

This marriage would be the culmination of a series of marriages, which had elevated Felix and his male forebears. His grandfather married into a fortune and acquired the title Count Sumarokov. His father married into the largest fortune in Russia and an even grander title, Prince Yusupov. Felix married a Romanov. The marriage took place in the Anichkov Palace, home of the Dowager Empress, Marie Fedorovna, on February 9, 1914. Felix and Irina set up their home in the Yusupov Palace on the Moika. They had a daughter, also named Irina.

During the next few years, the Prince became increasingly upset by the drinking and sexual antics of Rasputin. Felix was troubled by Rasputin's influence in the government, the impotency of the other members of the aristocracy to do anything about it, and the indifference of Tsar Nicholas and Empress Alexandra to what was happening. No one could penetrate the shield that the Tsar and Empress had erected around themselves and against any criticism of their friend, the mystic.

Felix's own father had been immediately dismissed as Governor-General of Moscow when, during an interview with the Tsar, he dared bring up the subject of Rasputin's influence. Finally, Felix decided it was necessary to remove Rasputin, and if no one else would do it, it was up to him. He enlisted the support of his close friend, Grand Duke Dimitri Pavlovich, and a convalescing officer of the Preobrazhensky Regiment, Ivan Sukhotin, whom he had met.

He set the stage by meeting with Rasputin, from time to time, in Rasputin's apartment or that of mutual friends, the Golovina family, a daughter, Munya, and her mother. They both believed in the mystic. Rasputin enjoyed Felix playing the guitar for him and singing gypsy songs. When all preparations were completed, Felix persuaded Rasputin to come to the Moika Palace the evening of December 16th, where he could meet Felix's beautiful wife Irina, a meeting eagerly sought by Rasputin.

Inspiration and the Plan

Duma Chamber
Tauride Palace
St.Petersburg, Russia
November 19, 1916

Prince Felix Yusupov had been mulling the assassination of Rasputin for some time. He attended a session of the Duma where he heard a fiery speech by Vladimir M. Purishkevich, a right- wing member. In his speech, Purishkevich savagely attacked Rasputin and his corrosive influence on the Tsar and Empress. The speech in the Duma chamber galvanized the Prince into action. The day after hearing Purishkevich's Duma speech, Prince Yusupov telephoned Purishkevich and made a date to call on him the following day.

Purishkevich had busied himself in winning the war, which had started in 1914, and this included outfitting a hospital train. He had remained silent about the disintegrating situation, both on the political and military front, until his recent lunch at supreme Military Headquarters. Here the generals greeted him, and the Grand Dukes urged him to tell the Tsar about the demoralizing state of affairs brought about by Rasputin. At lunch with the Tsar, he did so, however, he got no support from anyone present, each backed off rather than risk their privileges and positions.

The Prince made an excellent impression on Purishkevich when they met the next day. Purishkevich characterized Prince Yusupov as radiating elegance, breeding, and self- possession ...a man of great will and character, whom he felt was rare in Russians, particularly in the aristocracy.

They spoke for two hours during which Prince Yusupov expressed himself on what he felt about the current state of events and what needed to be done. He concluded by saying that the Tsar can't be influenced by pressure from outside, and that Empress Alexandra is really running the country because the Tsar is at military headquarters. Furthermore, the government won't do anything. Finally, he said that Rasputin needs to be removed, that there are people in Russia who will do it, and Prince Yusupov is one of them. Also, Felix mentioned, he has two other people who will join him.

He invited Purishkevich to come to the Yusupov Palace the next day to meet his confederates and hear his plan. When Purishkevich came the next day, he was surprised that Grand Duke Dimitri Pavlovich, cousin of the Tsar, was there. There was also a Preobrazhensky Regiment officer, Ivan Sukhotin, who was convalescing from war wounds. Prince Yusupov outlined his plan.

1, He would continue to ingratiate himself with Rasputin so that he could lure him to the Yusupov Palace without suspicion and kill him without tracing him to the conspirators.
2. To avoid noise, Rasputin would be poisoned.
3. The enticement for Rasputin to come would be an offer to meet Yusupov's wife, the beautiful Irina, daughter of the Tsar's sister.
4. The body of Rasputin would be thrown into the Neva River and weighed down with chains, and it would be washed out into the Baltic Sea.
5, The entire plot was to remain a dark secret and all pledged themselves to silence.

It was decided that another person was needed. Their first choice was Vasily A. Maklakov, a Duma deputy and a member of the Constitutional Democrats, a powerful political party. Purishkevich approached him, but he declined to join the group that actually would do the killing. However, he promised legal help if needed after the killing. At a later meeting, Maklakov also gave Felix a rubber-covered weight. Purishkevich later suggested a Dr. Stanislas Lazavert, who worked on his hospital train, be an additional member. This was agreed. During the following weeks the conspirators met to decide on a date, buy chains to weigh down the body, and find a suitable place to dump the body. The meetings were usually at the Yusupov Palace or Purishkevich's hospital train.

Purishkevich bought weights and chains at the Alexandrov Market. He and Dr. Lazavert scouted by car, locations at which to dump the body. The Prince and Grand Duke Dimitri scouted in another car.

Parishkevich and Dr. Lazavert found a hole in the ice next to an arch of the Petrovsky Bridge, which connected Petrovsky and Krestinsky islands, and this was selected as the body-dumping site. The date of December 16 was decided upon.

Murder Night

Prince Yusupov's Basement
Study/Dining Room
Yusupov Palace
94 Moika Embankment
St. Petersburg, Russia
Evening of December 16/17, 1916

The five conspirators gathered in the basement dining room in the Yusupov Palace at about 11 p.m. It had been a former wine cellar, but Felix had recently decorated it so that Rasputin could be lured and kept there, without being suspicious as to its real purpose.

The five conspirators - Member of the Duma, Purishkevich, Prince Yusupov, Grand Duke Dimitri, Lieutenant Sukhotin, and Doctor Lazavert - admired how the scene had been arranged. A final touch was to put a record of "Yankee Doodle Dandy" on the gramophone. It would be played in the study upstairs to mislead Rasputin into believing Princess Irina was entertaining. Dr. Lazavert supervised lacing the cakes and wineglasses with poison. Felix left for Rasputin's apartment with Dr. Lazavert as driver, outfitted in a chauffeur's coat, hat and gloves.

Felix arrived at Rasputin's apartment, number 20 on the third floor of 64 Gorokhovaya Street and went through the arch to the courtyard and up the back stairs to avoid the secret police in the main hallway. Rasputin was finalizing his dressing, including a blue blouse given him by the Empress. His maid and his two sleeping daughters were also there. Yusupov and Rasputin left by the back stairs and drove back to the Yusupov Palace. They went into the Palace from the side door by the snow-covered courtyard, and down the steps to the basement dining room.

For about two hours, Yusupov kept trying to get Rasputin to eat the poisoned cakes and drink the wine. Rasputin seemed to hesitate and asked about the noise and music upstairs. The Prince explained Irina was entertaining some friends, but they would soon leave. Rasputin asked the Prince to play some gypsy tunes, and he ate some of the cakes and drank some wine. *Nothing happened! The* Prince excused himself and went upstairs to confer with his fellow conspirators. After he returned downstairs, and after more cakes and wines, Rasputin complained only about some stomach queasiness. Felix returned upstairs where it was agreed the attempted murder couldn't be postponed. The Prince volunteered to shoot Rasputin.

Felix came downstairs again, distracted Rasputin into looking at a beautiful crucifix and shot him in the chest. The others came downstairs and moved Rasputin's body off a white bearskin rug so that blood wouldn't stain it. They even called Rasputin's favorite restaurant, Villa Rode, to inquire if Rasputin had arrived yet. This was to provide an alibi in case Rasputin had been seen at the Palace. The story was that Rasputin had left to go to the restaurant.

The doctor, the lieutenant, and Grand Duke Dimitri then drove off with the lieutenant in Rasputin's coat, to make any watching police believe Rasputin had left. Purishkevich and the Prince were left behind. The Prince returned to the basement dining room and you already know the rest from the beginning of our story.

Aftermath

Things didn't work out as planned after Rasputin was murdered. There wasn't a ground swell of demand for reform by the powerful in the military and government. None of those involved in the Rasputin murder was punished. Instead, the Tsar abdicated, the Provisional Government was established, and then the Communists came to power, as will be described in the next chapter.

A year and a half after the death of Rasputin, the entire Royal Family along with four of their remaining staff were murdered in a basement room in Siberia. Ironically, on their journey east, they passed under the window of Rasputin's home in Pokrovskoe while his wife looked down on them from a window.

None of those involved in the Rasputin murder was punished.

The Tsar sent Prince Felix Yusupov to his family estate at Rakitnoe. The Prince then went on to the warmer climate at the Yusupov estates in the Crimea. After the revolution, he left Russia with his family, the Dowager Empress Marie, and other aristocrats aboard a British warship, the dreadnought HMS Marlborough. He settled in Paris with Irina and their daughter. He managed to bring along some jewelry and paintings. Other measures of financial help came from French real estate, three books he wrote, and a lawsuit award from protesting a treatment of Rasputin's murder by a movie studio (MGM).

It was very far below the level of life he enjoyed in Russia, but was comfortable. He was even able to provide occasional help to other Russian expatriates. He and Irina sometimes went to dine with the Duke and Duchess of Windsor in their elegant Paris mansion. The Prince died in 1967.

Vladimir M. Purishkevich remained active in the White cause (the anti-Communists) in Russia and died only a few years later from typhoid.

Karl G. Heinze

Grand Duke Dimitri Pavlovich was sent to military duty in Persia. This probably saved his life, since thirty-seven other Romanovs were hunted down and brutally murdered. He later married a wealthy American heiress, had a son, divorced, and died in Switzerland. The son became mayor of Palm Beach, Florida, where I visited him a few years ago.

Dr. Stanislas Lazavert also ended up in Paris, where he later died. Lieutenant Ivan Sukhotin's end is not known. He most likely died serving in a White Army somewhere, and probably is buried in some long forgotten battlefield.

Anya Vyrubova also survived. She was taken from Tsarskoe Selo, questioned by the authorities, and eventually made it to nearby Finland. She died there in 1962.

The five conspirators in the murder of Rasputin had pledged not to talk about what had happened. This pledge was broken immediately. The link between the murder of Rasputin and the Yusupov Palace was on everyone's lips in St. Petersburg the very next morning. Purishkevich felt it necessary, within days, to write down his version of what happened, and, later, it was published.

After a few years, Prince Felix Yusupov also published a book covering the subject from his point of view and then followed with another book some years later. These accounts are the only known ones written by those directly involved. They are very similar and agree, for the most part, on the sequence of events and what happened. I have relied mostly upon Purishkevich's account, written shortly after the murder, for the facts of this story.

There was also a police report developed from the accounts of officials who observed the Yusupov palace; the coming and going of cars; people getting in and out; noises and voices; and shots fired. Recently, findings have been released from a report, compiled by the short-lived Provisional Government, based on interviews in 1917 with those concerned who could be located.

Based in part on this information, a new book, "The Rasputin File," by Edvard Radzinsky, was published in 2000. It discusses why the poison did not work; the other people who might have been in the palace; if someone else might have fired the fatal shots; and raises questions about the accounts of Yusupov and Purishkevich. Were these two

220

accounts a cover up to protect someone else? This new book certainly confirms that Rasputin still fascinates people today.

Rasputin's daughter, Maria, has also written books. However, while she was in the apartment when Prince Felix Yusupov came to fetch her father, she wasn't a witness to the rest of the evening's events. To date no new accounts from those directly involved have been discovered.

Arkhangelskoye, probably the most elaborate of the old Yusupov estates, is only about ten miles west of Moscow and can be reached today by bus. It is now a museum. Its colorful past is still evident in the main complex.

The palace had many fine paintings, statues and tapestries, many of which reflected the art collection of the former Prince Yusupov of the nineteen-century. He was Director of the Hermitage Museum and used his frequent travels to add to the collections of the Royal Family and for himself. On the grounds is a monument to Pushkin, Russia's great writer, who often visited. There is also a temple dedicated to Catherine the Great. The nineteen-century Prince Yusupov maintained a troupe of entertainers composed of his serfs (peasants attached to his estate). It was one of the best known and largest in Russia. On a signal from the Prince, the dancers would come out, drop their clothes, and stand nude. The building where they performed was handsomely decorated and equipped.

The estate can be visited today.

Baltic Sagas
Events and Personalities that Change the World!

Winter Palace Square
St. Petersburg, Russia

VII

Communism Triumphs in Russia
Women Factory Workers Topple Tsar.
Lenin and Bolsheviks Seize Power.

1917 - A Tumultuous Time in Russia

As described in our section on "Rasputin and the Prince," circumstances were not kind to the last Tsar, Nicholas II. His character and demeanor were not really suitable for the great authority he was destined to wield. He insisted on marrying a German princess he had chosen against the advice of his father, which seemed to have worked out personally but was a disaster for his reign. From the beginning, things went wrong. His coronation celebration in Moscow was marred by a riot.

The year 1905 brought a number of calamities starting with "Bloody Sunday," followed by the defeat of the Russian fleet by the Japanese. Next came riots and strikes. The Tsar was forced to establish a legislative body, the Duma, and share power.

About this time, the Tsar and Empress were learning that their son, Tsarevich Alexis, heir to the throne, born after four daughters, was a hemophiliac. This caused great anxiety in the Imperial family and contributed to their isolation. They established their main residence in the Alexander Palace at Tsarskoe Selo, now Pushkin Village. The notorious Rasputin gained great influence with the Empress, which later led to his often encouraging inappropriate and sometimes disastrous Government appointments.

The war with Germany, started in 1914, went badly due to lack of organization and leadership. Russian casualties were high, and the troops were poorly equipped. The Petrograd population was suffering from lack of food due to the diversion of the railroads for the war effort. The women, mothers and wives of the suffering men at the front, were particularly feeling the lack of bread.

Against this background, the 300-year-old Romanov dynasty had its autocratic iron fist removed from Russia's throat in only a few days by events that were sudden and largely spontaneous. The upheaval was led by a group of hungry and frustrated women who had been separated from their husbands and sons by three years of war. They had heard terrible stories of the soldiers' suffering and defeats and that the troops were demoralized. At home, these women couldn't get bread for themselves or their children. After work, they would stand in line for hours outside a bakery, tired and cold, and then often be told, " There is no more bread today."

The unrest started on February 23 in a few factories in the northern district across the Neva River from the central area of Petrograd. In a few of these factories, the women stopped working one day and poured into the streets shouting the single word, "Bread." They marched to nearby factories and shouted for the workers to quit work and join them. The throng surged toward the Bolshoi Sampsonievsky Prospect, the main thoroughfare leading to the Alexander Bridge and the heart of the city. The police set up a blockade at the bridge, but the demonstrators crossed on the ice of the frozen Neva River.

They headed for the Nevsky Prospect and Kazan Square shouting, "Bread," as they held rallies. In evening meetings, activists and agitators urged continuation of the strikes, and use of the slogan, "Bread and peace." The authorities downplayed the events of the day when reporting to the Empress, who was 14 miles away at Tsarskoe Selo, while the Tsar was at military headquarters.

Neither side yet understood the new militancy and deep resentment toward the Tsar by the workers. It wasn't realized that this outbreak was much more serious than a one-day strike. The authorities and the workers noted that the Cossacks showed no enthusiasm for charging crowds still made up mostly of hungry women. There were no obvious leaders among the workers, but they expressed a groundswell of resentment, nevertheless.

The next day the strike spread throughout the city. The Cossacks again refused to charge the demonstrators, who held several rallies at Kazan Square. The authorities began to muster the garrison soldiers to control the situation. There were fourteen regiments of soldiers throughout the city, but they were not the pre-war elite troops. After three years of war, most of the best-disciplined and loyal soldiers had been sent to the front. No one could be sure how these garrison troops would behave. Stores and restaurants closed early.

The third day, the strike spread to students, teachers and white-collar workers. Newspapers stopped publishing and banks didn't open. The police chief, Colonel Shalfev was killed charging demonstrators while his men hung back. Nicholas II, at military headquarters, was informed of the unrest and ordered the disturbances quelled.

Sunday, February 26, the fourth day of the strike, brought a break in the bleak weather. The skies were sunny and the streets were filled with people converging on the city center. All the bridges had been raised, but people crossed the Neva on the ice. Many demonstrators were killed when fired upon by Army training detachments. The men in these detachments, being instructed to be non-commissioned officers, were still loyal to the regime. The soldiers of many other regiments fired in the air over the heads of the demonstrators, and some even began to shoot their officers. The Tsar suspended the Duma.

This day was the revolution's turning point. The day's events demonstrated to the authorities that the loyalty of many of the Army's units couldn't be relied upon. The demonstrators, for their part, hardened their resolve and were determined to accept casualties, if needed, to bring down the Tsar.

The fifth day of what was now clearly a revolution saw the government in full retreat. Arsenals and police stations were overrun, arms were distributed, and bystanders were sometimes killed. Police and officers were concerned about being identified and tried to shield their faces. The number of loyal troops was being reduced fast.

Those troops that could be counted upon by the authorities were assembled at the Winter Palace. No one took steps to feed them, and they were scolded by the Tsar's brother, Prince Michael, for their appearance and for soiling the floor with their dirty shoes. The soldiers gradually deserted. Government ministers were now hunted down and arrested.

Tsar Nicholas II attempted to get through to his family at Tsarskoe Selo by train but failed because rebels disrupted railroad travel. The Tsar was advised to abdicate in favor of his son, Alexis. His brother Prince Michael would be regent. Nicholas agreed. The next day, Nicholas II changed his mind, deciding that he couldn't allow his sick son to be separated from his family, which he would as Tsar. Prince Michael also refused to rule. On Thursday, Tsar Nicholas II signed the Act of

Abdication in the drawing room car of the royal train while in the station at Pskov. He then went on to his family at the Alexander Palace at Tsarskoe Selo.

The fall of the Tsarist Government caused the people to turn to the remaining governmental body, the Duma, to run the country. The Duma was joined at their meeting place, the Tauride Palace, by another body, the Petrograd Soviet of Workers and Soldiers Deputies. This group was composed of leaders elected by the factory workers and soldiers and met in another room to monitor the work of the Duma. The Petrograd Soviet was modeled on a similar group that began in the turmoil of 1905. It was subsequently disbanded. The Petrograd Soviet wanted an end to the war, land grants for the peasants, an eight-hour workday, and Army reforms.

The Duma established a Provisional Government led largely by its middle class members. It pledged to continue the war, repeal limitations on freedom of the media, and allowed freedom of religion. Distribution of land was to be postponed. Prince Georgy Lvov, a landowner, became the first Prime Minister of the new government.

One man who served in both the Duma and Petrograd Soviet organizations at the Tauride Palace was Alexander Kerensky. Alexander Kerensky was a lawyer and socialist who had defended radicals in court and thereby gained a good reputation with workers. It is interesting to note that Kerensky was born in 1881 in Simbirsk, the same city where Lenin was born in 1870. Kerensky was elected to the Duma in 1912 and was thirty-six when appointed Minister of Justice in the new Provisional Government.

The year, 1917, proved to be a tumultuous period as various groups struggled to seize control from the Provisional Government. This finally culminated in October.

Assault on the Winter Palace

Winter Palace Square
Petrograd, Russia
October 25, 1917

There was a cold wind. Water puddles were scattered here and there from rain that fell earlier in the day in the square in front of the Winter Palace in Petrograd, Russia's capital. The name had been changed from St. Petersburg after the war started "because it sounded more Russian." The evening was dark, and, to keep away the chill, clusters of Red Guards and sailors were huddled around small fires.

Suddenly at 9 p.m., there was the boom of a cannon, fired from the cruiser Aurora moored nearby in the Neva River. The noise resounded throughout the city. It was a signal to the thousands of Red Guards and sailors in front of the Winter Palace to attack!

Since 6 p.m., the Palace had been surrounded. The waiting revolutionaries were ordered to be ready to move against the troops in the palace who remained loyal to the Provisional Government. The troops, protecting the ministers of the Provisional Government in the Palace, earlier in the day numbered about two thousand military cadets from army schools near Petrograd, a unit of Cossacks, a uniformed group of 170 women in a "Woman's Battalion," and an artillery battery.

These numbers had dwindled down during the day to about a thousand, consisting mostly of the military cadets. The field artillery battery from the Mikhailovsky School abandoned the Palace at about 4 p.m. and surrendered to the revolutionaries. General Bagoratuni, in charge of the Palace defenses, had also walked out and surrendered earlier in the day. Alexander Kerensky, Prime Minister of the Provisional Government, had left earlier to bring help.

At six p.m., Soviet representatives went to the palace to ask the remaining ministers of the government, gathered in the Malachite Room, to surrender. Since help was expected, they refused, and, instead, sat down to dinner in the small dining room next to the Malachite Room. The servants in the Palace, still dressed in imperial livery (blue uniform with red collars and gold braid), waited on the government officials.

At the Smolny Institute, Lenin was impatient at the failure to capture the Palace. Until the day before, he had been in hiding. It was then that he joined the other Bolsheviks at their small corner office on the third floor of the Smolny, which was their command post. While Lenin was in hiding, Trotsky had the Military Revolutionary Committee in continuous session for six days. This was the Bolshevik organization responsible for seizing control of the government by force.

When Kerensky cut the telephone lines to the Smolny on November 5, Trotsky reacted by calling this an attack on the Bolsheviks and their subsequent actions a defense. Trotsky immediately ordered food to be kept at the Smolny, posted guards, and set up a messenger service. He ordered seizures of the arsenal, radio station, telephone and telegraph building, power station, and some of the bridges. He mustered the support of factory workers and students armed and known as, "Red Guards." Rebel sailors and army units were rallied to the Bolshevik cause.

Since the Bolsheviks now controlled everything else, Trotsky was less concerned about the Winter Palace. He suggested the cruiser Aurora fire a volley of blanks to encourage surrender without damaging the Palace.

The sound of the Aurora's cannon fire at 9 p.m. started an exchange of machine gun and small arms fire between those inside and outside the Palace. The lights in the palace went out. In the dark, targets were difficult to see, and most of the shots went wild. The small arms fire was now joined by artillery using real shells fired from the Peter and Paul fortress across the Neva River and directed at the palace. The shells broke some Palace windows and knocked off some of its stone decorations. Nine palace guards and six attackers were killed but these were the only casualties here that day.

An eyewitness, the American journalist, John Reed, wrote a book entitled "Ten Days That Shook The World," that contributes to our knowledge of events in the palace that night.

At one o'clock, the attackers clambered over the firewood barricades, entered the palace, and crept around the many rooms and halls. They encountered a large number of packing crates which the Red Guards began breaking open with their rifle butts. They found carpets, linens, curtains, a bronze clock, and other palace furnishings. Before the soldiers could begin taking these items for themselves, somebody cried, "Comrades! Don't touch anything! Don't take anything! This is the property of the people!"

By this time, the Palace guards had dwindled down to only the military cadets; the Cossacks and most of the Women's Battalion escaped earlier. As the attackers crept through the unfamiliar corridors, the remaining cadets surrendered in small groups. Some members of the Women's Battalion had not left during the day and were found huddled in a back room. They were taken to the nearby Finland train station and sent to one of their camps. The palace servants stood around and tried anxiously to protect entrances to formerly forbidden rooms and areas.

Just after 2 a.m., the leader of the attackers, Antonov-Ovseyenko, reached the small dining room outside the Malachite Room and confronted the government ministers gathered there. They were arrested in the name of the Military Revolutionary Committee, marched out, and taken to the nearby Peter and Paul fortress.

The short era of the Provisional Government's rule in Petrograd was over. Lenin and his Bolshevik associates would now begin to put down rival political opposition, end Russia's participation in the World War, win the Civil war against defenders of the old regime (the "Whites"), establish a Communist government in Russia, and seek to impose communism on the rest of the world.

Lenin was the son of a respected and successful school administrator, who was well off financially and a minor nobleman. Lenin's father and his family had done well and risen far under the old government. Why and how did his son take the path of a revolutionary? How did Lenin become head of the government by October, after only returning to Russia in April?

Lenin Arrives at the Finland Station

Petrograd, Russia
April 16, 1917

Lenin had been anxious to return to Petrograd ever since he had received the news (in his one room apartment in Zurich, Switzerland) of the overthrow of the Tsar. He was eager to shape a new Russian government to his ideas. His Bolsheviks would lead this government. He was not happy with the Provisional Government, convinced that they were not going to do what he considered necessary: end the war, redistribute land, and give greater control to the workers.

His eagerness to end the war was well known to the Germans, and they were anxious to help send Lenin and his Russian revolutionary associates to Petrograd from Switzerland. If these revolutionaries could take Russia out of the war, it would end Germany's need to fight on the eastern front. Germany could then concentrate in the west. If Russia should engulf itself in a Civil war and weaken as a military threat, so much the better. Even though both sides wanted the revolutionaries to return to Russia, it took some negotiations to make it happen.

While traveling, the German authorities wanted the revolutionaries to be sealed off from contact with Germans while moving along their route. They believed it would prevent the revolutionaries from spreading their ideas in Germany. Lenin, however, did not want to give the impression he was accepting anything from the Germans.

Finally, everything was arranged, and Lenin and his party were placed on a sealed train that took them to the German coast. They crossed the Baltic Sea to Sweden on the ferry," Queen Victoria." In Sweden, a train took them around the Gulf of Bothnia before crossing the border to Finland, which then belonged to Russia. At the frontier town of Belo-Ostrov, between Finland and Russia, the train was stopped, as usual, for passport examination.

A great crowd of workers and some of Lenin's colleagues welcomed him to Russia. In future years, Stalin would represent that he was there also by commissioning paintings to portray the scene of Lenin descending the train and being welcomed by him.

Lenin was still apprehensive about how he would be treated in Russia, and considered that there was still a chance he could be arrested. However, he was assured that a great reception awaited him in Petrograd and that an arrest was not possible. He was carried on the shoulders of the workers to the waiting room where a speech by him was expected. He told them that the killing of soldiers must be stopped and that the workers and soldiers must bond together against the Provisional Government.

After the visa and passport formalities were successfully completed, the final leg of the journey to Petrograd began. The train carrying Lenin arrived at the Finland Station in Petrograd at 11:10 p.m. Lenin and his group had been traveling for seven days.

An even more enormous reception to welcome Lenin had been prepared by his colleagues in Petrograd. As soon as he stepped off the train onto the platform, a band played the " Marseillaise." Workmen had placed red banners in the main hall of the station. There were thousands of workers, sailors, and soldiers on hand. A number of the uniformed Guard Regiments, the Red guards, and the Baltic Fleet sailors were represented. Workers held up flags and torches. There was excitement, expectation, and impatience in the crowd. Searchlights from the Peter and Paul fortress swept the sky.

Lenin was escorted by a young ensign down a row of Baltic fleet sailors at attention. The ensign expressed the hope that Lenin would join the Provisional Government. Lenin didn't answer. While Lenin was trying to orient himself to this unaccustomed exuberance on his behalf, he was taken to the Tsar's former private waiting room.

In the private waiting room, members of the Petrograd Soviet waited for him. Lenin was wearing a round hat, his face was cold, and he was holding a bouquet of flowers that had been thrust at him. Nikolay Chkheidze, a leader of another political group, the Mensheviks, greeted Lenin first. He was well known to Lenin, but they didn't always agree. He welcomed Lenin and spoke of the need to defend the February revolution. He also knew that Lenin had his own ideas of what was to be done and was apprehensive of this leader of the Bolsheviks.

Finally, the crowd waiting outside could no longer be held back. They surged through the waiting room's glass doors, lifted Lenin to their shoulders and placed him on the turret of an armored car. Lenin looked over the crowd and waited for them to grow silent. Lenin, although tired, took energy from the charged atmosphere. He greeted the crowd and spoke with great vigor of the new order to come. He ended by shouting, "Long live the world–wide socialist revolution!"

Lenin was now 47 years old and physically unimposing. A short time before, he was living in a one-room apartment in Switzerland, far from Russia. He had never wavered from his belief that the revolution would come to Russia, but he had begun to think it might not happen in his lifetime.

This reception confirmed that although the revolution had occurred in his absence, there was a realization, both by these new men now in power and his own associates, that he would take an important part in shaping Russia's future direction. His years of writing, meetings, and speaking had established his position as a force with which to be reckoned.

The Finland Station continues to be the main railroad terminus for trains coming from the north to St. Petersburg. There is a statue of Lenin in front of the train station.

My daughter, Diane, and I returned to Finland, departing by train from this station in 1989. We had spent Christmas with relatives in Finland, and she wanted to see life in Russia under Communism, so we went there for New Year's Eve. We heard Gorbachev make the traditional New Year's Eve midnight radio address (by the leader of the Soviet Union), although we didn't understand what he said.

Vladimir Ilyvich Ulyanov (Lenin) 1870–1924

The man who arrived by train at the Finland Station in Petrograd the evening of April 16, 1917 would, in just over six months, take control of Russia. Eventually, his philosophy of government, Communism, would be spread to many other countries around the world, making him one of the most important personalities of the twentieth century. The man, Vladimir Ilyvich Ulyanov, is remembered as "Lenin."

It is one of the ironies of history that Lenin, who devoted his life to toppling the Tsar, was not in Russia when it happened and had not been in Russia for ten years. When the revolution came, he was in Zurich, Switzerland because he would have been arrested by the Tsar's secret police had he been in Russia.

He had waged a relentless and continuous campaign during his adult life by publishing books, articles, a newspaper, and making speeches, all with the purpose of replacing the Tsar with a people's government. He had spent his entire adult life studying, debating, and writing about how the Tsarist government should be smashed and replaced by a government based on the proletariat.

He was also constantly arguing with other revolutionaries who had their own ideas of a new government for Russia. He was now close to fifty years old. He had been imprisoned and exiled. He turned his back on what could have been a comfortable life for his views. The circumstances of his upbringing wouldn't have been expected to lead to his lifetime dedication as a revolutionary. How did he come to this life of a revolutionary on the run?

He was the son of a supervisor of education who was responsible for the entire Simbrisk province. His father had brought himself up to the level of a minor nobleman through academic excellence and hard work. All of his six children excelled in school, particularly the oldest boy, Alexander, and Lenin. Life in the Ulyanov household was comfortable and cultured. This came to an end in 1886 when the father died at the early age of forty-five. Lenin was sixteen years old.

The following year brought another blow to the family, the death of the oldest son, Alexander. He was hanged at Schlusselberg prison for complicity in an attempted assassination of Tsar Alexander III. Lenin's oldest sister, Anna, was also implicated and banished to a small town, Kokushkino, about one hundred and fifty miles from the family home at Simbirsk, and near Kazan.

Lenin had been a brilliant student and was headed for a university and a career in law when his brother was hanged. Whatever he may have planned to do with his life before the death of his beloved brother, seems to have been set aside. His life was now directed at bringing down the Tsar and establishing a new government.

In spite of Alexander and Anna's activities, which put the whole family under suspicion, Lenin was admitted to the University of Kazan. He was expelled after a few months for revolutionary activities and banished, thus joining his sister in Kokushkino. His mother and the smaller children also joined them. The idyllic family life in Simbirsk was over.

After the banishment sentence of Lenin and Anna was completed in 1888, his mother bought a farm in Samara, where the family spent the winters. The rest of the year they were in Kazan where Lenin studied at home because he wasn't readmitted to the University. In addition to reading to pass his degree requirements, he studied Marxism. His knowledge of German enabled him to translate Marx's Communist Manifesto into Russian. He took his examinations in 1891 and graduated first in his class.

With degree in hand, he went to St. Petersburg and registered for the bar in order to practice law. He dove headfirst into meetings with other revolutionaries and began his lifelong struggle against the Tsar. He also fought against competing ideologies through his writings and with his verbal powers of persuasion. He organized groups and attended meetings with those who would support his ideas. His activities often brought him to the attention of authorities. He was arrested in 1897 and, again, banished, this time to Siberia in 1898.

Nadezhda Konstantinovna Krupskaya, an active revolutionary whom he married around this time, joined him there. In 1900, after being released from Siberia, he traveled to Munich, London, and Switzerland. Nadezhda followed him, and they published a newspaper, Iskra (The Spark). He continued to write books setting out his ideas and quarreling with those who differed.

Lenin returned to Russia in 1905, lured by the important events taking place then, but fled through Finland two years later. He spent the next ten years in Paris and Switzerland, again writing and agitating for revolt. World War I particularly earned his scorn because it further seemed to enrich the wealthy. Beyond that, it added to the suffering of the poor while sending their sons and husbands to be killed at the front.

Bolshevik Second Revolution–October 1917

From the time he heard of the overthrow of the Tsar and the formation of the Provisional Government, Lenin was determined that a second Revolution would be necessary to overthrow the new Government and seize power for the Bolsheviks, and himself.

From the welcoming ceremonies for him at the Finland station, Lenin went directly to the elegant Kschessinskaya Palace for a late night meeting with the Bolshevik Central Committee and other senior party members, in all, about thirty people. The Bolsheviks had taken over this building as their headquarters. It was conveniently located near the Trinity Bridge and the Peter and Paul Fortress.

The Kschessinskaya Palace, until recently, had been the home of Mathilde Kschessinskaya, a prima ballerina. She had been the mistress of Tsar Nicholas II before his marriage, and later of the Grand Duke Andrew Vladimironick, a second cousin of the Tsar. Grand Duke Sergei Mikhailovich, the Tsar's uncle, was also her life-long admirer.

As the meeting began, Lenin immediately asserted himself and outlined his program for seizing power. He accused his associates of not doing enough to destroy the current regime. He declared what should be done immediately. It included - nationalize the land and banks, take possession of the aristocracy's assets, and establish the Soviets in power! He went on to outline how this should be done. He also proposed the name of the Bolsheviks be changed to Communists.

A crowd had followed them from the train station, and, from time to time, Lenin appeared on the Palace balcony to speak to them and shout slogans. In spite of his long absence from Russia, by the time the meeting broke up, he had reestablished his undisputed control of the party.

Since leaving Switzerland, Lenin had been busy developing his political thinking in light of the changing of power in Russia. Overthrowing the Tsar, who had occupied a lot of his thinking, had already been accomplished. The task that remained to be done was to replace the new Provisional Government with a government system reflecting his ideas, run by his Bolsheviks, and with himself as leader.

Lenin first presented these ideas in the late night meeting at the Kschessinskaya Palace and then developed them further, wrote them down, and presented them the next day at meetings in an upstairs meeting room, number 13, in the Tauride Palace.

The Tauride Palace was built at the command of Catherine the Great in 1783–1789 for Gregory Potemkin, her lover and special favorite. He conquered the Crimea (called "Tauris" in the ancient world) for Catherine and once tendered her a ball there with three thousand guests.

When Catherine's son Paul ascended to the throne, his hatred for his mother and Potemkin caused him to turn the beautiful and lavishly furnished palace into a stable. His son, Alexander I, restored it.

The Duma and the Petrograd Soviet now held their sessions in a large Tauride Palace hall. At these meetings, the day after his return, Lenin expressed his ideas first to a large gathering of Bolsheviks from all over the country, and then to the Petrograd Soviet. Finally, he was invited to another meeting that was meant to reconcile the Mensheviks, another left-wing party, and the Bolsheviks. Instead, Lenin's ideas, known as the "April Theses," created an uproar. They can be summarized as follows.

1. No rationalization of the war as necessary for defense.
2. Acceptance that the present government situation is only a transition period.
3. No support for the Provisional Government, which is to be denounced for failing to keep its promises.
4. Bolsheviks need to expand their appeal to the masses.
5. The goal is not a legislative parliament, but a Soviet of Workers and Peasants. The police, the army, and bureaucrats are to be abolished.
6. Land must be nationalized.
7. Banks must be nationalized and centralized.
8. Production and distribution are to be controlled by the workers.

9. There should be an immediate Bolshevik Congress to agree on a new program.
10. Restoration of a revolutionary International movement.

Lenin went immediately from being a "fellow revolutionary and arriving hero" at the train station, to a provocateur. Questions were raised as to why he had been allowed to cross Germany in a train and were the Germans bribing him. It began circulating that *"Perhaps he was a German spy!"* His own Bolsheviks wondered if he had gone too far, too fast. The Provisional Government recognized he was bent on their overthrow, and groups, relatively close to many of his views, were dismayed when they realized Lenin left no room for reconciliation or compromise.

Lenin himself was satisfied with the uncompromising positions he had taken. He now devoted himself to exhorting his followers, publishing newspaper articles, and giving speeches at factories and barracks to promote his views. He unrelentingly hammered out his main themes:

Peace for the soldiers!

Control of industry for the workers!

Land for the peasants!

All power to the Soviets!

Sweep away all those that stand in the way!

At this time, another revolutionary of great future importance to the Bolsheviks, Lev Davidovich Bronstein, known as "Trotsky," returned to Petrograd. He had been born in the Ukraine where he had achieved distinction in school and recognition for his intelligence. He became converted to Marxism before he was out of his teens and originally sided with the Mensheviks. He was a good writer and forceful speaker and soon assumed leadership positions. However, he was too independent to develop close personal ties to other revolutionaries. Over the years he was arrested, exiled, and spent time overseas.

He was in New York City writing for a Russian newspaper when the revolution in February occurred. He returned to Petrograd in May and joined the Petrograd Soviet. He became very popular because of his far-left leanings and speaking ability. He was cultivated by Lenin and elected to the Bolshevik Central Committee.

Also in May, Kerensky was named Minister of War, and, after touring the eastern front to encourage the soldiers, initiated a new offensive in July. It went well at first but poor supply lines and German reserves ended it. Desertions and the murder of officers increased. Continuation of the war was clearly not popular.

The Provisional Government had continued to press the war and was now losing support. Russian casualty reports continued to reach mothers and wives at home. Land reform failed to materialize. Inflation rose, and wages failed to keep pace. Industrial production fell, and food became short. Control from Petrograd of local governments throughout Russia was loose.

Finally, the defeat at the front encouraged an uprising on July 16 and 17 in the Petrograd streets, which the Provisional Government was still strong enough to suppress. It became known as, "The July Days." The Bolsheviks were blamed and their headquarters at the Kschessinskaya Palace searched and documents seized. Trotsky was arrested. Lenin was also faced with arrest, although he was actually in the countryside taking a brief holiday when the riots occurred. Lenin was also accused again of taking money from the Germans.

Lenin, perhaps remembering the fate of his brother, who was hanged after captivity, decided to adopt a disguise and flee. He shaved his beard and mustache, donned a wig, and passed himself off as a worker with the name, Konstantin Ivanov. From this time, until he returned shortly before the Bolsheviks seized power, he hid in a wide variety of places.

They included a haystack on a farm north of Petrograd, in an area called Razliv. He also lived in a number of apartments of supporters, most surprisingly that of the Helsinki Police Chief in Finland, who reported to the Department of Justice of the Provisional Government. During this time, Lenin continued writing and urged on the activities of his Bolsheviks in Petrograd through the use of couriers.

After putting down the July uprising, Lvov resigned as Prime Minister and Kerensky formed a new government. Kerensky had been the most popular man in the previous government because of his reputation for defending workers. The Provisional Government was soon faced with a new threat. This came in August from a right wing Army officer, General Lavr Georgievich Kornilov. He wanted socialists and communists arrested and the establishment of a more conservative government. He raised an army and marched on Petrograd.

Kerensky had to turn to the Petrograd Soviet for help. He was forced to defend his government by using army deserters and about twenty-five thousand Red Guards, the armed workers. The defense of the city was successful but revealed that Kerenky's position was dependant on workers, who were mostly sympathetic to the Bolsheviks.

Trotsky was released and became Vice-President of the Petrograd Soviet. The opportunity for a change in government favorable to the left sharply improved. The Bolsheviks formed a Military Revolutionary Committee to promote insurrection. Trotsky led it. This committee's objective was to increase unrest among the factory Soviets, military garrisons, and Navy ships. Lenin was still in hiding but kept in touch with events by newspapers and messengers. The Bolsheviks were now meeting in the Smolny Institute after being forced from the Kschessinskaya Palace.

The Smolny Institute is part of a complex of buildings on land that has a history dating back to Sweden's occupation of this area. Here, Sweden originally built a fort, Sabina, that a community of tar-distillers later replaced. Peter the Great later established there a Tar Yard, Smolny Dvor, for his shipyards. The Tar Yard was moved in 1723 and Empress Elizabeth built a summer residence there. When it burned down, she decided to establish a convent. The convent buildings were built around a Cathedral, the Cathedral of the Resurrection.

When Catherine the Great came to power, she decided to establish on the site, a school for ladies of noble birth. The additional building for this purpose was erected in 1806–1808. It included a large assembly hall, which takes up the first and second floor of the south wing. The school was known as the Smolny Institute. The building, in 1917, became the headquarters for the Bolsheviks and the Petrograd Soviet. After the Bolshevik revolution, Trotsky and Lenin both worked and lived there.

Unknown to the authorities, Lenin, after working his way back from Finland, had returned to Petrograd and was living in an apartment in the Vyborg district. A meeting of the Bolsheviks Central Committee was organized in the apartment of Nikolai Sukhanov, a Menshevik, who was not present. His wife, Galina, was a Bolshevik, and had given assurances that her husband would not be home. It was located close enough to his hideout for Lenin to attend.

It was the first meeting of the Bolshevik Central Committee Lenin attended since he had fled to Finland. There were only twelve members of the twenty-one Committee members present, due to difficulties in transportation and communication. Most wore disguises, including Lenin.

Lenin argued vehemently for an immediate armed insurrection. He felt now was the right time. His confidence was bolstered by his conviction that the German workers would revolt after the Bolsheviks seized power in Russia. After a spirited night of debate, his motion was ratified, ten votes to two. It was also decided to establish a Political Bureau (Politburo) to provide day-to-day guidance in the rapidly changing political situation. Its members were Lenin, Trotsky, Stalin, Sokolnikov, Zinoviev, Kamenev, and Bubnov.

Kerensky had his own spies and contacts and was wary of an insurrection. He sensed a takeover attempt might be made soon. Kerensky decided to move first to prevent a seizure of power by the Bolsheviks. On October 24, he ordered a battalion of shock troops from Tsarskoe Selo to march to Petrograd. He also sent for artillery to come from Pavlovsk and ordered the cruiser Aurora to sea. He had engineers cut the telephone lines to the Smolny Institute, and publication was halted of the Bolshevik newspaper, Rabochy Put, which was edited by Stalin.

When Trotsky learned of the suspension of the Rabochy Put newspaper and the cutting off of the telephone service to the Smolny, he was jubilant. Now he could justify his insurrection as a defensive measure and caused by the government's injustice. The Bolsheviks even felt that, *"Kerensky could be accused of being a counter-revolutionary!"* Trotsky immediately took countermeasures.

Motorcycle couriers were established to maintain contact with the factory Soviets, the Army and Navy Committees, and other supporters.

Karl G. Heinze

Red Guards were sent to the newspaper, Robochy Put, to protect it and allow it to resume publication. Red Guards were posted to protect the Smolny Institute. Passes were required for admission. Food was brought to the Smolny to permit an extended stay by occupants.

The Navy Committee, from the cruiser Aurora, asked if they were to go to sea as ordered by the government. They were told to ignore the order. Trotsky huddled around maps of Petrograd with members of the Military Revolutionary Committee and designated strategic targets for Bolshevik troops, mainly Baltic sailors and Red Guards. A meeting was called of the Bolshevik Central Committee.

While the revolutionaries plotted, the elegant men and women of Petrograd went to the Alexandrinsky Theatre to watch Alexei Tolstoy's play, "The Death of Ivan the Terrible." Others, in evening clothes were at the Maryinsky Opera to hear Fedor Chaliapin in "Boris Godunov." There were no outward signs of commotion, as in previous disorders. The military were in their barracks and no groups of workers roamed the streets.

Lenin in his secret apartment wrote a letter urging immediate steps to take over the government. It included the exhortations, *"We must not wait! We may lose everything!...The government is tottering...To delay action is the same as death."* He left his secret apartment in the Vyborg district the evening of October 25 and made his way to the Smolny. When he got there, the takeover by Bolshevik troops of the main telegraph office, the post offices, the Neva bridges, the Central Bank, the power stations, and other strategic locations was nearly complete. Few shots were fired.

Only the Winter Palace where Kerensky had convened a meeting of the Government Ministers had still not been captured by nightfall. However, Kerensky himself had left the city earlier to try to find and motivate loyal troops to protect his government.

As already described, on October 26 at 2 p.m., the Bolsheviks finally took the Winter Palace. Trotsky, Lenin and the other Bolsheviks presented the Petrograd Soviet with a fait accompli takeover of the Provisional Government during a very late night meeting. They didn't concern themselves with a walkout by those members who disagreed with them. Lenin was asked to write a proclamation. Lenin's proclamation read:

"To the Citizens of Russia. The Provisional Government has been overthrown. State power has passed into the hands of the organ of the Petrograd Soviet, the Military Revolutionary Committee, which stands at the head of the Petrograd proletariat and garrison. The cause for which the people have been fighting–the immediate proposal of a democratic peace, the abolition of the landlords' ownership of land, workers' control over industry, and formation of Soviet Government–this cause is assured. Long live the workers, soldiers and peasants' revolution!"

It had all gone so quickly and smoothly that Lenin was to remark later that the Party, "found power lying in the streets and simply picked it up."

Lenin's first decree concerned the nationalization of land, which he followed with a call for an end to the war with Germany. "Commissars," replaced government ministers and the Bolsheviks filled the positions. Lenin became President of the Soviet of People's Commissars and Trotsky was placed in charge of Foreign Affairs. There were eleven other appointments, but everyone understood that Lenin and Trotsky held the real power.

Although Lenin, Trotsky, and the Bolsheviks had overthrown the Provisional Government, appointed Commissars to take over from Ministers, and had started issuing Decrees, they were under no illusions that their new position was secure. Censorship of the press and all other media came quickly.

Kerensky was at Gatchina, about twenty miles from Petrograd, and hoped to recapture the city with Krasnov's Cossacks (cavalry from southern Russia). Both Kerensky and Lenin were not sure of the loyalty of any of the soldiers in the area around the capital. Lenin tried but couldn't get garrison troops to leave the city and march to the front.

Lenin assumed personal control of the Bolshevik military efforts by ordering its headquarters to be moved to the Smolny. Trotsky also threw himself into the battle for the city by giving speeches to garrisons and factories urging defense of the new Bolshevik government. During a speech to the Petrograd Soviet, he was asked why he wasn't out there with the Red Guards. He replied, "I'm going now," and marched out.

Finally, a series of engagements at the heights of Pulkova near the city decided the issue for the moment. Bolshevik agitators had infiltrated Krasnov's Cossacks and the Cossacks finally decided there was no reason to fight for Kerensky. The Cossacks accepted safe conduct back to their homes on the Don. The immediate threat to the Bolsheviks ended, but there was more fighting to come.

There had long been a festering demand for a new legislature. The "Provisional" in Provisional Government reflected the general understanding that a more permanent government would be established as a result of the Constituent Assembly. One of the motivating factors for Lenin, hoping to get the Bolsheviks into power quickly, was to avoid having the new government subordinated to this new Assembly. He favored having locally elected Soviets represent the masses.

However, Lenin, finally but reluctantly, convened a Constituent Assembly. It met in January 1918. Bolsheviks received only twenty–five percent of the vote. Lenin dissolved it, and it never met again. The other left leaning parties now became alienated from the Bolsheviks, but Lenin no longer cared.

Lenin knew that peace with Germany was essential if the Bolsheviks were to govern. Continuing to send badly organized Russians to be slaughtered would bring down his government just as it had the governments of the Tsar and Kerensky. Negotiations with Germany dragged on until March, with Lenin hoping for the revolution in Germany that didn't happen. Finally, on March 3, 1918, the Treaty of Brest-Litorsk was signed, but at a great cost to Russia.

Finland, the entire Ukraine, the Baltic States, Poland and other territories were lost. The Allies felt betrayed and made plans to intervene in Russia. The former army officers who had fought for Russia for many years felt betrayed and thought that the Bolsheviks were working for the Germans. The Cossacks were concerned they would lose their land and privileges. These men formed the White Army to oppose the Red Army of the Bolsheviks.

Another immediate result of the peace with Germany was moving Russia's capital, after two hundred years, from Petrograd back to Moscow. Lenin was afraid that the Germans might still make a sudden thrust at Petrograd and felt that Moscow, deep in Russia, offered a more secure haven.

The Communists, led by Lenin, reestablished terror as the way to assert their authority. A decree was issued setting up the All-Russian Extraordinary Commission for Fighting Counter-Revolution and Sabotage. It became known as CHEKA. Its stated purpose was to protect the revolution, and it killed people not only for what they had done, but also for who they were or had been. This sometimes meant killing whole sectors of society.

Many thousands of people from all walks of life - women, children, anyone who stood in the way of Bolshevik rule - were seized and killed. A reign of terror was unleashed when Lenin, after making a speech at a factory, was wounded by a pistol shot by a woman.

Lenin was a brilliant student and studied government all his life. By any standard, he was an educated man, and yet, he reverted to barbaric means to enforce his rule. When he came to power in a modern, and what should have been a more enlightened world, terror was continued as an instrument to maintain rule in Russia. When seventeen-year-old Lenin had heard the news of his brother Alexander's hanging, he had declared, "I swear I will revenge myself on them." Thirty years later, he kept his promise.

Tsar Nickolas II, his wife, five children, and four remaining members of their household were taken at night into the basement of the house in which they were imprisoned. There they were shot at point–blank range, stabbed by bayonets if they were not dead yet, and their bodies dumped in a pit. Thirty-seven other members of the Romanov family were hunted down and killed.

Censorship, secret police, killing of the opposition, meaningless elections, and rule by dictatorship were a page out of Russia's dark past. In 1570, Ivan IV, Tsar of Russia, invited the leading citizens of Novgorod to a banquet. They had been slow to accept his rule after he had annexed the city. After they were conveniently convened in one room, he gave a prearranged signal, and they were all slain. On another occasion, he struck and murdered his own son. He also established Russia's first secret police known as the "Oprichniki." He earned the epithet of, "Ivan the Terrible."

Over a hundred years later, Sophia, Peter the Great's half-sister, came to power as Regent, by using the Streltsy, the county's military force at that time. They murdered the family members and supporters of young Peter and his mother. When he finally ascended to the throne himself, Peter the Great took his revenge, and went on to kill thousands by brutal means to achieve his ends. He even had his son and heir, Alexis, murdered.

The Russian rulers had always used the civil authorities, secret police, Cossacks, and government troops to enforce their rule by imprisoning, torturing, and killing. Unhappily, the Russian people would continue to suffer this fate under the Communists. This is a severe indictment of a form of government that promised to improve the life of working people in Russia and all over the world.

Internal Strife and Lenin's Legacy

The Civil War, the internal strife in Russia, which followed the signing of a peace treaty with Germany, involved a great many different factions each of which had its own agenda. The major factor that united Lenin's enemies was that they were all, "anti-Bolsheviks." The Allies wanted Russia back in the war to handicap Germany with an eastern front. Different national interests and various entry points into Russia divided their efforts. The British sent troops north to Murmansk, and the Japanese landed in the far eastern areas of Russia. The United States sent troops to both Murmansk and the Far East. The French came in through the Black Sea.

When World War I ended, a major reason for intervention was removed, leaving only a sense of loyalty to former allies. Concerns about Bolsheviks sustained a diminishing interest in further fighting.

The Russian right - officers from the Old Russian Army, former property owners, and Cossacks, who had formerly enjoyed special political privileges - wanted to set the clock back. They were called, "Whites." They hurt their cause by giving recaptured land back to the former owners, usually the aristocrats. This prevented them from getting support from the vast majority of the population, the peasants. Left-leaning political parties and their supporters wanted a socialist government but not the Bolsheviks.

The Czech Legion was another group that added to the muddle on the White side. It was made up of deserters from the Austro-Hungarian Army, and they were supposed to leave Russia by traveling eastward by way of the Trans Siberian railroad. When the Bolsheviks attempted to disarm them, the Czechs seized the railroad and became another enemy of the Bolsheviks.

After a few years of fighting, the Red Army under Trotsky was shaped into a formidable fighting force, and its better position in the heart of the country slowly improved its fortunes. Unified White action was made difficult by the basic ideological split between left and right leaning factions. By 1920, the Bolsheviks had prevailed.

In February 1921, the sailors stationed at the Kronstadt naval fortress rebelled. These formerly ardent supporters of the Bolsheviks, who had given great support to the Bolsheviks in the overthrown of Kerensky's government, became disillusioned with the Bolshevik repressive measures and rule of the Bolshevik dictatorship. Their new slogan was, "The Soviets without Communism."

They had an open-air rally and drew up a long resolution demanding a more flexible kind of socialism with more freedom. Some workers in Petrograd went out on strike in sympathy with the sailors. Trotsky arrived with full powers to quell the rebellion. Striking workers were shot.

When the sailors at Kronstadt wouldn't surrender, they were subjected to artillery and aerial bombardment. Vast numbers of Red Army troops in white capes attacked across the ice each day. The sailors finally surrendered and twenty-five hundred sailors were shot, most without trial. Thousands more were sent to die in labor camps in Siberia.

Peter the Great built the Kronstadt Navy Base on Kotlin Island to be the main headquarters for his fleet and to guard the nearby city of St. Petersburg. There, in a park, is a large statue honoring Peter the Great, founder of the Russian Navy. Also remembered here in a small museum, are other famous explorers and contributors to the Russian Navy, who set out from here. Vitus Bering, a Dane, for whom the Bering Strait between Russia and Alaska was named, is probably the best known.

When I visited the base in 1996, a former crew member of a Russian nuclear submarine escorted me around. We could see a number of submarines tied up at a pier about a hundred yards from where we were allowed to go. Judging from the seagulls nesting on them, they didn't seem to be in active service. Farther away, on a different pier in another direction, we saw several large surface ships. We judged them to be cruisers, and they looked ready to go to sea.

We also visited the formerly beautiful Kronstadt Cathedral, where Russia's sailors used to worship before sailing off to ports all over the world. When we went inside, we saw it had been partitioned into office space by use of plywood panels.

We were told that the base continues its tradition of being heavily involved in research for new technical advances for the Russian Navy. We were restricted as to where we could go. Access to the base is not promoted among foreign tourists, but I wanted to go there and was able to visit with no problem. It is accessible by public transportation. There is now a land connection from the mainland on the north side. A connection is also under construction from the southern mainland, but budget considerations are delaying it.

After the Kronstadt rebellion in February 1922, Lenin had less than three more years to live. In March 1922 his health started to fail, and two months later he suffered the first of three strokes. He spent most of his time after the first stroke at a former millionaire's mansion in a town called Gorki, twenty-three miles from Moscow. He died in January 1924. He was 53 years old. His remains were later placed in a specially built mausoleum in Moscow's Red Square.

Lenin's ideas on government had a great impact on much of the world, not only Russia. He was certainly one of the leading figures of the twentieth century. It took most of the remaining century after his death to discredit the legacy of his ideas. The embers smolder still in a few parts of the world.

Baltic Sagas
Events and Personalities that Changed the World!

Former Rocket Research Institute
Peenemunde, Germany

VIII
Space Age Begins
At Pennemunde

First Successful Space Launch

Launching Table, Test Stand VII
Rocket Research Institute
Peenemunde
Baltic Sea Peninsula in Northern Germany
October 3, 1942

"X minus three"

It was a clear and cloudless day. There were three minutes to go until noon when the giant A-4 rocket would be launched from its firing table next to Test Stand VII. It stood forty-six feet high and, with fuel, weighed about 14 tons. The rocket was still connected by two cables to the ground - one to the measuring instruments in the nearby shelter and the other providing electric power. The rocket was painted in alternating rectangles of black and white so that if the rocket were spinning after launch it would be quickly apparent. To prevent spinning, four fins at its rear protruded from its otherwise aerodynamically, streamlined shape. The steering gyroscopes were already running.

The loudspeaker, connected to the intercom system, continued the countdown,

"X minus two"

The staff making final adjustments on the rocket took refuge in the shelter, and the working platforms were withdrawn. Dr. Walter Thiel, in charge of the test area, had developed the launching schedule. He now joined the senior propulsion and guidance engineers and technicians in the Test Stand measurement shelter. Here, they would monitor the rocket's status and performance on a large array of instruments and gauges. They could observe the rocket through a periscope from inside the shelter. A team of engineers from the Siemens firm was focusing a television camera.

"X minus one"

After a final check of all the monitoring instruments, the launching staff concurred the rocket was ready to go. A green smoke shell was set off and rose in the sky to signal, "10 seconds until launch!" The propulsion engineer pulled the first of the three main switches.

"Ignition"

Sparks started coming out of the nozzles at the rocket's tail and bounced off the blast deflector. They scattered onto the concrete platform holding the launching table.

"Preliminary stage"

The propulsion engineer pulled the final two switches. The sparks became a flame and then a jet stream of reddish-yellow combustion gases. This stage was scheduled to last 3 seconds. The two cables detached and fell to earth. Batteries now powered the rocket.

"Rocket has lifted"

The rocket's main power stage was now activated and its powerful turbopump was spinning at 4000 revolutions per minute, producing 540 horsepower, and forcing 33 gallons of alcohol and oxygen per second into the combustion chamber, generating tremendous thrust.

The rocket climbed straight and steady with increasing acceleration and left behind only a white dust cloud. The flame spitting out of the rear was almost a long as the rocket itself. A tremendous roar filled the air.

Only five seconds had passed since ignition of the preliminary stage. The rocket stayed on its vertical course for only 4.5 seconds and then began to tilt eastward toward the Baltic Sea. A planned tilt of 50 degrees would provide maximum range. The rocket continued to pick up speed and now was going about 650 miles per hour. Most importantly, the fin-stabilized rocket *was not spinning!*

"Sonic velocity"

For the first time, a liquid propellant rocket achieved supersonic speed!

"Thirty- three...Thirty-four...Thirty- five"

The seconds since launch were being called off over the intercom as the rocket was speeding away from Pennemunde and over the Baltic Sea, at a height of about 6 miles and at twice the speed of sound. As the rocket expended fuel, it became lighter, and this, plus the thinner air resistance, accelerated its speed and climb rate. The bright flame shooting out behind it was still visible to observers but getting smaller. The varying air currents at the different heights through which the rocket was passing at over 2000 miles per hour caused a vapor trail behind it to zigzag. This became known as, " frozen lightning."

"Brennschluss"

Brennschluss (Burn-finish) occurred after fifty-four seconds, when a radio signal closed the valves supplying fuel to the rocket motor. The rocket engine shut down and the exhaust flame disappeared. Now there was only a thick, white vapor trail. The rocket's momentum continued to hurl it on its upward trajectory northeast over the Baltic Sea.

"Success!"

For the first time in history an automatically controlled rocket had been hurled into space on a pre-planned course.

A few miles from the launch site, hundreds of workers came down off the rooftops from where they had been watching on the buildings of the Research Institute. They crowded around on the streets and lawns congratulating the senior staff members and each other for this monumental scientific feat. One of the first persons to reach the street from the roof of the assembly workshop of the Development Works was Dr. Wernher von Braun, the Rocket Research Institute's Technical Director. He rushed over to greet Colonel Walter Dornberger, Commanding Officer of the Institute. Colonel Dornberger had followed the launch from the roof of the Measurement House. His friend and

Karl G. Heinze

Commanding Officer of the Army Experimental Station Peenemunde, Colonel Leo Zanssen, had been with him.

They drove to the launch site. Here there was great excitement among the test crews who were gathered around Dr. Thiel and the senior engineers. Already everyone was discussing future improvements.

Amidst the excitement, Colonel Dornberger called for quiet in order to hear the reentry of the rocket into the earth's atmosphere after its descent from nearly sixty miles up. The countdown continued.

"Two-ninety four...Two- ninety-five...Two- ninety six..."

"Impact!"

The rocket had come back through the atmosphere without disintegrating and hit the water. It was outfitted with a dye marker so as to be spotted from the air. A search plane guided a launch to the spot in order to plot the point of impact, which was about 125 miles away from the launch site.

In the evening, Dornberger hosted a small celebration, at which he made the following remarks, reported in his book, V-2.

"The history of technology will record that for the first time a machine of human construction, a five-and-a-half-ton missile, covered a distance of a hundred and twenty miles with a lateral deflection of only two and a half miles from the target. Your names, my friends and colleagues, are associated with this achievement...a speed of thirty-three hundred miles per hour...a height of nearly sixty miles...

The following points may be deemed of decisive significance in the history of technology: We have invaded space with our rocket and for the first time - mark this well - have used space as a bridge between two points on the earth; we have proved rocket propulsion practicable for space travel."

This day's achievement required the focused attention of many learned and brilliant scientists and engineers. They worked in and connected many diverse technological fields – aerodynamics, mechanical engineering, electronics, guidance systems, and chemistry, opening up completely new scientific fields. A complex research facility that grew from a small testing site near Berlin had been established on the remote shores of the Baltic Sea and housed thousands of workers.

How did this come about?

Wernher von Braun (1912-1977)

The first successful launch of the giant A-4 rocket on October 3, 1942 resulted from the close collaboration of a team of highly trained and motivated scientists and engineers. However, one man in particular, who was only thirty years old at the time of the successful test firing, Wernher von Braun, surely deserves his rightful place as the pivotal figure in successful space rocket development. He was the Technical Director at Peenemunde. After the war, his rocket team went to the United States to continue work on rockets, and subsequently, space exploration.

Wernher von Braun was born March 23, 1912, the son of a German government official, who was relocated frequently. That meant his son, while growing up, attended a number of different schools. He was an indifferent student. Upon his religious confirmation, his mother gave him a telescope to encourage his curiosity, and he developed an interest in space astronomy.

In 1925, young Wernher read a book, *The Rocket into Interplanetary Space*, by Herman Oberth. Wernher was handicapped by not being able to understand the mathematics in the book. The motivation to understand what was described in the book made him apply himself at school, and he advanced to the head of his class. He went on to enroll as a student at the Berlin Institute of Technology.

At this time he also joined the German Society for Space Travel. Through this association, he met Hermann Oberth and assisted him in testing liquid-fueled rockets. After a few months, Oberth left Germany to return to his German speaking settlement in Romania. Wernher von Braun now helped establish a small development station for liquid fuel rockets called, "Rocket Field Berlin" sponsored by the German Society for Space Travel.

In 1932, von Braun received his degree in Mechanical Engineering and went on to the Graduate School at the University of Berlin to study physics and work on a Doctorate. His leadership and devotion to space travel by this time was acknowledged by the small group of men devoting their spare time to this work. When the Society began to experience financial problems, the German Army's Ordnance Department stepped in and offered its support through the efforts of a German Army Officer, Captain Walter Dornberger.

Walter Dornberger, born in 1885, was an army officer technologically trained in ballistics and in charge of solid fuel rocket development in the Army's Ordnance Department. In 1932, he was commander of Experimental Station West at Kummesdorf, an army proving ground about seventeen miles south of Berlin. The Army was interested in rockets. Fortunately for Germany, the Treaty of Versailles, the peace treaty ending World War I, had not prohibited them to Germany. During World War I, the German Ordnance Department had developed a cannon capable of hitting Paris from 125 miles away. They hoped to extend the range of this Paris Gun, called, "Big Bertha," through the use of rockets. Dornberger had served in World War I, been commissioned, and retained in the small 100,000 men army after the war.

Dornberger recognized the potential of liquid fuel rockets and arranged a research grant at the University for von Braun. About this time, the Society for Space Travel had been disbanded, and the army did the only work permitted on rockets. Von Braun received his doctorate in 1934, and his thesis was based on developmental experiments with 300 and 600 pound thrust rocket engines. Although von Braun's interest in rockets was as a means of space travel, the Army's interest and willingness to provide funding was strictly based on its use as a weapon. The military's interest was in weapons of war, in tanks and bombers, not civilian cars and airline travel.

In his book, V- 2, Dornberger describes the first, liquid fueled rocket testing that took place at Kummersdorf in December 1932. Additional facilities had been built at the experimental station to accommodate the new rocket testing. Captain Dornberger and von Braun, now a civilian employee of the Army, had added a mechanic, Heinrich Grunow, and an engineer, Walter Riedel, to help them.

This first team assembled on a cold night, December 21, 1932. They had placed a newly developed rocket in their recently completed test stand. The test stand had concrete walls 18 feet long and 12 feet high

257

formed in a "U" shape with metal doors as the fourth wall. Riedel measured the pressure of the rocket's engine in the control room and was to open the valves to release oxygen and alcohol at the proper moment. Von Braun was holding a 12-foot long rod with a can of gasoline on the end. He would light this under the rocket to ignite the fuel, when Reidel called out that the pressure was correct. When the moment came, Reidel called out, von Braun lit his match, Dornberger ducked behind a nearby tree, and then, "there was a swoosh, a hiss, and – crash!"

The searchlights went out, debris filled the air, and the new test stand was wrecked. Disappointment at the rocket's failure was offset by the test group's realization that they had survived the explosion.

During the next two years, work was conducted on the whole range of technical projects needed to achieve success in rocket development - injection nozzles, motors, different combinations of propellants, stability and control considerations, and so forth. Contributions were often made in these areas by outside engineers who offered their knowledge. Finally, in December 1934, two rockets, designated A-1 and A-2, were successfully test fired.

Funds were a constant problem. Finally in March 1936, General Von Fritsch, Army Commander-in-Chief, was persuaded to visit the Kummersdorf testing area. He was impressed enough to ask, "How much do you want?" This encouraged Dornberger and von Braun to make plans to expand their rocket testing facility beyond the facilities at Kummersdorf and look for a place away from the urban area of Berlin where longer flights could be attempted. Also, they were interested in a place where larger ground facilities could be built and secrecy maintained.

Peenemunde

During the holiday season in December 1935, twenty-three year-old Wernher von Braun was visiting relatives in northeast Germany. He was looking for an enlarged test site for the Army's new, secret, experimental rocket station. His grandfather often went hunting at the northern end of Usedom Island on the Baltic Sea. It was ideally suited for providing a long, firing range over water. The site was called Peenemunde.

General Kesselring, Chief of Aircraft Construction, finally made possible the purchase of a large tract of land, the building of ground facilities and housing at a remote location. He agreed to have the Air Ministry participate in the funding. The new Rocket Research Institute, to be located at Pennemunde, now moved swiftly ahead.

By May 1937, most of the Kummersdorf staff had been moved to Peenemunde. Eventually, the people there would total ten thousand. Included in the number was a group of people, mostly women, who handled the vast amount of data which was generated with their slide rules. Their large displays of trajectory information used so much paper they became known as "the wallpaper girls." It has been estimated that German's commitment to the space rocket development was proportionally equal in size and resources to the USA's commitment to developing the atomic bomb, considering the differences in the relative size of each country's total economy.

There is a small island just six miles offshore in the Baltic Sea northeast of Peenemunde called Greifswalder Oie. The first rocket firings were conducted there in December 1937.

The objective was to produce a rocket that would exceed the Paris Gun's range of 80 miles while carrying a 23-lb. payload of high explosives. The specifications, for the rocket agreed upon, were a payload of 1 ton and a range of 172 miles. For every mile traveled, a two to three feet deviation, short or long, was felt acceptable, along with a two to three feet lateral deviation. It also had to fit through existing railroad tunnels as it traveled over land. A sleek, forty-six foot projectile emerged from these specifications.

Although the design objectives for the final rocket, designated A-4, had been set, initial testing was with a smaller rocket, designated A-3. However, Dr. Rudolf Hermann, who had a wind tunnel in Aachen to test designs, found problems with the design of the A-3. Although expensive, it was decided that Peenemunde should have its own wind tunnel. Dr. Hermann, with some of his associates, came to Peenemunde to supervise construction of a wind tunnel and direct its operation.

The A-3's continuous failures finally resulted in a decision to abandon it and develop a new design to be designated A-5. It was to provide a testing platform for the much larger A-4 rocket. In October 1939, the newly designed A-5 was successfully launched and achieved a range of eleven miles with a seven and a half mile altitude. The successful design features were now incorporated into the A-4, and work on getting it ready to launch was accelerated.

At last the A-4 prototype was launched on June 13, 1942, but the propellant system failed, and the rocket went out of control and crashed. The armaments chiefs for the three branches of the armed forces - Field Marshal Milch, Admiral Witzell, and General Fromm together with Albert Speer, Minister of Munitions - were on hand for this test.

A second A-4 launch test was conducted August 16 and was also not successful, but the rocket did exceed the speed of sound for the first time. This unsuccessful test was also observed by a number of high-ranking officers and officials, and its failure was a great disappointment.

The next test was critical. During this development period, Albert Speer and the army helped keep the rocket project funded by providing production contracts for the facility.

Finally, on October 3, 1942, the third A-4 rocket launching was a complete success. It rose to over fifty miles and traveled one hundred and twenty miles.

Fuhrer Headquarters: Hitler Gets Interested

East Prussia
July 7, 1943

Nine months after the successful test firing of October 3, 1942, Dornberger and von Braun were summoned to Fuhrer Headquarters for a 5 p.m. meeting with Hitler.

Hitler had been advised of the rocket program's progress and the successful October launching by Albert Speer, Minister of Munitions. Hitler was becoming more receptive to new weapons and ideas as the Russian campaign began to deteriorate. Before this, anything beyond his World War I experience, such as jet planes, atomic bombs, and rockets met with disinterest. The debacle at Stalingrad had occurred earlier in the year, and an entire German Army had been destroyed. The Africa campaign had also been lost. The Allied air raids were taking their toil day and night, and realists understood the tide had turned against Germany.

The last time Hitler had met with the rocket team was in March 1939 in Kummersdorf, and he had never visited Peenemunde. His previous interest in rockets had not been very great and could be best described as skeptical. Today's meeting was taken to be an opportunity to arouse his enthusiasm. A film had been put together, since the successful October launching, hopefully, to make him optimistic about the rocket's potential. Models of some of the rocket's launching devices and related equipment were spread out on a table.

Long after 5 p.m., the doors to the projection room, where the meeting was to be held, finally flew open and someone cried out, "The Fuhrer." Hitler walked in with Keitel, Jodl, Speer, Buhle and their personal aides.

By this time, Hitler was spending most of his time in shelters, and the change in his physical appearance shocked Dornberger. Hitler was bowed over and tired looking. After exchanging greetings, the lights were lowered, and the film began. As always, the film made an impression of power and imposing size as the giant rocket appeared from behind giant gates, one hundred feet high, for static tests. Then the rocket was loaded on a Meillenwagen, a transporter for field use. After showing how the rocket could be driven around, it was raised to a vertical position and fueled.

Finally came the awesome sequence of launching. Wernher von Braun delivered a commentary during the film. Dornberger added how the weapon could be further improved, and mentioned the necessary preparations and resources now required.

Hitler began getting excited. He went over to the table to examine the models and thanked them. Discussions followed about firing from bunkers compared to mobile transporters. Hitler, as usual, favored buildings and construction. Hitler also asked about larger rockets. He was told that this would take 4–5 years to develop. Hitler now began to think of this as a weapon that could "win the war!" He said the program would get top priority. He apologized for not believing earlier that the rocket work would be successful. He then left the meeting.

After an evening meal and entertainment by Speer, the rocket group returned to Peenemunde. They were happy their work was recognized and appreciated, and they were pleased that Hitler's blessing would get them needed resources. At the same time they were apprehensive that the A-4 rocket's likely influence on the war's outcome might be exaggerated.

British Air Raid

Rocket Research Institute
Peenemunde
Baltic Sea Peninsula in Northern Germany
August 17–18, 1943

The air-raid sirens first sounded at about eleven-thirty at night. Most of the people at the Rocket Research Institute were sleeping. The sirens often disturbed the sleep at the Rocket Research complex because the British bombers usually assembled over the Baltic before heading south to Berlin.

"Allied formations massing over the central Baltic, north of Rugen. Direction of approach not yet known," was the report of the local air defense headquarters.

Peenemunde's strategy was not to fire on allied aircraft until it was clear that the rocket station was the target. The idea was to avoid drawing attention. As usual, the first wave of bombers flew over Peenemunde heading for Berlin. This was meant to draw off the German fighter aircraft.

However, this time the British bombers had also targeted the Rocket Research base at Peenemunde. As the bombers started their bombing run on Peenemunde, its air defense batteries started firing at their attackers. It was thirty-five minutes after midnight.

Damage was initially thought to be quite heavy. Many members of the Research staff and workers were killed or wounded during the bombing. The settlement area where the technicians and engineers lived had been specifically targeted. The test stands, development area, the pre-production works, the power station, oxygen plant, and the town of Transsenheide, where many construction workers lived, had also been targeted. The harbor and the air base located at Peenemunde

Karl G. Heinze

West were not hit. A major casualty was Doctor Thiel and his whole family. Chief Engineer Walter was also dead. A total of 735 lives had been lost. Forty- seven bombers were shot down by anti -aircraft batteries and night fighters.

A more careful assessment by the rocket staff, after the raid, gave more cause for optimism than the first estimate. The test fields, special wind tunnel, and the Measurement House were not hit at all. Work was resumed after four to six weeks because of the immense amount of help received. By repairing only essential buildings, and with camouflage, an effect was created of complete destruction. For the next nine months, there were no more raids on this target.

264

Rocket Production and Deployment

The successful test firing of the A-4 rocket in October 1942 did not lead to its systematic and immediate deployment as a weapon. Instead, when Hitler began to tell the people around him the A-4 could win the war, control of it became the chief objective of the various power circles surrounding him.

The Army's Weapon Development Group, through its representative, Dornberger, had financed and guided the rocket to its present stage and wanted to control its production and deployment. However, to get the priorities for materials and manufacturing was almost impossible, given the conflicting interests of those closest to Hitler. Albert Speer, Minister of Munitions, and Heinrich Himmler, Reichfuhrer of the SS, were in much more powerful positions to get the rocket produced and control its deployment.

Albert Speer had been appointed to head the Reich's Todt organization, which had charge of all construction that had to do with the war effort. Hitler had appointed Speer to this position when Fritz Todt died in an airplane mishap. Speer was close to Hitler, because Speer had trained as an architect, and his entry into Hitler's inner circle was due to the continued fascination the dictator had for this field. Later, Speer also became Minister of Munitions. The construction of coastal rocket launching sites, and production of the weapon itself, now got Speer involved more directly with the Peenemunde rocket project and its personnel.

Albert Speer now introduced Gerhard Degenkolb to Colonel Dornberger and the Peenemunde rocket project. When Dornberger asked how Degenkolb could help with obtaining the vast resources needed to produce the A-4 rocket, Speer told him that Degenkolb had achieved a great reputation in getting locomotives produced. When Dornberger told Speer that locomotives were not the same as a new, highly technical weapon such as the A-4, Speer shrugged his shoulders and urged cooperation with Degenkolb. Degenkolb established a rocket production committee in the Ministry of Armaments and War Production. What Dornberger feared was the loss of time that developing a new organization would mean, going from the successful test firing of the A-4 rocket to its operational use. This proved to be a legitimate concern.

Heinrich Himmler, Reichsfuhrer of the SS, and, next to Hitler, Nazi Germany's most powerful and feared leader, first visited Pennemunde in April 1943. His planned visit prompted Colonel General Fromm and General Leeb, Head of the Army's Weapon Department, to be on hand. It wasn't possible to fire an A-4 that day, but lectures and ground tests were conducted. Himmler advised Dornberger that their rocket was a frequent topic of discussion in the Fuhrer's circle, and that its growing importance made it of great concern to the German people and not just the Army.

Himmler expressed concerns about security, but General Fromm tried to assure him that the Army could handle it provided there was a prohibited zone around the area. This was agreed upon, and Himmler left by airplane after again expressing his interest in the rocket work and in doing more to help the project. He proposed to come again soon, spend the night and have private talks. About this time, Dornberger's good friend and Commanding Officer of the base, Colonel Leo Zanssen, was relieved of his duties. His tenure at Peenemunde had been under pressure for some time from forces outside the Army for whom he maintained control of the rocket complex.

About two months later, Himmler came again. He was unaccompanied and drove his own, small, armored car. Local police officials had accompanied him, but, after dinner he dismissed them. Dornberger, von Braun and others of the senior staff now sat around with Himmler and talked about the early days at Kummersdorf. They spoke about their worries in getting production priorities for the A-4 rocket, space travel, and individual fields of activity of senior staff members.

Himmler listened carefully. The time Himmler spent in talking to the senior rocket group was undoubtedly being used to assess their zeal in pressing the project forward as a means of delivering destruction. His spies probably had been advising him of the talk among the scientists of post-war space exploration. This was anathema to Himmler and his henchman, who realized what losing the war would mean for them.

The next day, two A-4's were launched. The first failed. The second fired successfully. Himmler left after the second launching, and promised to speak to Hitler about better priorities. If Hitler responded favorably, he promised to provide more help himself.

Von Braun had an aircraft at his disposal, which he flew himself. He would go to people and places involved in the work at Peenemunde. Upon returning from such a trip one evening, a few months after the last Himmler meeting, he was handed a note directing him to immediately report to Reichsfuhrer Himmler at his headquarters. He flew there. Himmler advised him, in a very cool manner, of the urgency of getting the A-4 operational quickly. Von Braun attempted to make Himmler understand that something as complex and technical as the A-4 rocket couldn't be bulldozed along.

Possibly, Himmler was using this private meeting to assess the chances of getting von Braun to shift his loyalties from the Army to the SS. In this he failed, but it wasn't long before Himmler made it clear that he meant to take control of the A-4 rocket, and that he wasn't going to allow himself to be crossed.

Less than a month later, on March 15, 1944, the Gestapo arrested Dr. Wernher von Braun. Von Braun had been asleep in his bachelor quarters when there was a loud knocking at his door and three Gestapo agents took him off to the police station in Stettin, about 70 miles away. Two close associates of his, Klaus Riedel, in charge of the design offices, and another engineer, Helmut Grottrupp, were already there. When the three men compared notes, they realized what had happened.

At a party a few nights before, the three had been speculating about space flight after the war and were overheard by a planted Gestapo agent. Later, they learned this agent was a dentist and the girlfriend of a Gestapo officer. The three men were accused of delaying the development of the A-4 as a war weapon by distractions about space travel. In addition, von Braun was accused of treason. It was charged that he kept an airplane in readiness so he could fly to England with the secrets of the rocket program. The three men were to be brought before a Gestapo court, and they wondered if they might be hanged or shot.

After two weeks confinement, Dornberger succeeded in getting Albert Speer to convince Hitler to intervene in order not to upset final development of the A-4. Hitler signed a decree ordering the rocket men released, and Dornberger took it to the court, which promptly complied with Hitler's command. All charges were dropped!

On August 8, 1944, Himmler appointed one of his own people, SS Brigadier Kammler to the position of Commissioner General of the A-4 program. With the power of Himmler behind him, Kammler stepped up efforts in getting the A-4 rocket weapon produced and into action against the allies. The weapon was renamed the V-2 for, "Vengeance Weapon # 2," by Dr. Josef Goebbels, Minister of Propaganda. The V-1 had been an earlier weapon. The first use of the V-2 against London was on September 8, 1944. During the next two months, 850 rained down on London.

To protect rocket production from air raids, Hitler decreed that the manufacturing facilities be moved to a massive underground facility near Nordhausen in the Hartz Mountains. Control of V-2 rocket production was put in complete charge of the SS, under Hans Kammler. In all, an estimated fifty-eight hundred V–2 rockets were launched, but their total destructive payload was very minor compared with the payload from a single allied air raid. It had taken too long to get the V-2 produced and deployed to contribute much to the war effort.

In his book, Crusade in Europe, Eisenhower is quoted as follows:
"It seemed likely that, if the German had succeeded in perfecting and using these new weapons six months earlier than he did, our invasion of Europe would have proved exceedingly difficult, perhaps impossible. I feel sure that if he had succeeded in using these weapons over a six-month period, and particularly if he had made the Portsmouth-Southampton area one of his principal targets, Overlord might have been written off."

Americans Acquire German Scientists

In April 3, 1945 the Peenemunde staff was ordered evacuated to the south as the Russian Army drove west and appeared likely to overrun the Rocket Research complex. The Gestapo now guarded the Peenemunde rocket group, and there were rumors circulating that Himmler might use the rocket staff and their vast amount of technical data as bargaining chips to his advantage. However, in the confusion of the final days of the war this didn't become possible, and Himmler committed suicide.

All the allies, including the Soviets, by now realized the worth of the German scientists, because of their large lead in many technical fields. In Washington, the decision was reached to bring these men to the United States. A U.S. Major, Robert Staver, was assigned the task of locating these men, now in the very large Thuringia area, where some three million people lived. Complicating the matter was that, although the U.S Army held the area now, it was due to be a Soviet area of occupation and the Red Army was expected in a few days. Also, Major Staver had no official authorization to offer these men employment. There was the question, too, of whether the scientists would be agreeable to journeying off to an unknown place.

What helped persuade them were reports of Russian atrocities in Berlin and other parts of Germany. Major Staver and three cooperative German scientists spread out looking for the scientists using lists they had compiled and working against the time the Russians would arrive.

Convincing the scientists to evacuate to the U.S occupation zone to the west proved difficult until Wernher von Braun, who had surrendered to the Americans earlier, was brought in to help. His standing with the scientists quickly persuaded them, and more than one hundred and twenty agreed to go. They were rounded up by cars and trucks, often with only 15 minutes notice, and taken to the railroad station at Nordhausen. After some last minute delays in getting a locomotive, the train left less than six hours before the Soviets arrived.

On November 16, 1945, five months later, the U.S.S. Argentina arrived in New York harbor with the German scientists, to very little fanfare.

Along with the German scientists and engineers led by von Braun, a large number of V–2 rockets, parts, and associated technical data also went to the U.S.Army's Proving Grounds at White Sands, New Mexico. However, Walter Dornberger, now a Major General, was sent to prison in England. Eventually, he was released and joined his former rocket colleagues in the U.S.A. Here the newly assembled rocket team, now joined by American scientists, fired rockets and accumulated new information, particularly atmospheric data.

Von Braun was often asked about how his group had become so knowledgeable about rockets and accumulated such a lead over the rest of the world. He usually answered, "After all, if we are good it's because we've had 15 more years of experience in making mistakes and learning from them."

However, he also expressed surprise that the efforts of an American, Robert H. Goddard, who also did work on rockets, were not better known. Von Braun said that Goddard had foreseen a lot of the ground gone over in rocket development by the Germans. Goddard had also launched rockets, although not of the size and scale achieved at Peenemunde. "Until 1936, Goddard was ahead of us all," said von Braun. Von Braun became an American citizen in 1955.

A Russian scientist, Konstantin Tsiolkorsky had also theorized and written about rocket propulsion earlier, but he never went on to build rockets. The Russian interest in rockets was sharply felt in October 4, 1957, when a small satellite named Sputnik was launched. Immediately, interest in rocket development to conquer space became a priority, and a competition developed between the democracies and communism.

Von Braun and his associates were quickly directed to get the U.S.A. into space, and when the Russians put a man in space, the race was joined. Eventually, the USA put its first man, Alan Shepard in space, followed later by a circle of the globe, and then, in 1969, Neil Armstrong was the first man to step on the moon.

The vast resources available to von Braun and the space program in America finally achieved the dream of space travel!

During this time, von Braun served as Director, Marshall Space Flight Center. In March 1972, he transferred to the National Aeronautics and Space Administration (NASA) as Deputy Associate Administrator. He went on to private industry in 1972, and, due to ill health, retired in January 1977. He died in June 1977.

I had the opportunity to hear Doctor Von Braun speak just a few years before he died. He was the featured guest at a luncheon in New York City at the Metropolitan Club. A friend of mine, who was a member of the Club, invited me to attend the luncheon with him.

What I remember of Dr. von Braun's remarks that day was that he exhorted the audience to continue to support continued space exploration. Although he had an accent, his English was good and his delivery forceful. His personality was friendly and confident.

Dr. Wernher von Braun didn't receive much recognition at the close of the twentieth century, when they were compiling lists of the century's leading lights. The circumstances of his time and place in his early life made him part of the German war machine, and, for many, this was hard to forgive. However, not only Adolph Hitler, but also Jack Kennedy, employed his genius.

Long after many of the people and events of the twentieth century are distant memories, perhaps Earth colonists at distant planets and explorers to all parts of the universe will remember him and his work.

Peenemunde Update

A few years ago, I rented a car in Copenhagen, Denmark and drove east along the Baltic coast. I was interested in seeing the former East German Baltic cities and planned to go as far east as Peenemunde, location of the former Rocket Research Institute. I had no idea of what I would find there.

I drove on to the island of Usedom on a late Friday afternoon in August and headed north to the peninsula that was the site of the former rocket complex. By the time I got near there, I had trouble finding a room. South of Peenemunde the island of Usedom is still quite rural and unspoiled with beautiful beaches, which Germans enjoy in the summer. I finally found a Spartan room in what appeared to be a former camp, probably built for company workers in communist days. They also offered a simple dinner–stuffed cabbage, potatoes and pudding. Since there was no TV and little to do, I went to sleep about 9 p.m.

The next morning, I drove to the rocket complex and looked around before the museum building opened at 9 a.m. There were still buildings standing that reflected damage from the World War II air raids. I drove into a car park nearby and joined a bus group that was being taken around by a guide. The car park was quite small. Except for this bus group, there were few other visitors. The main part of the rocket base is about three by five miles, but we were only taken around the central part.

When the Russians got to Pennemunde in 1945, they took whatever equipment was there, along with the technicians that had remained behind, and shipped them to the Soviet Union. The complex was then used as an airbase and home base for East Germany's Baltic Fleet.

The Guide took us to a former air raid bunker where there was a model of the testing station with lights that highlighted various facilities when you pressed the appropriate buttons. There was also a model of Test

Stand VII, where the first V-2 was successfully launched. A film of various successful and unsuccessful rocket test firings was shown. Souvenirs of model rockets, videos, slides, and booklets were offered for sale. The guide pointed out a number of airplanes (MIG's) and rockets that were on display outside, including a V-1 and V-2 (the former A-4). Next we were taken to the waterfront behind the power station, where two missile ships of the former East Germany navy could be boarded. These were going to be sold or scrapped. The vessels appeared to be well designed and formidable, particularly for duty in the restricted waters of the Baltic.

We also saw the building that housed the Research Institute engineering offices. Photographs and pictures of the rocket-testing era lined some of the walls. However, not all places were available for viewing, and we didn't get to see the area of the test stands and the airdrome, which were located some distance away.

Across the Baltic Sea, in Stockholm harbor, just a few hundred miles away, is a museum that houses and tells the story of the nearly 400-year-old remains of a Swedish warship, the Vasa. In 1628, it capsized and sank about thirty minutes after it started on its maiden voyage from the wharf below the Royal Palace. For hundreds of years, it rested on the harbor bottom until discovered in 1961. It was then raised, preserved and displayed in its own building with special lights, computer directed guides, exhibits, etc.

In contrast, Peenemunde's Rocket Research Institute preserves its history in a small, old building, now serving as its museum. Here one of mankind's extraordinary technological achievements was born and a new age started. Near it are a few other wrecked buildings. If there is hesitancy in doing more to tell Peenemunde's story, because of the war nature of the rocket work, maybe we need to remember the Vasa probably sunk because it was top heavy with cannons.

What I did see at Peenemunde was highly absorbing and fascinating. I believe the former Rocket Research Institute at Pennmunde is the doorway through which man entered space for the first time. As the years go by, perhaps others will see it this way and do more to present the unique Peenemunde Space story in a way that will encourage visits, and, subsequently, an understanding of what was accomplished here.

Baltic Sagas
Events and Personalities that Changed the World!

Suomenlinna – Sveaborg Fortress
Helsinki Harbor, Finland

IX
Winter War 1939
Finland Attacked!
Soviet Union Humbled at First
World Watches as Finland is Crushed

Dedicated to Saima Markus
A widowed mother who left her home in Karelia
to remain a Finn.

Finland's Lot—Between Two Powerful Neighbors

Although every country is unique in its own way, Finland is unique in a number of special ways. Although usually clustered with the Scandinavian countries of Sweden, Denmark and Norway, its history is quite different. Finns were never Vikings, didn't emigrate north from Western Europe, don't share the same language root, don't have a royal family, and were more isolated. Long ago, the people occupying Finland were separated by the northern climate into small pockets of people, widely scattered throughout their northern area.

Self-reliance is a strong trait among Finns that contributes to the special Finnish character. It is described by the Finnish word, sisu. Sisu is a kind of combination of guts and stubbornness. This is how someone explained it, "If someone knocks you down, and you know that if you get up you'll get knocked down again, and you still get up, that's sisu."

Their widely scattered small communities prevented the Finns from developing their own unifying government. This helped Sweden take over the area and administer it as a colony for hundreds of years. Sweden extracted from Finland not only taxes and goods but also manpower for its army. During Sweden's era as a great power, it is estimated that over a third of the men in its military were Finns. The Swedes governed from Turku, which started as a trading post on Finland's southwest shore.

Turku was the leading city in Finland for a long-time and is still very important today. It is historically significant, particularly in helping to understand the Swedish period in Finnish history. Turku also has a special charm that age and experience sometimes bestows. It reflects its heritage as the former capital, when the Swedish governor presided at Turku Castle. The old Castle dates from about 1280 and is still open today as a museum and for exhibitions. Some of its large halls have been restored and are used for special events.

The Turku Cathedral is also nearby. It was consecrated in 1300 and is still the seat of the Archbishop of Finland. It is the repository of many tombs of prominent people in Finnish history and has a museum containing items of importance in Finland's religious history. When visiting the cathedral, a good place to start is at the two frescos facing the altar. One depicts Bishop Henry, an Englishman, baptizing Finns for the first time. He came with the Swedes on a crusade to convert the heathen Finns. The other shows Mikael Agricola, Bishop of Turku and an important figure in bringing the reformation to Finland, offering the Finnish translation of the New Testament to the King of Sweden.

Sweden, during this time, competed with the Russian City of Novgorod for control of the lands around the eastern Baltic Sea, the region known as the Gulf of Finland. The city of Viipuri came into being about this time in the area, near Lake Ladoga, known as Karelia. Other castles and strongholds were also built to protect Swedish interests in the eastern areas. Later, King Gustav Vasa of Sweden, in order to draw trade from the Hanseatic City of Tallinn, ordered four Finnish villages to move to the area of the Vantaa River and establish Helsinki. However, Helsinki continued to trail far behind the capital, Turku, in importance. During these years, Finland was often coveted by other Baltic powers, and Sweden was forced to defend its ownership.

Tsar Alexander I acquired the Duchy of Finland from Sweden in 1809 as part of the Tilsit agreements he made with Napoleon. Finland became a Duchy under the direct control of the Russian Tsar. The Tsar wanted Finland's capital closer to Russia, and he moved the capital from Turku to Helsinki three years later. A great fire destroyed much of Helsinki just before his decree and necessitated that a new city be built. It resulted in the lovely metropolis, with broad boulevards and splendid buildings, that exists today. A Finnish Parliament was instituted and the country enjoyed more self-rule than under Sweden. Later, Alexander III and his son Nicholas II restricted Finland's self-rule.

When Russia ended its participation in World War I, Finland became independent. It resisted being pulled back into Bolshevik Russia by fighting and winning its own internal Civil War, the War of Liberation. Finns took solace from a slogan they embraced, "We are no longer Swedes, we will not become Russians, so let us be Finns."

Although World War I had ended with its participants sickened by its carnage, in the 1930's war clouds again gathered over Europe. After Adolph Hitler became German Chancellor in 1933, he set out to regain the lands the country lost as a result of the First World War. As trench soldier himself in the war, he was particularly sensitive to the humiliation the country and its people felt due to the Versailles Treaty. He planned to use this emotional appeal to motivate the country in support of his plans.

In large part, the harsh Versailles Treaty peace terms reflected the demands of the French Premier, Georges Clemenceau. French national pride had been stung by the humiliation of France's defeat in the 1871 Franco-Prussian War. The continental rivalry between France and Germany was rearing up again.

After expanding Germany's Army, Hitler first took control of the Rhineland, a formerly demilitarized zone. A Berlin-Rome Axis treaty with Mussolini came in 1936. A union of Germany with Austria was followed by Hitler's demand for the Sudetenland, the western part of Czechoslovakia. Czechoslovakia mobilized.

British Prime Minister Neville Chamberlain interceded and prevented immediate war by flying to Munich and securing an assurance that this would be Hitler's last territorial demand. He returned to England waving a paper and saying he had assured, "Peace in our time." It was not to be. Hitler next demanded that Poland restore Danzig to Germany. Mussolini, watching Hitler's success with adding territory, seized Albania. Hitler now negotiated a non-aggression pact with Stalin to remove the threat of the Soviet Union in the East. He attacked Poland a few months later. Britain and France, who had a pact to support Poland, declared war on Germany two days later.

Germany's lightning war, "blitzkrieg," defeated Poland in less than three weeks. The Soviets invaded and took eastern Poland. The pact with Germany also gave the Soviets a free hand in the Baltic States, and they began to assert themselves there. Stalin was now quoted as saying, "I understand Finland's wish to remain neutral...this is not possible."

Kremlin-Demands from the Soviet Union

Moscow, Soviet Union

The Finnish delegation had arrived on November 3 for what was to be the final attempt to avoid hostilities with the Soviet Union. Less than a month after the Soviet Union attacked and annexed eastern Poland, Finland was invited to send a delegation to Moscow. The subject of the meeting for the Soviets was security for the Soviet Union from an attack against it through the Gulf of Finland, or through Finland itself. The subject for Finland was maintaining its cherished independence. There had already been two previous meetings in Moscow, and this was expected to be a final attempt to avoid war.

First Moscow Meeting–October 12, 1939

At this first meeting, Stalin and Molotov (the Soviet's new Foreign Minister), were both present. Joseph Stalin (1879—1953) emerged to replace Lenin as dictator of the Soviet Union in 1924 and used his key Communist party positions to fortify his authority. He proved adroit in slowly gathering into his hands the power of making appointments to high party and government positions that would insure personal loyalty to him. In the 30's, prominent political and military figures were subjected to trials as Stalin consolidated his power. Most of the old party members not beholden to him were eased out, died off, or were executed.

Vyacheslav M. Molotov (1890–1986) was an early and long time Bolshevik who enjoyed high government positions most of his adult life. In 1911, he helped found the communist newspaper, Pravda. He had served as pallbearer for Lenin and was a close advisor to Stalin. In the next twenty-five years, he would represent the Soviet Union at most major international conferences, first with the Nazis and then the Allies.

Juho Kusti Paasikivi (1876–1958) was the leader of the Finnish delegation and the country's minister to Stockholm. He had studied in St. Petersburg, spoke Russian, and had negotiated the Treaty of Tartu in 1920, bringing peace between Finland and the Soviet Union. He was close to 70 years of age but tough and cheerful. His attitude toward the Soviet Union was even-handed; he neither sympathized with nor hated communism. He believed that Stalin's interest was not ideological but concerned with military security.

Stalin demanded that Finland lease Hanko, a small town on Finland's west coast, to the Soviets for use as a military base. Also, he wanted a number of islands in the Gulf of Finland ceded to the Soviet Union. He wanted to move the frontier of Finland to the north, five or six miles away from Leningrad.

In return, Stalin offered Finland land of greater size in Russian Karelia, which sat next to Finland's border and was north of Lake Ladoga. Paasikivi replied to Stalin that he would have to consult Helsinki.

At a meeting two days later, Paasikivi said that the new border was not possible for economic reasons. Stalin said that his soldiers were concerned about the use of the Gulf of Finland as an invasion route, and they didn't concern themselves with economics. Paasikiv asked, "Who would attack Russia?" Stalin mentioned that either Germany or England was a potential enemy.

Second Moscow meeting–October 23, 1939

At the second meeting, the Finnish delegation included Vaino Tanner, who shortly thereafter became the Finnish foreign minister. At the start of the meeting, the Finns protested about Soviet military overflying Finland, but Stalin and Molotov ignored this. There were a number of conferences during the next few days, but nothing substantial was changed except that the Soviets reduced the number of troops they proposed to station at Hanko. Tanner wrote to the Swedish prime minister for support, but his reply indicated not to count on Sweden's help.

Prior to the Finns arriving in Moscow for the third, and, what everyone understood would be the last, meeting, Molotov revealed to the Supreme Soviet the Soviet's demands of Finland. One Soviet delegate, present at the meeting said, in reference to Finland expecting help,

"Poland, too, had a guarantee." Molotov's speech was reported throughout the world, making it difficult for the Soviets to back down now without losing face. This put greater pressure on the Finns, and they almost cancelled their trip. Further reflection caused them to try once more to prevent hostilities.

The meeting on November 3 ended with Molotov remarking, "We civilians can't seem to do much more. Now it seems to be up to the military. It is their time to speak."

November 4, 1939–6 p.m.

On November 4, the Finnish delegation was asked to come to the Kremlin at 6 p.m. At this meeting Stalin said, "The Soviet government is the only government that would tolerate an Independent Finland. The Czarist government would not tolerate it, nor would the Kerensky government. But the Soviet government demands protection for its borders. For this reason, the problem of the Finnish Gulf is important. The Soviet government will not change its mind about needing Hanko." Paasikivi replied, " I am afraid Hanko cannot be given up under any circumstances."

Stalin now pointed to a map and, to the surprise of the Finns, began pointing to other islands in the Gulf and asking, "Do you have any use for these?" This new interest in other islands wasn't something the Finns could deal with on the spot. There was some further discussion and then the Finns brought the meeting to a close, saying, "We have gone as far as we can with our proposals, but, with basic principals at stake, we know what course we need to follow."

Situation on the Eve of War

The staggering contrast between the armed forces and the industrial resources of Finland, compared with the Soviet Union, was almost beyond comprehension. In 1939, Finland's population was about 4,000,000 people. The Soviet Union was around 170,000,000 - over forty to one. Finland could muster an army, including reserves, of about 300,000. The Soviet Union had millions.

The Soviet Union had an arms industry capable of producing tanks, armored cars, airplanes, artillery, and all the necessary small arms. Ammunition and other supplies could be produced in an endless stream. Finland had very little military equipment, lacking particularly modern arms, such as tanks and airplanes. What equipment it did have was, for the most part, old.

The recent German blitzkrieg in Poland, coordinating mechanized and fast moving infantry, tanks, artillery, and air support, was a discouraging example of the reliance in modern warfare on a preponderance of these weapons. At the start of the war, Finland protected the most direct Soviet Union invasion route, north of Leningrad, through the Karelian Isthmus, a ninety-mile front, with about 150,000 troops organized into nine divisions and other units. They relied heavily on a defensive position, called the Mannerheim line, which was a series of bunkers, barbed wire, artillery emplacements, tank traps, and trenches constructed primarily of earth and felled tree. Behind this was a less well-prepared, reserve defensive line.

Opposing them, in the beginning, were twenty-six Soviet divisions totaling over 400,000 men. They had about 1500 tanks and armored cars and superiority over Finland in artillery of about five or six to one.

On the northern six hundred mile front, from Lake Ladoga to the Arctic Ocean, the Soviet Union deployed about 200,000 Russians against about 60,000 Finns. Again, the Russians had a great equipment advantage. As the war went on, the Russians drew on their endless manpower reserves to throw greater numbers of fresh troops into the war.

What Finland did have was soldiers defending their homeland and capable of individual acts of great heroism. They would be fighting in dense forests and brutal weather conditions, to which Finns were accustomed, and would be lead by a well trained, experienced, and battle tested warrior, Marshal Carl Mannerheim.

The Soviet Union's strategy was to punch into Finland's southern heartland through a massive attack up the Karelian Isthmus, which is north of Leningrad. Other troops were to cut Finland in half by an attack through its central waist and reach the Sea of Bothnia. At the same time, air raids were to frighten and demoralize civilians and disrupt economic and political life.

Finland's strategy was to:
1. Dig in behind defensive positions, and, finally, the Mannerheim line, inflicting intolerable casualties on the enemy. They would withdraw only when forced.
2. Shift reserves and commanders to reinforce endangered areas.
3. In the north, use the dense forest, lack of roads, and the brutal climate to harass and tear apart the invading Russian columns.
The Finns also hoped that civilians would be resolute in face of air attacks, and that help would come from other nations.

Special mention needs to be made of one way in which Finland stretched its manpower. Women auxiliaries, called Lottas, took over many of the duties usually performed by men, thereby releasing soldiers for the front. About 100,000 of these women served, acting as sky watchers, or in the medical, communications, and food service areas.

The name Lottas goes back to the war between Sweden and Russia in 1808/1809. A Finnish officer reporting to the front had brought his wife, Lotta, with him. She came to be held in great affection by the soldiers, as she would write letters for the wounded, cooked, and provided a touch of home.

World opinion was overwhelmingly on the side of Finland. The Soviet Union clearly was the unprovoked aggressor in its demands on Finland. The sharp discrepancy in size between the two nations and the Soviet air attacks on civilians disgusted the whole world. Russian air attacks on trains carrying civilians from Viipuri, near the front lines, to Helsinki were particularly loathsome.

Volunteers to help Finland came from several nations: 8,000 from Sweden being the largest group. They also came from many other nations and totaled about 11,500 in all. Nearly 300 assorted aircraft were sent to them by six nations. Ten nations sent material, mostly artillery, small arms, blankets, ammunitions, etc. This help was all welcome but wasn't enough to make a real difference in the war.

Three major powers were already at war in Europe. Germany was fighting against England and France, and they all had an intense interest in the hostility between Finland and the Soviet Union, aside from sympathy for Finland. Their interest was based primarily on securing a geographic advantage by establishing a foothold in the Scandinavian countries.

There was also interest in the raw materials being supplied from this area for Germany's war effort, particularly Swedish iron ore. Finland had to balance a need for getting real help in its war with a deep concern for what allied or German troops on its soil would ultimately accomplish. Would it make all Finland a battleground and crush the small nation, no matter how it ended? Finland decided the price was potentially too high. In the end, the allied powers and Germany were kept away.

The United States, particularly, expressed sympathy for Finland. Finland had enormous good will in America, stemming in part from appreciation for being the only country to repay its World War I debt in full. However, except for some Finnish-American volunteers, an offer to mediate (rejected by the Soviet Union) and some relief aid, little else was forthcoming.

Marshal Carl Gustaf Mannerheim (1867–1951)

Ironically, the man who commanded Finland's military in all three wars that Finland fought against Russia in the twentieth century, served in the Russian Army for the first twenty-seven years of his military career. The Russians trained him as a cavalry officer; he fought for Russia in two wars; and he achieved a very high rank.

He was born in Finland to a noble family with ties to Sweden. He learned self-reliance at an early age, when his impoverished father left his family and fled to Paris. Young Mannerheim decided on a career in the military. Service in the Russian Army came about when he was expelled for rule infractions from the Finnish Cadet School at Hamina, in 1886.

A military training facility is still located at Hamina today. Mannerheim attended the Finnish Cadet School here, which has served since 1920, as the Finnish Reserve Officers School. Just outside the school is a monument to the Finnish officers killed in action in the 1939–1944 wars. Hamina was a fortress town, under construction by Sweden, when it was surrendered to the Russians in the 1741–1742 war.

Hamina is located about one hundred miles east of Helsinki, on the Gulf of Finland. Its central bastion now provides a stage for cultural events. There is an art gallery and a number of interesting tourist attractions, including the town museum where the Russian Empress, Catherine the Great, and the Swedish King, Gustavus III, negotiated in 1783.

To gain acceptance to the Tsar's Russian army, young Mannerheim now applied himself to improve his scholastic record. He pursued the necessary academic credit to get accepted into the Nikolai Calvalry School in St. Petersburg, from which he graduated with honors in 1889.

His attention to professional training, and his personal demeanor and bearing, soon brought him choice military duties. These duties sometimes brought him in close contact with the royal family. His early assignments included service in a Guard Regiment, the Chevalier Guards. Its honorary Colonel was the Empress. In his *Memoirs,* the Marshal describes the uniform of the Chevalier Guards, which included, "tight, white buckskin breeches which were put on wet over one's bare skin." At the coronation of Nickolas II in 1896, he was selected as one of four officers standing near their majesties during the Moscow ceremonies.

His early military career also included service in the part of Poland that was occupied by Russia. His interest in horses and social skills later on helped gain him acceptance in Polish aristocratic circles beyond those usually accorded Russian officers. Being a Finn and not a Russian, undoubtedly, also played a part.

During the 1905 Russia-Japanese war, he saw active duty. Shortly after returning to St. Petersburg from this war, he was sent on a special two-year mission to observe conditions in the Russian lands just north of India, in China. He traveled 3,200 miles, mostly on horseback, and ended his trip in Peking. A few years later, he was back in the field in Poland as commander of the 13th Uhlan Regiment.

After World War I started, he commanded increasingly larger formations. His military performance also won him decorations, including the Cross of St. George and a Romanian order. By 1917, he was in command of the 6th Cavalry Corps as a Lieutenant General.

Then came the abdication of the Tsar and an increasing breakdown of discipline within the Army. Late in 1918, sensing it might be a good time to get a clearer picture of events away from the battlefront, Mannerheim requested medical leave in Odessa, on the Black Sea. He had previously gone there during the war for medical care. He traveled from there to St. Petersburg encountering some difficulty, as normal order was breaking down.

Mannerheim was in St. Petersburg in November 1917 and viewed the Bolshevik revolution up close. He was dodging Red Guards who were hunting down former high-ranking officers in the Tsar's army. He went to Helsinki and quickly saw that it was a perilous time if Finland were to retain its newly declared independence. There were still Russian ships, from its Baltic fleet, in Helsinki and 40,000 armed Russian soldiers in garrisons spread around the country. Finns who supported the Bolsheviks were organizing themselves into militant Red Guards. They planned to take over Finland with the support of the Russian garrisons and fleet. If successful, these Red Finns planned to have Finland rejoin the Russian Empire, now under the new Bolshevik government. Mannerheim was in favor of an independent Finland and firmly against the Bolsheviks.

Mannerheim was asked to take charge of the military forces being organized to keep Finland independent. The Red forces had established themselves in southern Finland in the large cities of Tampere, Helsinki, and Viipuri. The forces supporting an independent Finland, called, "Whites," were concentrated in Vaasa on the Gulf of Bothnia. Mannerheim successfully organized and hastily trained a White Army. It included returning "Jaeger" troops, Finns who had been training in Germany. Swedish volunteers, many of whom were well trained, also came. Some members of the Finnish government also prevailed on Germany, still at war with the Allies, to send help. Mannherheim was skeptical of German help. He felt this would line up Finland with what was becoming the losing side in the struggle between the major powers. It would also reduce chances of Finland getting post war help from the Allies.

Mannerheim's White Army succeeded in capturing Tampere, and then Viipuri. German troops, who had landed at Hanko, captured Helsinki. In May 1918, a ceasefire was negotiated and a formal Tartu Peace Treaty was signed in 1920.

Mannerheim disagreed with the government on how much German involvement there should be in organizing and commanding the Finnish Army in the future. This led to Mannerheim resigning his command in May 1918. He made a farewell speech to the army, then traveled to Sweden, France, and England.

When Germany surrendered to the Allies in November 1918, Mannerheim was vindicated, and he was invited to become Regent of Finland. However, he lost the presidential election in 1919. He retired from public life and became Chairman of the Finnish Red Cross, interesting himself in work benefiting children. In 1931, he accepted the Chairmanship of the Defense Council and held this post until 1939. He was appointed Field Marshal in 1933.

When the Winter War between the Soviet Union and Finland began, he was asked again to become Supreme Commander of Finland's armed forces. He was now 72 years old but didn't hesitate to put himself in the service of his country. He was uniquely qualified for this command position, in many respects. He knew the Finnish Army and its personnel very well. He had the highest regard for the men in the ranks and knew Finland's best weapon was their spirit, resourcefulness, courage, and skill in making use of the weather and terrain. His own long experience in command also enabled him to make shrewd choices of commanders for the various theatres of operation and adjust to changing situations.

He also understood the Russian military and their likely behavior. Russian soldiers were brave but would become discouraged when faced with poor organization and unknown situations. They needed good leadership, especially in Finland's harsh weather and unfamiliar terrain. Mannerheim knew the leadership of the Red Army would be in the hands of those more adept at political, rather than military, skills. Many of the best officers had been killed during World War I and then in the Bolshevik revolution and the Civil War that followed. Stalin's purges in the 30's removed more trained officers.

A Russian victory would depend on attacking with vast numbers of soldiers (with little concern for casualties), and a preponderance of military equipment.

Mannerheim set up his headquarters in a schoolhouse at Mikkeli, about 85 miles northwest of Viipuri. Here, he organized his staff, and developed the defensive Finnish military strategy.

Soviet Union Attacks!

The initial Soviet ground attack poured across the Finnish frontier at the Karelian Isthmus on November 30, 1939. At this stage, the Russians were well fed, warm, and confident. They hadn't even been issued overcoats. The war was anticipated to last less than two weeks. They expected to be greeted by grateful Finns happy to be liberated from capitalistic servitude. The soldiers were singing and carrying leaflets and gifts of money and clothing. Behind them came political commissars to ensure their enthusiasm. They were still singing, advancing arm in arm, when they hit the first mines.

These first Soviet troops soon encountered what they came to call the, "dirty tricks of the Finns." There were mines placed in unlikely places, including manure piles and water buckets which exploded when moved. To regain their confidence, the Russian infantry began to depend on advancing behind their tanks. To combat the tanks, the Finns used Molotov cocktails - bottles of kerosene and gasoline. The cocktail was ignited by setting fire to a gasoline-drenched rag stuck into its neck, and then thrown at an opening in the tank.

The Finns had also developed a wooden box mine, which, being magnetic, was difficult to detect. The Russians sent their soldiers, armed with spikes, ahead of the tanks, where Finnish snipers would kill them.

Finnish anti-tank groups hid in camouflaged foxholes. From there, tanks could be attacked with Molotov cocktails, or a log or crowbar could be shoved into tank treads. When the tank crews emerged, they were met by machine gun fire. The Finns developed a wide range of methods to disable Russian tanks, which usually depended on the heroism of individual soldiers. As the days went on and the cold winter set in, the Russian troops got hungry, cold, tired and discouraged. They failed to meet friendly Finns, "happy to be liberated," as they had been told to expect.

In the beginning, the Russians also made the tactical mistake of rotating their attacking troops each day. A unit would move forward in the morning, advance a mile or two, and, in the evening, return to its starting point. The next day another unit would be sent forward. As the Finns withdrew from their forward frontier area and took up their positions on the fortified Mannerheim line, a stalemate developed. Having already encountered so much resistance in the frontier area, the Russians were hesitant to attack this much-publicized and dreaded line of fortifications.

At the eastern end of the southern Finnish defensive position, at Toipale, the Russians attempted mass infantry charges supported by tanks, which were repulsed with enormous losses. This battle continued until December 20. Finally, the Russians withdrew, and the Finns surveyed the battlefield, which revealed fifty-eight destroyed tanks, thousands of dead soldiers, abandoned rifles, grenades and ammunition. A Finnish counterattack was attempted, but failed. Activity, for now, consisted of sporadic artillery fire from both sides.

Back in Leningrad, the Russian military staff re-evaluated their original ten to twelve day victory timetable and wondered at the resourcefulness and fighting spirit of the Finnish soldiers.

Finnish Anti-Tank Team

Five Miles West of Lake Ladoga
A Few Miles inside Finnish Frontier
Karelian Isthmus
December 1939

The temperature dropped a few degrees almost every day, and it was already down to ten degrees tonight. It was quite dark now; daylight only lasted for about eight hours this time of the year. Snow had fallen again, as it had most days since early November, and the battlefield in front of the Finnish defensive line was covered. A hundred meters in front of the Finnish trenches, new snow covered the sludge kicked up by the Russian attack two days earlier. Since then, the Finnish troops had been laying new mines in front of their positions and repairing the damage done to their trenches by Soviet artillery. An attack was expected in the morning. The Russians' two days of rest provided time to replace their casualties and destroyed equipment.

This sector of the front was about four hundred meters wide and was bordered on the east by a small stream flowing in a northwesterly direction from Lake Ladoga. It eventually joined a larger stream that went on to the Gulf of Finland. Soon, it would be frozen solid and able to support troops and tanks, but, for now, the stream and marshy ground provided a natural barrier to Soviet activity from that direction.

On the western side, there was a dense stand of trees, boulders, and undergrowth, all of which would hamper an attack from that direction. However, the ground in between these two natural barriers had been cleared for farming and, consequently, provided the Russians with an open space through which to attack.

Under cover of darkness, Vesa and Ilkka, a two-man Finnish anti-tank team, crept forward about two hundred meters beyond the Finnish trenches. The cold weather was not a problem for these two soldiers.

They had learned to ski, play hockey, and hike through the woods in the cold Finnish winter for most of their lives. They were dressed in layered clothing to retain their body heat. Vesa wore a warm woolen sweater, knitted by his mother, under his jacket and over it a white cloak. The Finnish soldiers wore white cloaks to blend them into the snow-covered terrain. Ilkka also wore a woolen sweater, knitted by his girlfriend, who was serving as a Lotta.

For the Russians, who had come to the Karelian Isthmus just a few weeks ago, it was very different. They hadn't been provided with proper clothing. They huddled around their campfires at night to keep warm. When they attacked, they bunched up behind their tanks. They tried to avoid exposing themselves to small arms fire which came from an enemy sheathed in white, making the Finns almost invisible against the snow.

Vesa had only been on active duty in the Finnish Army for nine months. He had received three months of training, mostly in the use of a hand held machine gun. Ilkka had been in the Army longer than Vesa and had been trained to destroy tanks by moving in close and heaving a Molotov cocktail into any opening. It took great courage to get close enough to a tank that was firing its machine gun at you, followed by the enemy infantry running and firing at you from behind it.

Vesa and Ilkka were dug into a small crevice behind a tree. They were at the edge of the forest next to the open ground and had covered themselves with branches and snow. There were six Finnish anti-tank teams forward of their lines, three in the forest and three on the marsh side. Vesa and Ilkka were the farthest forward on the forest side.

About 10 a.m. the Soviets started directing artillery bombardment toward the Finnish trench positions. It was about noon when Vesa and Ilkka heard the clanging of the Russian tanks coming from the south. In about fifteen minutes, they saw the first one. As the first Soviet tank went by, Vesa and Ilkka stayed low and out of sight. There were about thirty tanks in three lines across the 400-meter front in this attack. The tanks led the attack in front of about six hundred Soviet infantry. The soldiers were close together and just behind the last row of tanks. Suddenly, Vesa and Ilkka heard machine guns. They saw flames from the leading Soviet tank near the tree line. They also heard the Finnish trenches erupt with anti-tank and other cannon fire on the tanks in the middle.

A tank in the third line suddenly came up just opposite them. Ilkka leaped up and ran toward it. The crew in the tank didn't see him because they were directing their machine gun fire at the anti–tank team that had attacked the lead tank. Ilkka threw his lighted cocktail bomb into the driver's viewing slit, then dropped and rolled away, back to the cover of the forest. Vesa opened fire on the closest Russian infantry, keeping them from firing at Ilkka. The Russian soldiers fell down in the snow or scattered. The tank caught fire, and, as the crew jumped out, Vesa cut them down with his machine gun.

The anti-tank teams, mines, and artillery fire from the Finnish trenches disabled about a dozen Soviet tanks. The Finns continued to concentrate their heavy guns on the tanks while their infantry directed small arms fire at the Soviet infantry. After an hour of hard fighting, the remaining Russian tanks turned around and followed their fleeing infantry.

When it was clear the Russians were finished for the day, the Finnish anti-tank teams returned to their trenches carrying their dead and wounded. Both Vesa and Ilkka survived the day's action. Their experience had helped them time their attack just right so that neither the tank they attacked, nor the other tanks were able to get a clear shot at them. The Russian infantry never really got close to them nor could they see Vesa and Ilkka in their white cloaks.

Two of the other Finnish anti-tank teams weren't as fortunate. One cocktail thrower was killed before he could get close enough to his target; his team member was wounded by infantry fire. Both members of another team were killed by machine gun fire from a tank in the center of the line. Just as the tank turned, the gunner saw them in the open and gunned them down. The Finns had taken about twenty casualties, six dead and fourteen wounded. The Russians lost the twelve tanks, almost all their crews, and nearly a hundred infantry.

Finnish ordnance specialists and the trench troops searched the battlefield before dusk to collect equipment and ammunition that could be turned against the Russians.

Northern Battles in Freezing Cold

The war on the nine hundred mile front, extending north from Lake Ladoga to the Arctic Sea, was very different from the Karelian Isthmus. There was no Finnish defensive line due to the great distances and the limited number of Finnish troops available. The Finnish tactics were to use their understanding of the terrain and their experience with winter. They would hit and run, harass the Soviet columns as they tried to advance, and let the weather help wear down the bunched up Russian soldiers and equipment.

The winter weather conditions in the forests of northern Finland are brutal, and the 1939/40 winter was particularly severe, the coldest since 1828. Few armies had ever been asked to fight this far north, and the Russians had no experience or training in this harsh climate. The Russian columns, as they crossed the Finnish frontier with their tanks, armored cars, and artillery, faced snow levels over their heads, few roads, frozen lakes, and a largely unseen enemy.

The Russians had to tramp the snow down to move ahead. The Finns would fell tree trunks across the roads of their expected route in order to delay the Russians. The Finns would weaken the ice on frozen lakes, in advance of the Russians, causing their heavy equipment to break through and often drowning the crews. If Russian tanks were parked on a frozen lake, the Finns would pour water on the tank treads at night and immobilize them.

The Russian soldiers didn't have appropriate winter clothing. Their horses suffered from the cold and lack of fodder in the snow-covered ground. Lubricants in their equipment froze.

The experienced Finns, in their layered outfits, were dressed for the severe weather. Their white sheets and cloaks blended with the snow to camouflage them. The Finns were experienced hunters and good marksmen. One Finnish sniper, Corporal Simo Hayha, was credited with killing five hundred Russians. The Finns moved on skis they could remove quickly. They were relentless in their sudden attacks. In the winter, this far north, daylight lasted for only a few short hours. As night fell, these sudden attacks were particularly frightening.

The Finns hid behind tree trunks and boulders. Sometimes, they would get close to a Russian tank, throw a Molotov cocktail at an air intake or an open hatch, and shoot the crew as the fire and heat drove them out. One effective weapon with which the Finns were equipped, a Suomi submachine gun, was used with devastating effect.

A tactic the Finns developed was to divide the Russian columns into isolated clusters of men and equipment. This was called a *motti*. Inside the mottis, the Russians huddled for warmth around their immobile tanks to gain protection from the tank's guns. They ate their horses and looked forlornly to the skies for support and supplies from their air force.

All the while, Finnish soldiers, individually or in small groups, would sweep in, get off a few killing shots, and disappear. The Russian artillery, even if they finally were manned, loaded and fired, had no real target. The Russians became hungry and exhausted. Their casualties were enormous, and morale plummeted.

The Russians once managed to overrun a Finnish field kitchen that had hot sausage soup still cooking on the stove. The hungry and exhausted soldiers immediately gave up fighting for food. Many of them were killed with Finnish sausage in their mouths when the Finns swiftly counterattacked. This engagement became known as the, "Sausage War."

After the Russian attacks in the Karelian Isthmus stalled, the Russians next directed their offensive activities to an unfortified area on the northern side of Lake Ladoga. This major battle just north of Lake Ladoga became known as the battle of Tolvajarvi. Marshal Mannerheim hadn't expected too much pressure in this area. He thought the Russians would have trouble keeping their troops there supplied. However, the Russians had been improving the road network on their side of the border. They surprised the Finns by pouring in more troops than Mannerheim thought likely. If the Russians broke through here and swung west around Lake Ladoga, they could come in behind the Mannerheim Line.

Marshal Mannerheim decided he had to use his reserves to meet this threat, even though his first concern was guarding the Karelian Isthmus. To command the Finnish forces against this dangerous new threat, Mannerheim sent Colonel Paavo Talvela. Colonel Talvela had studied the possibility of an attack in this area during his military training. He knew the terrain well. The Russian divisions attacking here were the 139th and 75th, with a total of 45,000 men supported by tanks, artillery and mortars. Working in the Finns' favor was that more than half of the 139th division had received no training, and about a third were new recruits.

When Colonel Talvela reached his new command area on December 10, his first action was to reorganize the scattered and retreating Finns there. He and his subordinate, Lt. Colonel Aaron Perjure, began to meld their newly arrived reinforcements with the local Finns they had gathered. They immediately planned a series of counterattacks to break the momentum of the attacking Russians. The Russians, after their initial attacks, were also becoming increasingly scattered in the unfamiliar and snow covered forests and icy lakes. Often engaged by the Finns at night, the untrained Russians became confused. Sometimes the Russians, in their confusion, fired at each other. At times, the Russian airplanes fired at their own troops.

The less heavily armed but more mobile Finns kept attacking and pushing the Russians back, inflicting heavy casualties. In the unfamiliar forest and cold weather, the Russians fought at a disadvantage since their heavy equipment could not be properly utilized. The camouflaged Finns, in their white cloaks, were almost invisible to their enemies. They moved quickly on their skis, succeeded in pushing the Russians back, and captured large stocks of abandoned enemy equipment. The surviving Russians finally got back to the east bank of the Aitto River and remained there for the duration of the war. The Russian threat in this area was over. The Tolvajarvi victory was an important strategic victory and a welcome boost to Finnish morale.

One of the most important battles fought on the northern frontier was for the village of Suomussalmi and the area around it, which included two large lakes. This small village of four thousand people at Finland's waist was the gateway to Oulu, 150 miles to the west on the Gulf of Bothnia. Soviet capture of Suomussalmi was the key to cutting Finland into two parts.

Karl G. Heinze

The Russians deployed two powerful divisions for this task. The 163rd division was made up mostly of Mongols who were not well trained but thought to be good soldiers. The other division, the 44th, had been sent from Moscow and was made up of top-flight Ukrainian soldiers. This division was expected to lead the coming victory parade at Oulu. The two divisions had 48,000 men, over 150 tanks and armored cars, and over 300 cannons. The two divisions were to invade Finland separately. The 163rd was to advance first and then receive supplies from the 44th, when they joined up.

The defending Finns had 17,000 men, lightly armed but mobile. They meant to prevent the two divisions from joining up. The Finns had burned and abandoned Suomussalmi and taken up more advantageous defensive positions nearby. They felled trees, dug trenches, and hid behind boulders.

The 163rd division was ordered not to occupy Suomussalmi, since it offered no shelter or supplies. However, when the first soldiers of the strung-out column of the division reached Suomussalmi, they decided to occupy it. From here, they launched attacks against the Finns to the west. The Russians suffered heavy casualties and decided to retreat to the village and wait there for reinforcements and supplies from the 44th division.

The Finns now attacked the strung out column and the Russians gathered themselves into small pockets of men, mottis, which soon ran out of supplies. The Finns constantly harassed these separate pockets. The Russians' hands and feet began to suffer from frostbite; they became exhausted and hungry. When they despaired of being reinforced or supplied, they began to throw away their weapons and fled east, scattering across the frozen lakes or through the deep snow. They left behind 5,000 dead and their equipment. The 163rd Division was eliminated as a fighting unit.

After the 163rd Division had been annihilated, the Finns turned their attention to the Russian's 44th division, which had crossed the frontier and was now slogging its way up the Raate Road through the cold snow and ice. The Russians were finding this a far different experience then marching through the broad boulevards of Moscow behind a band playing stirring, martial tunes with crowds cheering and waving flowers. The Finns now had not only the exultation of their recent

296

victory to encourage them, but the spoils of war from the 163rd Division–Russian trucks, artillery, and most important, anti-tank guns.

The 44th Division was now concentrated in a five mile stretch of the Raate Road. They also had clusters of troops stretched out fifteen miles back to the Soviet Union frontier. Tanks patrolled between the troop concentrations.

First, the Finns felled trees as barricades against the tanks. Next, they suddenly attacked the concentrated head of the column with a strong force immediately causing the Russians to stop their forward movement, lose spirit, and forget offensive action. They dug in at the side of the road where they had been attacked and waited for the next move from the Finns.

This enabled the Finns to regroup their forces, most of which had recently been in the battle of Suomussalmi. The Russians didn't realize that these were many of the same Finnish troops that had recently defeated the 163rd division. The Russians gave the Finns credit for more overall strength than the Finns possessed. With the 44th Division now bogged down on the icy road and crowded with thousands of troops in a narrow five-mile corridor, its troops grew confused, cold, hungry, and exhausted.

The Russian tanks often crushed their own men and material, trying to maneuver out of the narrow road. Before long, they ran out of fuel and their engines froze up when temperatures fell to minus 40 degrees F. Food ran out. Many of the Russians didn't eat for five days. When they attempted to flee from their dug-in positions, the Finns, or their own commissars, shot them.

As the division disintegrated, a captured Russian confessed he didn't understand the reasons for invading cold, dark Finland. He said you couldn't even see the Finns, yet they were everywhere. Leaving the protection of the campsite meant certain death. He also realized, by looking around, that the Finns had little to gain from the Soviet form of government.

The Russian soldiers in the north were also told they were there to liberate the Finns from capitalist servitude, but the Finns were not showing much gratitude. Soviet political commissars accompanied the Russian troops and shot anyone showing a lack of fighting zeal. The commander of the 44th Division, General A. E. Vinogradov, and a number of his subordinate commanders, were later executed by orders of the Soviet High Command.

Marshal Mannerheim, describing the battles of Tolvajarvi and Suomussalmi, later wrote, "They were to prove the most remarkable ones from the tactical point of view and because they were of decisive importance for the morale of the Finish nation. Further, they give the most realistic picture of the pitiless conditions under which the Winter War was fought."

Change in Soviet Command and Strategy

After the unsuccessful December attacks, the Russians made a change in commanders in January, 1940 and concentrated their efforts again on conquering Finland by sweeping up the Karelian Isthmus. The new commander in charge of the Karelian Isthmus forces was Marshal Timoshenko, who had recently participated in the occupation of Poland and had good relations with Stalin. During January, the Russians concentrated on artillery and air bombardment of the Isthmus while they regrouped their ground forces. The Russian ground troops were reorganized and reinforced, and behind the front, they received extensive training in coordination of artillery, armor, and aviation.

On February 1, a strong Russian offensive began in the Karelian Isthmus with the major effort headed toward the center, near the city of Summa. The opening attack started with a massive artillery barrage. At noon, five hundred tanks attacked followed by infantry masked by a smoke screen. Five hundred airplanes supported the attacks. The action lasted throughout the night.

On February 6, an even larger Soviet attack was launched and on a wider front. The coordination between Russian artillery, tanks, and infantry had been much improved since December. Observation balloons helped direct the artillery fire and coordinated the ground attacks. The Russians continued to crowd masses of soldiers into narrow attacking corridors, and their casualties were still high. On February 11, the front was extended farther, and the Russians attempted to turn the flanks of the Finnish defenders by attacking across the now frozen Gulf of Finland to the west and across the ice of Lake Ladoga.

The Finnish forces, having to contend with growing fatigue, now had a broader front to defend. The lack of reserves and reinforcements exacerbated these problems, making the situation extremely difficult. At a high cost to the Russians, of enormous casualties and destroyed tanks, the Finns were forced to withdraw to defensive positions farther back. The Finns continually regrouped to meet the areas of heaviest attacks. Commanders were moved from place to place, while reorganizing defending forces and adding men and equipment where they could be found.

Young Finnish soldiers, still training in the rear, were rushed into battle along with newly formed ground units made up of sailors. Volunteers from Sweden and Norway were sent north to replace Finnish troops that could then be sent to the Karelian front.

The battles in the Karelian Isthmus were a continuous effort. There was a pattern of massive Russian artillery barrages, together with aircraft attacks, followed by great numbers of tanks and infantry. There was a large destruction of Russian tanks by anti-tank guns and Molotov cocktails. In addition, casualties of their infantry from machine guns, and other weapons, were enormous.

In spite of inflicting these heavy losses on their enemy, the Finns, under the sheer weight of the Russian advance, had to withdraw to defense positions farther back. A key difference was that the Russians could quickly replace their losses, while the Finns no longer could. A Finnish attack on February 26 using thirteen, light Vickers tanks couldn't break through the Russian tanks and anti-tank guns. All were finally destroyed.

After the unsuccessful Finnish tank attack, the Russians again began a massive artillery bombardment in one sector. The Finns anticipated Russian ground troops would soon follow. When this didn't happen, the Finns on night patrols found hundreds of dead Russian soldiers on the battlefield. The artillery barrage had been directed short, and the Russians had annihilated their own men. From the condition of the newly lubricated weapons they recovered, the new uniforms, newly shaved faces and general good health and appearance, the Finns concluded that these Soviet soldiers had been sent to the front very recently. The Soviet continued to press forward and captured islands in the inlet in front of Viipuri by attacking across the ice. They succeeded in piercing the Mannerheim line and splitting it.

The strength and construction of the Mannerheim line received considerable attention from participants and onlookers of the Winter War. To explain their lack of quick progress up the Karelian Isthmus, the Soviets compared it to the French Maginot Line and greatly exaggerated its construction, crediting it with having reinforced concrete emplacements. One official Russian communiqué called their final piercing of this defensive position, "a deed without parallel in the history of the war."

Marshal Mannerheim terms this, "complete nonsense." The Mannerheim Line, according to him, was a series of machine gun nests connected by trenches. Its main strength consisted of, "the courage and stubbornness of the Finnish soldiers."

The Finnish cities of Helsinki, Viipuri, Hanko, Kotka and others were subjected to Soviet air attacks. The Soviet air arm was not effective in its attempt to intimidate the civilian population. The Finns defended themselves with their small air force and with anti-aircraft artillery from the ground. At the start of the war, the Russians had an estimated 3,000 aircraft against 96 Finnish planes. During the war, the number of Finnish planes rose to 287.

In the beginning, the Soviet airmen were rushed into action with insufficient training and were not that much help to their ground troops. When Soviet planes attempted to drop supplies to isolated troops in the north, they were seldom effective. The supplies sometimes fell into Finnish hands. They also failed to do much damage against Finnish ground troops, at first, because the Finns blended into the snow or were too close to Soviet positions. In the final push up the Karelian Isthmus, the now-more-experienced Russian air arm coordinated their efforts more effectively with their ground troops.

The well-trained Finnish pilots shot down 240 Russian planes. Including losses to anti-aircraft fire, the Soviets lost 684 planes (confirmed), and perhaps as many as 925, against only 61 Finnish planes lost.

War Ends - March 12, 1940

While the battle raged on in the Karelian Isthmus, the politicians were active. Mannerheim recommended peace be the immediate objective. Aid from Sweden, if it came quickly, would be the next best thing. Help from the Allies was a last resort, since Finland's plight was not their main concern. The French and British now offered to send a force of 100,000 men. The Finns were skeptical of this offer of help. They felt the Allies wouldn't reach the battle zone in time to do much good and, instead, would take up strategic positions in Scandinavia. Preventing Swedish ore from reaching Germany was still high on their list of priorities. Attempts to get Germany and Italy involved in the peace progress were unsuccessful.

By this time, Stalin was ready to end the Winter War in order not to create a war zone in Scandinavia, so close to the Soviet Union. Also, the weather would soon turn warmer, making it more difficult for the Russians in the south who were attacking across the ice on the Gulf of Finland. The biggest problem for the Finnish military now was the length of the fighting front and their shortage of troops to defend it. A Finnish peace delegation was sent to Moscow on March 6, and, after five days, a Peace Treaty was signed.

When peace finally came on March 12, after Finland had resisted for 105 days, the nation was stunned. There was mourning for the 24,923 dead or missing and 43,557 wounded. It was a heavy price for a nation of only 4,000,000 people. The Finnish people also were deeply concerned over the Soviet Peace Treaty that had been imposed.

The peace treaty was much harsher than the conditions for peace that the Soviet Union had outlined less than four months ago. The Soviet military had dead and casualties in the hundreds of thousands, lost aircraft estimated at almost one thousand, and over two thousand tanks and armored cars destroyed.

Molotov remarked, when the terms were being settled, "Since blood has been shed against the Soviet government's wishes and without Russia being to blame, the territorial concessions Finland offers must be greater than those proposed by Russia in Moscow in October and November of 1939."

The Soviet Union took Viipuri, Finland's second largest city; its largest lake, Ladoga; the Saima Canal; the entire Karelian Isthmus, the largest Artic port, Petsamo (denying Finland access to the Arctic Ocean); and Hanko. The losses totaled 22,000 square miles and were home to 12 % of Finland's population. The people were given only two weeks to evacuate.

The timber industry in Karelia, with its sawmill factories and its wood finishing plants, was included in this area. Loses were also huge in the chemical industry and in power plants.

Finland had been defeated, but not conquered.

Aftermath

Hitler and his generals paid close attention to the Winter War and formed their opinions about the Soviet's military capabilities accordingly. Hitler compared the speed with which the German Army overran Poland (under three weeks) with the Soviet's taking 105 days to get Finland to sue for peace.

However, Hitler didn't take into account the lessons learned by the Soviet military from the Winter War and other considerations. Fighting in the cold was something the Soviets now took into much greater account. Also, if attacked, the Soviets would be fighting from defensive positions and stretched out supply lines would be the problem of the Germans. Most important, it would be the Russians who would be defending their homeland. Finally, the Soviet landmass was so much larger than Poland, and its resources in manpower so great; a blitzkrieg victory would become very elusive.

Looking at what the Winter War cost Finland in land, resources, and in dead and wounded, compared with Stalin's demands before the hostilities, one has to ask, "Was it worth resisting?" We can only speculate, since we can't know for sure what might have happened. If the Finns had decided on giving up several miles of the Karelian Isthmus, a thirty year lease on Hanko, and a few islands in the Gulf of Finland, would that have been the end of it? Almost surely Stalin would have asked for more in the months ahead, particularly if the Finns demonstrated a disinclination to fight.

In the months after the signing of the Peace Treaty, Stalin did make more demands of the Finns. He demanded that all Finnish state and private property taken from Karelia and Hanko be returned. This included giving seventy-five locomotives and two thousand railroad cars to the Soviets. Also, the nickel mine concession in Petsamo should be transferred from Britain and the new ownership was to include the Soviet Union. The Aland Islands should be demilitarized. Finland was also struggling to resettle the hundreds of thousands of Finns from

Karelia who wanted to remain Finns. Adding to the tensions, a Finnish civilian aircraft was also shot down.

However, events overran the way the situation might have played out, what with the start of the German and Russian conflict in 1941. Finland joined in the hostilities to recapture its lost territories. Mannerheim was appointed Marshal of Finland in 1942. When Finland, at the end of World War II, again needed to make peace with the Soviet Union, it had to pay substantial reparations in material goods, ships and industrial equipment. These reparations are credited with helping Finland to industrialize and laid the foundation for the highly educated work force and modern enterprises that exist today.

Nikita Khrushchev, who became head of the Soviet Union, in his book, *Khrushchev Remembers,* notes, "You might ask, why didn't we seize Finland during World War II, when the Finnish army was virtually wiped out? Stalin showed statesmanly wisdom here. He knew that the territory of Finland wasn't relevant to the basic needs of the world proletarian Revolution."

It's also likely that if Stalin had tried to make Finland a satellite, as he did the nations of Eastern Europe, it would have meant prolonged guerilla warfare. Soviet propaganda efforts during the Winter War were singularly unsuccessful. They tried to set up a "people's government" headed by a Marxist Finn, Otto V. Kuusinen, who had been living in Russia. The Finns laughed at it. Soviet leaflets, battlefield loudspeakers messages, and radio broadcasts made no impression on the Finns.

Perhaps, Stalin's grudging respect for the Finnish will to resist kept his troops out of the country after World War II. Finland was the only continental European country that the enemy didn't occupy in World War II.

Marshal Mannerheim again directed the Finnish military in World War II. He steered it through the shoals of German and Soviet hostilities but didn't pursue territorial gains beyond recapturing Finnish territory lost in the Winter War.

When World War II ended, Marshal Mannerheim was no longer in good health. In his remaining years, and still today, he stands high among Finns, in spite of past disagreements with government policy and former political leanings of some Finns. Although always a little aloof, he is now referred to affectionately as, "Marski."

A large equestrian statue of Mannerheim stands as a memorial to him near the post office on Mannerheimintie, Helsinki's main thoroughfare. To my mind, Mannerheim's real memorial is the independent and free country of Finland he fought so hard to maintain. The freedom and high standard of living that Finns have enjoyed since 1918 confirms their sacrifices were worthwhile. Comparing Finnish life with their close neighbors, the Russians, so long under communism, provides a visual benchmark for the merits of democracy.

I've spent Christmas in Finland a number of times and then gone on to another nearby Baltic location to celebrate New Year's. For New Year's 1988/89, when Communism still prevailed in the Soviet Union, I went with family members to Leningrad. The sharp contrast between the gaily-decorated store shelves in Helsinki, filled with high quality holiday foods and gifts, and the limited and less attractive offerings in the uninviting communist city stores was startling and depressing.

One of Helsinki's finest restaurants, the Savoy, is located on the downtown Esplanade. It is a roof-garden restaurant and is reached by four special elevators. The restaurant was designed in 1937 by one of Finland's foremost architects, Alvar Aalto, and still looks contemporary today. It has a silver plaque and a picture of Mannerheim at the corner table where he often had lunch.

You can order his favorite foods, which are available every day. You should start your meal with cold schnapps, "Marski's shot," in a frozen glass, filled to the brim in the old Russian Army style, upon which he insisted. When he was asked how this custom came about, Mannerheim replied that it went back to the days when he served in the cavalry of a Russian Guard Regiment. Part of their salary was paid in vodka, one drink at breakfast and two with dinner. Since the Army paid for these drinks, the soldiers wanted them as full as possible. Mannerheim's hand was steady, and he liked to test the hand of others.

He also enjoyed starting his meals with a dish called,"Vorschmack." Lamb and beef are first roasted with onions. They are then ground together with herring and anchovies and heated with garlic and water. After simmering and adding seasoning, it is served with sour cream and a boiled potato. It has a distinctive flavor I enjoy. The evening before having the "Mannerheim" lunch at the Savoy, we had dinner at a neighborhood place. The bartender told us that the corner table at which we were sitting is where Lenin sat when he fled to Helsinki in 1917. History is in nearly every corner of the Baltic.

Mannerheim's former home in the fashionable embassy district of Helsinki is now a museum. It is filled with items from his long and far ranging career. Not far from Mannerheim's former home is Helsinki's outdoor waterfront market. From here you can take a short boat ride to the former island fortress of Suomenlinna – Sveaborg, built by the Swedes starting in 1748. Here you can visit museums that depict the Winter War and display many of the weapons used. There is also one of the area's best restaurants, the Valhalla, in one of the former fortifications, but it's only open in the summer.

Mannerheim wrote his memoirs, "The Memoirs of Marshal Mannerheim," after he retired. It is an account of someone who lived in interesting times - an old Chinese wish for a happy life. It is also a good read, and I recommend it to you.

In the pantheon of Baltic Sea personalities who helped change the world, Mannerheim's place is assured.

Baltic Sagas
Events and Personalities that Changed the World!

Old Town Waterfront
Medieval Crane from 1444 in Background
Gdansk, Poland

X
Soviet Communism Fails
Decline Begins in Gdansk Shipyard

World War II Ends

World War II ended in Europe with the Soviet Union's armies astride Eastern Europe and in Germany's capital, Berlin. In the north, its troops were just short of Lubeck on the Baltic Sea, in the west, and at the Adriatic Sea, in southern Europe. In central Germany, they occupied the country about 100 miles to the west of Berlin. Germany was split into two zones with the Soviet Union occupying "East Germany," and the United States, Great Britain and France dividing "West Germany" into three zones with each occupying their own zone.

Berlin, now in the heart of East Germany, was also occupied by the four former allied powers. Access to Berlin by the United States, Britain, and France was by highways through Soviet-controlled East Germany, and by air. All the eastern European countries overrun by the Soviet Union's troops had Communist governments installed. Most painful was the failure to establish a free, democratic government in Poland, where the attack by Germany had triggered Great Britain and France's declaration of war in 1939.

Stalin even kept for the Soviet Union the eastern part of Poland, annexed as its spoils from the Soviet-Nazi pact of 1939, along with the Baltic states of Estonia, Latvia and Lithuania. When the other allies complained of Poland's lost land, Stalin suggested Poland receive land from the eastern part of Germany, with the remarks, "After all, they lost the war." Joseph Stalin was proving to be as much of a conqueror as Hitler.

The end of World War II allowed Great Britain, France, Holland and Belgium to regain control of their overseas colonial empires from which they had been cut off. During the war Churchill had remarked to Roosevelt that he had not become the King's Prime Minister, "to preside over the dissolution of the British Empire." The pre-war power structures, however, proved impossible to maintain.

In the years following the war, the colonies of the former European powers, one by one, slipped out of their shackles. As these overseas resources were lost to these former world powers, they gradually diminished in influence and the world came to recognize only two "superpowers" in the post-war era, The United States and The Soviet Union.

When Roosevelt died in April 1945, the Vice-President, Harry S. Truman, became President of the United States. He attended the Potsdam conference in Germany with Stalin and Churchill, during which Clement Atlee replaced Churchill as British Prime Minister. Of the major, wartime allied leaders, that left only Stalin Atlee had been Deputy Prime Minister and was familiar with the affairs and positions of the British government.

Harry Truman had not been so well briefed. He had seldom seen President Roosevelt and had not been told of the atomic bomb development or the growing problems with the Soviet Union. In spite of this, he quickly demonstrated both a willingness to make tough decisions and the strength of character and resolve necessary to lead the free world.

After an urgent plea to surrender was rejected, Truman ended the Pacific War by dropping an atomic bomb on Hiroshima, Japan and quickly followed this with an atomic bomb on Nagasaki. Japan surrendered, and Stalin seized Japan's Sakhalin Islands, which Russia still holds. Although the killing of hundreds of thousands of Japanese, mostly civilians, is still debated today, Truman based his decision on sparing the hundreds of thousand of American casualties (it was estimated) an invasion would have cost.

Harry S. Truman invited the wartime Prime Minister of Great Britain, Winston Churchill, to make a speech at Westminster College, Fulton, Missouri on March 5, 1946. The speech included the following:

"From Stettin in the Baltic to Trieste in the Adriatic, an iron curtain has descended across the Continent. Behind that line lie all the capitals of the ancient states of Central and Eastern Europe. Warsaw, Berlin, Prague, Vienna, Budapest, Belgrade, Bucharest and Sofia, all these famous cities and the population around them lie in what I must call the Soviet sphere."

It marked the beginning of the cold war.

On the Baltic Sea, only the western end and a few Finnish ports remained free. The coasts of East Germany, Poland, the Baltic States, and Russia were behind the so-called Iron Curtain. Communism was entrenched from Rostock, East Germany to Leningrad, Soviet Union. Such famous, former Hanseatic cities as Gdansk, Kaliningrad, Klaipeda, and Riga were all behind the Iron Curtain.

Cold War Highlights

The headlines for the next four decades would keep score of the ebb and flow of the fortunes of the United States and the free world, and the Soviet Union and its Communist supporters.

"The Truman Doctrine"- March 12, 1947 Economic aid for threatened nations was announced today.

"The Marshall Plan"– June 5, 1947 Secretary of State George Marshall at commencement exercises at Harvard University announced a European Recovery Program to help the war ravaged economies of Europe get back on their feet.

"Soviets Close Highways to West Berlin" – June 26, 1948 President Truman immediately begins the Berlin Airlift to take food, medicine, and even coal by round-the-clock flights to the city.

"North Atlantic Treaty Alliance"– April 4, 1949 The formation of a defense alliance for Western Europe (NATO) was announced today.

"Soviets Explode Atomic Bomb" – August 29, 1949

"Communists Take Over China" – October 1, 1949

"North Korea Invades South Korea" – June 25, 1950

"Death of Joseph Stalin Announced" - March 5, 1953
After the death of Stalin, there was a struggle for power in the Soviet Union. After a few years, Nikita Khrushchev (1894-1971) emerged as the Soviet Leader. His rule was to be a dynamic period in the Soviet Union and in its relations with the United States. At a Soviet Party Congress, he made a secret speech that denounced the policies of Stalin. He began to loosen some of the tight control on public expression and closed the forced-labor camps. In spite of these

progressive actions, he was a confirmed Communist, convinced it was the best system and determined to make it succeed.

Nikita Khrushchev visited the United Nations in New York City in 1960. He took off his shoe and banged it on the table in front of him. "We will bury you!" he declared. He convinced many Americans that he meant it. Scenes of nuclear devastation and the pictures of the victims at Hiroshima and Nagasaki were still fresh in our minds.

I was working at Procter & Gamble in downtown Cincinnati in 1960 and living in a small bedroom community, Terrace Park, east of the city. There were only about 500 families and one policeman. The residents were mostly college educated and upwardly mobile "yuppies." After Khrushchev's threat at the UN, fear of a nuclear attack led us to call a town meeting to decide what to do.

After much discussion, we authorized a bond issue for a million and half dollars to build a community nuclear shelter. The newspapers reported that we were the first community to do this. We were not the last. The plan was to build the shelter into the side of a ravine and persuade Kroger, a large supermarket chain, to use it as a warehouse for their grocery inventory. In case of an attack and a prolonged stay, the groceries would serve as our food supply until the radiation danger passed.

Meetings were held to outline rules as to how much time would be given those working in downtown Cincinnati to get to the shelter if an attack came during business hours. Also, how would we prevent residents of nearby towns from filling the shelter and crowding out Terrace Park residents? Was training in the use of defensive weapons to be part of the plan? Considerable heat was generated by those attending some of these meetings.

During this time, the cold war and threat of nuclear attack was vividly real. A friend of mine at work, who lived in another town, showed me a shelter he was helping to build in the basement of a neighbor's house. Their two families would use it. Others were doing the same thing. Stock piling food at home was common. Large buildings had signs directing people to the nearest "FALLOUT SHELTER." Schools conducted drills to show children what to do in the event of a nuclear attack. Newsreel pictures of the mushroom cloud hung over us all.

During this scary time, in 1959, the U. S. Government constructed a massive nuclear shelter at the Greenbrier resort in West Virginia. It provided shelter for 1000 members of the government. This facility's existence was finally revealed in 1992. Today, it can be visited as a tourist attraction.

The Cold War headlines, with Khrushchev in charge of the Soviet Union, continued.

"Bay of Pigs – Cuban Expatriates Defeated" – April 17-19, 1961

"Soviets Erect Berlin Wall" – August13, 1961

"Cuban Missile Crisis - Soviets Remove Missiles! – October16-28, 1962

The risky move by Khrushchev to put missiles in Cuba seemed to be the final straw for the Communist leadership in the Soviet Union. Khrushchev was retired. Things calmed down. Leonard Brezhnev became head of the Soviet Union. The Terrace Park Nuclear Bomb Shelter Bond was never issued and the shelter never built.

After the Cuban Missile Crisis, the next major confrontation between the forces of Democracy and Communism was fought out in Southeast Asia, in what had been the French colony of Indo-China prior to World War II. After the French failed to regain control, the country was split into North and South Vietnam. The French withdrew.

The United States took on the burden of preventing North Vietnam from taking over the entire country. After a long ruinous struggle, one that politically divided the people of the United States, a peace treaty was signed and America's military left. Without military opposition from the United States, the North Vietnamese finally marched into South Vietnam's capital, Saigon, and the painful Vietnam era finally came to a close.

Soviet Communism Up Close

At the height of the cold war, in 1965, I made a visit to the Soviet Union to see up close how the people lived under a Communist form of government. We traveled as part of a group of ten people, visiting six cities in various parts of this large country–Moscow, Volgograd, Rostov, Sochi, Kiev, and Leningrad. The tour was organized by the official government tourist agency, Intourist. This report is based on the journal I kept of that trip.

It was raining slightly when we arrived in Moscow, our first Soviet city, on an evening in late May. I decided immediately to see nearby Red Square, the location of Lenin's Mausoleum, and the focal point of so many newsreels of Russia. When I reached the area in front of Lenin's Mausoleum, with the Kremlin immediately behind it, there were two soldiers marching with rifles on guard at the tomb.

There were very few people in the dark, large square. Off to the side was a uniformed policeman and, nearby, three young couples were strolling and singing. One boy had a guitar. As I was watching them, a young man approached me, and a second young man soon joined us. They asked, in broken English, if I wanted to exchange some rubles for American dollars, and if I wanted to sell my jacket. I was surprised, particularly with the policeman nearby. We had been warned repeatedly against engaging in any financial dealings outside official channels in Russia, since the currency was state-controlled and the exchange rate fixed by the government. Foreigners had been arrested and detained for private financial dealings. I shook my head, " No," and walked away. The drizzle, the darkness, the proffered financial deal, and the setting, made this an exotic introduction to my first night in the Soviet Union.

We learned from our Intourist guide that her work was considered a good job. It usually went to nice-looking, personable women in their late twenties or early thirties, who were well regarded by the government. In this case, our guide, Valentina, was apparently selected for this work because her father had died defending Moscow in World War II, and been decorated for heroism. The English language training received by the guides, at least in 1965, must have come from British sources because their accent, and books they had studied, came from there.

The second day in Moscow we were taken to Red Square to see Lenin's Mausoleum. There was a long line stretching from the front all the way around the Kremlin wall. Because we were tourists, our guide placed us in front of the line and the Russians who had patiently advanced to this position, made room for us. We filed into the building and, in a subdued light gazed at the remains of Lenin in a glass sarcophagus. After Stalin died in 1953, he had been laid alongside Lenin, but was removed after Khrushchev's secret speech to the Twentieth Party Congress in 1956 denouncing Stalin's crimes.

On one occasion, I asked our Intourist guide to explain "Communism" to me. She said Lenin explained it by saying, "Each worker contributes according to his ability, and each worker receives according to his needs." She explained they hadn't arrived yet at this stage but were working toward it. The system today was "socialism." Even in 1965, I thought Lenin was better at making a revolution than in understanding human nature. The Americans I knew were willing to work hard and put in long hours to make a better home and life for themselves and their families, but I couldn't see them doing this for others beyond their own family.

The second city on our tour was the "Hero City" of Volgograd, which had been re-named Stalingrad from Tsarstin, until Stalin was downgraded in Khrushchev's famous speech. The German Sixth Army had besieged the city in World War II, referred to in the Soviet Union as "The Patriotic War," and its successful, bloody defense had been costly to both sides. The city had been almost completely destroyed but had been rebuilt. The surrender of the entire German Sixth Army here, in 1943, was a turning point of the war in Europe.

We next went to Rostov, "Gateway to the Caucasus," and an important trade center. The 1965 Noble Prize for Literature winner, Mikhail Sholokhov, author of, "And Quiet Flows the Don," used to live nearby. The Don Cossacks, well known for their horsemanship and singing, are identified with this area.

Our next stop, Sochi, is the largest Soviet recreation and health resort on the eastern coast of the Black Sea. There are a million visitors here a year. It has a climate similar to the Riviera and resembles it physically. Sochi is a beautiful place, and we had the best room and food of our trip. Our stop here seemed to be designed to allow us to relax, as well as go sightseeing.

Marina was our Intourist guide here, and the guide I remember best. Marina was an attractive, large woman, the wife of an Army officer stationed in Leningrad. She was sent to the Sochi resort area to accompany her mother, who was recovering from an illness. Marina was good-natured and cheerful but also sensitive to any comments that might reflect critically on her or the Soviet Union.

On one bus ride, I was sitting alone in the back, and, after a while, Marina joined me. We started talking about how Russian people live today compared with life under Stalin. These were among the comments she offered.

"Stalin was too interested in self-glorification and encouraged a cult of personality. He set up concentration camps, which we didn't know about. However, his head of the secret police, Lavrenti Beria, was responsible for much of the cruelty. Stalin's pictures, statues, etc., were quickly removed, many overnight, after his denouncement at the Twentieth Congress. Lenin is a saint and will always be revered. Khrushchev was a good man who got too old for such a big job and made mistakes, particularly in agriculture, where he shouldn't have meddled. There was a fear he might have started another cult of personality."

Little is known about the leaders of the country. Marina gets her news from the English newspaper, the Daily Worker. We had a wonderful time in Soshi, which I attribute in large part to Marina's sunny disposition and ebullient personality.

Our next city, Kiev, is the capital of the Ukrainian area and is one of the oldest cities in Russia. It was the gateway through which Christianity was introduced to the nation. Kiev had a lot to offer in understanding the history and development of the country.

On the first full day here our tour took us to the banks of the Dnieper River, upon which the Vikings used to sail south in order to trade for the riches of Constantinople. On the heights overlooking the river, there was a large statue of Saint Vladimir (960–1015) holding a cross. It was he who had brought Christianity to Russia. As Grand Duke of Kiev, he had decided that his pagan nation would never grow, prosper, or participate in the advances of civilization unless it converted to one of the world's great religions. Also, the population of his growing kingdom was so diverse in its languages, customs, and beliefs that it needed something to pull it together. A common religion would help to do this.

Vladimir himself was a hard drinking, lusty man who had sacrificed many humans on pagan altars. He considered many religions carefully but gradually eliminated all but one. He rejected Islam because it forbids drinking, and Roman Catholicism because it would make him subservient to the Pope. The Jewish religion was rejected because it hadn't protected its followers from being scattered. The Greek Orthodox Church with its beautiful icons and services, centered in Constantinople, appealed strongly to Vladimir, whose emissaries had been sent there to observe for him. In 988, Vladimir was baptized into the Greek Orthodox Church. Two years later, all his subjects were baptized in the Dneiper River, for which Vladimir was canonized. The Russian Orthodox Church evolved from this beginning.

Of all the places we visited, Kiev gave me the greatest understanding of how much the Russian Orthodox religion must have permeated life in this country. To reduce its authority and importance to the people, Communism was determined to stamp it out, reflecting Lenin's belief, "Religion is opium for the people." Under the Soviets, churches were neglected and allowed to fall apart, or converted to other uses. The more prominent ones were sometimes converted to museums.

At lunch that day in the dining room of a new and large hotel, we saw the American pianist, Van Cliburn, at a nearby table. He was probably the most popular American among Russians at that time. A few years before, in 1958, he had come to Moscow as a twenty-four year-old contestant in the first Tchaikovsky International Competition. His playing won the gold medal and, instantly, he became the toast of both America and Russia. It had been expected that a young Russian would take the prize and not a Texan.

A ticker tape down Broadway in New York City greeted him upon his return to America. Ever since, he has been in great demand for concerts and recordings. He was boyish-looking, tall, and handsome, which added to his appeal. We nodded to him, and he encouraged us to come over to his table. We exchanged a few pleasantries before excusing ourselves.

Many years later, Van Cliburn's special place in both the United States and Russia, was again confirmed. After a strenuous concert schedule he had taken a ten-year sabbatical, during which he didn't play publicly. He was lured back to the stage by an invitation from President Ronald Reagan to play at the White House in 1987, during a visit there by Mikhail Gorbachov, head of the Soviet Union. After this appearance, Van Cliburn resumed giving public performances. In 2001, he was a Kennedy Center honoree.

Leningrad, our last stop, is one of the most beautiful and best-planned cities of the world. For over two hundred years, it was the capital of Russia and the center of its economic, political, social, and cultural life. It is still the second largest city in the Soviet Union.

Russia's great artists, writers, composers, performing artists and painters, graced its public and private theaters. The great ballet dancers - Nijinsky and Pavlova - were trained here. The composers Tchaikovsky and Rachmaninov worked here. Dostoyevsky, Gogol, and Pushkin were part of the literary scene at various times. The leading countries of the world maintained embassies here, and many of the world's largest businesses had branch offices on the city's main thoroughfare, the Nevsky Prospect.

Most of these activities ceased with the 1917 revolution, and the city's status as Russia's hub was reduced when the capitol was moved to Moscow. However, the buildings, monuments, and parks, reflecting its imperial days, remain. Some were damaged in World War II, when the city was surrounded and the scene of heavy fighting. Stalin elected to have the city resist, and millions died in its defense. Many of these died of malnutrition and the shortage of fuel and medical supplies.

When we were there, it was the time of the "White Nights." This far north it is dark for only a few hours a day and there is a kind of twilight throughout the evening. The streets were fairly dim, to save electricity, but there were large electric signs with Communist slogans on a number of buildings.

We started our sightseeing in Leningrad at the Winter Palace, by going up the Ambassador's staircase. The Winter Palace itself has over one thousand rooms and is only one of the buildings in the Hermitage museum complex next to the Neva River. The museum is so large that we could see only some of its treasures. We did, however, see two of the world's thirteen paintings by Leonardo De Vinci; Rembrandts; a Michelangelo statue; Peter's throne room; Alexander Nevsky's massive silver sarcophagus; and a great deal more.

We were interested in seeing that the Soviets kept the famous equestrian statue of Peter the Great, although a Tsar, in its honored place in Decembrist's Square. Peter's role, in establishing Russia as a great European power, apparently outweighed his often brutal and autocratic treatment of his Russian subjects.

After our Leningrad visit, we flew back to Moscow to connect with our Air France flight from Russia to Paris. Two disquieting incidents happened at the airport, which gave me some additional insights into the mindset in the Soviet Union at the time. I saw a beautiful lacquered balalaika displayed at an airport shop. I purchased one and it was brought out from the stockroom. While I was walking away from the counter with the balalaika wrapped in paper, I tore the paper off one end to confirm that it was what had been displayed at the shop. When I did this, I saw that it was damaged, and so I turned right around to exchange it. The young girl who sold me the instrument refused to believe I hadn't done the damage myself, in the few minutes while I was walking away. She called over two of her colleagues and showed it to them. One, in particular, got very indignant and insisted that everything that left the place where it was produced was perfect. After I continued to insist on an exchange, they finally relented, giving me a new one. We all inspected it immediately at the counter.

The second incident involved my journal. During the entire trip around Russia, I kept a journal in a blue loose-leaf binder and wrote six or so pages of my impressions each day. I always kept it near me so I could update it whenever time permitted. The uniformed official checking our passports noticed the binder and asked what it contained. I told him, and he asked to see it. After leafing through it, he called over another official, who started going through it page by page. I assumed the second official was called over because he knew English.

I was starting to get a little apprehensive since my entries were straightforward, including both good and bad. We might miss our plane, if this dragged on much longer, and who knows what else? I might have gotten really worried if I hadn't been in the Soviet Union for almost three weeks. Suffice it to say, there is a little less fear of "the devil you know." Finally, the official snapped the journal closed and waved us off as we said, "Dosveedahnya" (goodbye). It turned out to be only the first of many visits.

The Russians we met were very curious about how we lived; our home; how many children we had; and what we thought of Russia. Did I have an automobile? How old was I? They seemed eager for direct information from the source.

The Soviets seemed to be concentrating on building a militarily powerful nation and had less interest in the everyday needs of their citizens. Tanks and rockets were being produced rather than automobiles. Complaints about deficiencies in new housing construction were expressed shortly after occupancy–the elevator wasn't working, concrete was cracking, the hall lights were out, and so fourth. In older buildings, kitchens and baths were often shared. We saw this for ourselves when we occasionally visited the homes of local people we befriended. Housing was still a big problem, twenty years after the war.

We missed America's free enterprise system, the benefits of competition, and our emphasis on giving customers what they wanted. Consumer preference research, competitive promotions, choice (Coca-Cola versus Pepsi or Chevrolet versus Ford), product innovation, and convenience sizes weren't part of the culture here. People had enough to eat, but it wasn't particularly good quality, with not much variety. Bread, butter, fish, and cabbage soup were good but the poultry was scrawny and the meat generally tough. Everyday consumer products that add to the quality of life–perfumed soap, facial tissues, soft towels, and stylish clothes, among other things, were missing.

When Russians see a queue, they often quickly join it, because something scarce may be available. Even if you don't need it, maybe a friend does, or you can trade it for something you need more urgently.

To buy something, you first get on line for a slip from a clerk, then join another line to pay for it, then a third line to receive the item.

The tyranny of the Tsars has been replaced by the totalitarianism of the Soviets. The Government controls all media, education, and organizations. It means only the "Party line" is disseminated and tolerated.

Shipyard Strike in Gdansk

Lenin Shipyard
Gdansk, Poland
Thursday, August 14, 1980

Poland was one of the Eastern European countries where a Communist regime had been established since 1945. World War II started in what was then the, " Free City of Danzig," when Germany attacked it in 1939. The city, at the end of the war, was given to Poland and renamed Gdansk.

The city has a very long history, going back a thousand years. It was formerly a possession of the Teutonic Knights, whose former headquarters fortress, Marienburg, is located in nearby Malbork. Gdansk was then a Hanseatic port and had changed ownership between Germany, Poland, and even Sweden. Since 1945, the old city has been restored, and the City Hall, churches, and merchant homes again reflect the Hanseatic era. Dating from 1444, there is a historic, picturesque large crane on the waterfront. said to be capable of lifting four tons. St. Mary's Basilica, also located in the old city, is the largest brick church in the world and took 159 years to build. It can hold five thousand people.

In 1980, the Lenin Shipyard, on the Gdansk waterfront, had 15,000 workers and was the largest employer in the city. In 1970, the shipyard work force here had stopped working, to protest employment conditions. That uprising had ended badly with the military called out to subdue the strikers. A number of workers had been killed.

Lech Walesa, an electrician, had participated in that strike as a twenty seven-year-old. His continued involvement in trying to improve working conditions since then had marked him as troublemaker and led to his firing from the shipyard in 1976. During the intervening years, he had picked up work here and there to support his wife and large family. He also attended meetings of the KOR (Committee for the Defense of the Workers), a group of educated Poles who passed along their knowledge of underground activities such as printing leaflets, negotiating tactics, and organizing.

Walesa had arrived early this day outside the twelve-foot high wall surrounding the shipyard. He planned to climb over the wall, helped by some of his friends, to support his former co-workers who planned to confront the authorities today and persuade them to give the workers a voice in their working conditions and pay. The place Walesa had selected to scale the wall was near shipyard Gate #2.

The area around the gate was now crowding up with thousands of resentful workers talking among themselves and refusing to work. The workers had smuggled in posters demanding the reinstatement of a popular worker, Anna Walentynowicz, who was recently fired. Her firing had been the catalyst for a number of frustrations troubling the workers. Food prices had been increasing again and the workers were being squeezed. They wanted a pay raise.

The head of the shipyard, Klemens Gniech, climbed on a bulldozer and promised the men that if they returned to work something would be done. As the crowd of workers thought this over and wondered what to do, a short, stocky, angry man with a mustache climbed on the bulldozer roof and shouted down to the director, "Remember me?" It was Walesa, who had gotten into the shipyard over the wall. He told the director his lies were, "no longer believed." Not all the workers remembered Walesa from his earlier days in the shipyard, but many did and trusted him. Walesa quickly formed a Strike Committee and had the director send his limousine for Anna Walentynowicz.

Walesa and the other workers had learned from the 1970 strike and didn't intend to go into the streets where the police or military could attack them. They also planned to use what they had learned about how to negotiate. They expected to achieve better results than in 1970. Walesa and his Strike Committee presented the director with five demands.
1.   He and Anna were to be returned to work in the shipyard.
2.   An increase in pay.
3.   An increase in family allowance.
4.   No reprisal for strikers
5.   A monument to the 1970 uprising victims.

Anna Walentynowicz had been a worker in the shipyard for nearly thirty years, first as a welder and then as a crane operator. She had been orphaned during World War II. Her husband had died later leaving her with a son. She was a small, kindly woman and thought of fondly by her fellow workers for bringing them small presents and food. She had been a Communist but became disillusioned and began to participate in activities to improve worker's conditions. Meetings of the KOR were sometimes held in her apartment, where Walesa had met Anna at one of the meetings.

August 7, she was fired from the shipyard for distributing political leaflets. This was only months before her retirement. It added to the incidents, which had been accumulating and ignited the unrest among the workers. Although others did the organizing and negotiating, Anna was considered the heart and soul of the shipyard uprising.

Strike Takes A New Turn

After the negotiations at the Lenin Shipyard started, other Gdansk workplaces and the nearby Gdydia Shipyard also stopped working. They sent representatives to the Lenin Shipyard to observe developments. On Saturday, August 16, 1980, after two days of negotiations, the shipyard director refused to consider anything more than the monument already agreed upon, a pay raise, and to rehire Walesa and Walentynowicz. Most of the Strike Committee was ready to take this offer and many workers began to leave for home. Over the factory loudspeaker, the director announced the end of the strike. A resolute call for workers' rights was petering out to become merely a wage increase settlement.

When the representatives of the other work places saw that the Lenin shipyard strike was fizzling out, they felt betrayed. They became angry and began shouting. Henryka Krzwonos, a streetcar driver, seized the microphone outside the negotiation hall and vented her fury over the abbreviated settlement. Upon leaving the hall, Walesa, immediately took in the atmosphere, climbed on an electric yard truck and drove around extorting the workers to stay in the yard. Many did and others came back. The Strike Committee was reorganized to include more shipyard workers who wanted to go beyond the original five demands and to add workers from other work places.

What had been a local strike now galvanized into something much larger. The new demands grew to twenty-one and embraced improving rights for Polish workers everywhere. The new demands included not only the right to independent unions, but freedom of speech and release of political prisoners. No longer was this a matter of just working concerns, it was about freedom from repression for all Poles.

The Solidarity movement began at this moment. It was a great leap forward!

The next day, Father Henry Jankowski came from a nearby church and celebrated a mass just inside Gate # 2. There were thousands of workers present and Father Jankowski blessed a wooden cross they had made. Walesa carried it to the spot where the monument was to be erected and cemented it into place. Word of what was happening in the shipyard had spread to the whole city, and the workers were now gaining support from the general population.

On bicycles and carts, people arrived with cabbages, potatoes, bread, cheese, other food, drinks, and cigarettes. A committee was organized in an improvised kitchen to prepare meals for those inside the shipyard. KOR advisors started up a publication and called it, "Solidarity," a word often used by Walesa. The first issue of twenty thousand sold out quickly. Alcohol was banned. Violence or damage to shipyard property was avoided. Nothing was done to invite physical reprisals.

The gates were decorated with flowers, pictures of the Pope and the Virgin Mary, and the Polish flag. Slogans appeared on the factory walls, "21 x Tak" (21 times yes), "YLKO SOLIDARNOSC" (ONLY SOLIDARITY). The workers slept where they could, on tables and benches or on the ground. The summer weather was helpful in this situation.

As the days went on, and the work stoppage continued, the number of factories halting production and sending representatives to the shipyard grew to two hundred and fifty. An Inter Factory Strike Committee (MKS) was formed to coordinate the demands of the other factories.

Mass was said every day at five o'clock. After mass, those worker representatives from outside the shipyard returned to their own factories to report on the discussions. Each day, Walesa climbed to a spot above the crowd and reported to the thousands gathered to hear him. He was in his element–he told jokes, prayed, sang, and shaped the mood of the crowd. Although he was only one of the negotiators, he was the one who could pull on the crowd's emotions and stir them. When he finished talking, he would raise his arms and make the "V" for victory sign with his fingers. Outside the negotiating hall, Anna Walentynowicz and others, spoke to the workers to keep them unified and committed.

The firms represented in the shipyard negotiations grew to five hundred. Although the authorities cut off telephone communications, word of what was happening in Gdansk was spreading throughout Poland, not only from leaflets, but also from Radio Free Europe. Other industrial cities were joining in the work stoppage. Worker committees were set up in Szerecin, Elblag, and smaller cities.

There was still a concern among the workers, remembering 1970, that the authorities might use force, or that the Soviet Union would intervene. A number of academics had addressed an appeal to the authorities to avoid bloodshed. On Friday, August 22, two of those who had signed the appeal, came to the shipyard and were gratefully welcomed by Walesa. He told them they were needed to support the efforts of the workers who lacked some of the skills required for negotiations. In response, six advisors came the next day.

The situation now alarmed the authorities sufficiently that Edward Gierek, Poland's Communist Party Secretary, sent Mieczyslaw Jagielski, a Deputy Prime Minister, to the negotiations at the Gdansk shipyards. Jagielski and his associates arrived by train. They moved through the loud and crowded shipyard to the glass enclosed room in the hall where the talks were to be held.

The first day of talks did not go well. Jagielski took a hard line, insisting the strikes must stop. Walesa wanted to go over their twenty-one demands, item by item. Also, Walesa wanted two KOR activists, Jacek Kuron and Adam Michnik, released. Jagielski returned to Warsaw without any agreement.

The next two days, Monday and Tuesday, also produced no results, and Jagielski refused to even discuss the idea of free trade unions. The crowd of workers surrounding the hall was growing restless.

On Wednesday, outside the shipyard, developments took place that sharply impacted the talks. The miners in Silesa and the workers at the steel town, Nowa Huta, went on strike. They set up a workers' factory committee and drew up their demands. Cardinal Wyczyski made an appeal for caution, saying that a prolonged strike would harm the nation. The government broadcast this appeal on TV, but Walesa and Poland's normally faithful Catholics didn't heed the Cardinal.

Next day, offsetting the Cardinal's caution, the Bishop's Council released a statement that backed up the workers. In support of the

Gdansk uprising, the circle of Poles was now spreading to include workers, the educated class and the clergy from all over Poland.

On Thursday, Jagielski began to yield some ground to the right to strike and freedom of the press. On Friday, Jagielski didn't come to the shipyard. Rumors circulated about the likelihood of the government using force. One problem for the government in imposing a military solution was that there were too many targets (the striking factories). They were spread all over Poland. In the shipyard, Walesa was at his best: magnetic, steadfast, determined, singing the national anthem, and calm. He was strongly supported in his resolve by Anna Walentymonicz, Andrej and Joanna Gwazda, Bogdan Lis, and others.

On Saturday, Jagielski returned, and there was genuine give and take on the worker's demands. Releasing the KOR activists became a sticking point, but the strikers would not abandon them. Jagielski went back to Warsaw to consult with the Communist Central Committee, but the atmosphere suggested that the next day things would be brought to a head.

The mood in the shipyard the next day, Sunday, August 31, was peaceful, and there was an expectant calm. The crowd sensed an historic moment was going to take place. Immediately, after he arrived at the shipyard, Jagielski announced the KOR detainees were to be released. He agreed to all the workers' demands. There was a singing of the national anthem. In the hall, there was a signing ceremony. Jagielski said that there were no winners or losers. Walesa greeted the jubilant crowd, shook his fists, and announced a mass to be broadcast the next day.

A number of things contributed to bringing about this basic and historic improvement in reducing Communist repression in Poland.

1. The Lenin Shipyard strikers' resolve gained growing support throughout Poland from workers (even from those who didn't do manual labor), the church, and the intellectuals.

2. The strikers communicated the events at Gdansk, providing all Poles with a stake in what was happening.

3. Poland was a deeply religious, Catholic society. In 1978, the election of the Archbishop of Krakow, Cardinal Karol Wojtyla, as the first Polish Pope, had heartened Poles everywhere.

4. Poland had a long tradition of rebellion against authority imposed from outside nations. Poland had a culture and language that prompted it to survive as a nation, in spite of numerous conquerors and frequent border changes.

5. The times worked against the Communist authorities. By 1980, the devastation of World War II was wearing thin as an excuse to explain food and other civilian goods shortages. The free world had moved on and those under Communism could see it wasn't delivering.

6. The Soviet Union had advised that it would not intervene militarily. The Polish authorities couldn't allow a work stoppage to continue that would cause the facilities to remain idle. In the end, the Polish Communist authorities were left with the option of giving ground or brutal repression that would be observed by the entire world.

Putting the reforms sought by the Polish people into a written agreement and having them signed by the Communist authorities was a great victory. The next important step was implementation, and this proved more elusive. Disagreements within the new national union, Solidarity, soon surfaced. Moderates competed with radicals for leadership. How fast and hard the union should push for reform became an ongoing issue. The economy continued to deteriorate. A new strike was threatened. A general, Wojciech Jaruzelski, became the new Prime Minister.

Walesa's stubborn nature began to erode his former, enormous popularity. His inclination to make decisions without consultation, his new apartment, and his travels abroad invited criticism. Walesa won the election as Chairman of the union's National Committee in 1981 but with only 55 % of the vote.

In December 1981, General Jaruzelski declared Martial Law. Walesa and other union leaders were arrested. Later, Walesa was released. In July 1982, Martial Law was lifted. In October 1982, Walesa was awarded the Noble Peace Prize. He didn't go to collect it in Oslo, being concerned that he wouldn't be allowed to return to Poland.

In 1990, Walesa was elected President of Poland. However, he was defeated for this position in 1995. He is no longer in the center of political life in Poland, but he certainly has a place in history, both as a leading personality in the Baltic and in the world.

A New Day in the Baltic

While the struggle for power sharing went on in Poland in the 80's, events elsewhere were also affecting the worldwide balance of power. The Soviets had invaded Afghanistan in 1979, and they were getting bogged down there. The Soviet troops were finally taken out of there in 1989. In 1985, Mikhail Gorbachev was elected General Secretary of the Soviet Union Communist Party and called for new policies of Glasnost ("Openness") and Perostroika ("New thinking").

In Communist China, after Mao Tse-Tung died in 1976, there was a movement by his successors to loosen the grip of state control and allow more economic freedom.

In 1980, Ronald Reagan, who called the Soviet Union the, "Evil Empire'" was elected President of the United States. Ronald Reagan added his voice to the other American Presidents who had stood up for West Berlin's freedom. Harry Truman had instituted the Berlin Airlift in 1948 to help keep West Berlin free. John F Kennedy had confirmed America's commitment to West Berlin by proclaiming there, in 1962, "Ich bin ein Berliner." President Ronald Reagan, on June 12, 1987, in front of the Berlin Wall, demanded, "Mr. Gorbachev, tear down this wall."

The Berlin Wall came down on November 9, 1989. It was the most dramatic event to mark the unraveling of the Soviet Union's post World War II empire. This was followed by the Soviets pulling their troops out of East Germany and returning to Russia. The Soviet Republics, one by one, declared their independence from Russia. Only the St. Petersburg area and the small sliver of Kaliningrad, isolated from Russia by newly independent Belarus, give Russia access to the Baltic Sea.

It's been over twelve hundred years since the Baltic Region dramatically announced its entry into the world's consciousness with the Viking raid on Lindisfarne Monastery in 793 A.D. Tumultuous events in the region reached an apogee in the twentieth century, when all the countries there were affected by the Communist takeover of Russia in St. Petersburg, and after that, World War II. Only Sweden avoided being embroiled in the general conflagration, and even it had to step gingerly to avoid commitment to one side or another. The era after World War II saw the Baltic countries split into opposite political sides.

Today, there is a new day in the Baltic. The countries that share its shores are no longer divided into east and west. The former Soviet bloc countries, Estonia, Latvia, Lithuania, and Poland are free to elect their own leaders. East Germany has been reunited with West Germany. The Baltic area is at peace.

Now-a-days, Baltic nations emphasize economic development rather than territorial ambitions or extreme political changes. They serve as an example to many parts of the world, where old antagonisms still prevail.

Selected Bibliography

The Viking are coming!
Allan, Tony. *Vikings, The Battle at the End of Time*. London, Duncan Baird Publishers, 2002.

Fitzhugh, William W. and Ward, Elizabeth I. ,eds. *Vikings, The North Atlantic Saga*. Washington and London, Smithsonian Institution Press, 2000.

Guy, John. *Viking Life*. Hauppauge, New York, Barron's Educational Series, Inc., 1998.

Margeson, Susan M. *Viking*. New York, Dorling Kindersley Ltd., 1994.

The Teutonic Knights
Lamb, Harold. *The Crusades*. New York, Doubleday, Doran, & Company, Inc, 1930.

Michener, James A. *Poland*. New York, Random House, 1983.

Sieniewicz, Henry K. *The Teutonic Knight*s. New York, Hippocrene Books, 1993.

Przybyszewski, Father Boleslaw. *Saint Jadwiga–Queen of Poland 1374–1399*. Translated into English by Professor Bruce MacQueen, London, Veritas Foundation Publication Centre, 1997.

The Hanseatic League
Zimmern, Helen. *The Hansa Towns*. London, G. P. Putnam's Sons, 1907.

Peter the Great
Jackson, W. G. F. *Seven Roads to Moscow*. London, Eyre & Spottiswoode, 1957.

Klyuchevsky, Vasili. *Peter the Great*. London, MacMillian & Co., Ltd., 1958.

Massie, Robert K. *Peter the Great*. New York, Ballantine Books, 1980.

Tolstoy, Alexey. *Peter the First*. New York, Signet Books, 1961.

Catherine the Great

Catherine II. *The Memoirs of Catherine the Great.* London, ed. Dominique Maroger, Macmillian, 1955.

Coughlan, Robert. *Elizabeth & Catherine.* New York, G.P. Putnam's Sons, 1974.

Courtiers, by one of her. *Memoirs of Catherine II and the Court of St. Petersburg during her reign and that of Paul I.* Paris-New York, The Grolier Society, Limited Edition.

Madararariaga, Isabel de. *Russia in the Age of Catherine the Great.* New Haven and London, Yale University Press, 1981.

Mager, Hugo. *Elizabeth, Grand Duchess of Russia.* New York, Carroll & Graf, 1998.

Montefiore, Sebag. *The Life of Potemkin.* New York, Thomas Dunne Books, St. Martin's Press, 2000.

Rasputin and the Prince

Almedingen, E. M. *My St. Petersburg.* New York, W.W.Norton & Co.

Fitzlyon, Kyril, and Browning, Tatiana . *Before the Revolution.* Woodstock , New York, The Overlook Press, 1978.

Fulop-Miller, Rene. *Rasputin The Holy Devil.* The Viking Press, 1928.

King, Greg. *The Man Who Killed Rasputin.* Carol Publishing, 1996.

Massie, Robert K. *Nicholas and Alexandra*, New York, Dell Publishing, 1967.

Moynahan, Brian. *Rasputin.* DaCapo Press, 1997.

Oakley, Jane, *Rasputin-Rascal Master.* New York, St. Martin's Press, 1989.

Purishkevich, V.M. *The Murder of Rasputin.* Ann Arbor, Michigan, Ardis, 1985.

Rasputin, Maria. *My Father.* New Hyde Park, New York University Books, 1970.

Rasputin, Maria, and Barham, Patte. *Rasputin, The Man Behind the Myth.* Englewood Cliffs, N.J., Prentice Hall, Inc.,1977.

Radzinsky, Edvard. *The Rasputin File.* New York, Doubleday, 2000.

Wechsberg, Joseph. *In Leningrad.* Garden City, New York, Doubleday & Company, Inc.,1977.

Youssoupoff, Felix. *Lost Splendor.* New York, G.P. Putnam's Sons, 1953.

Youssoupoff, Felix. *Rasputin: His Malignant Influence and Assassination.* New York, Dial, 1927.

Communism Triumphs in Russia

Payne, Robert. *Lenin.* NewYork, Simon and Schuster, 1964.

Reed, John. *Ten Days That Shook The World.* New York, The Modern Library, 1919.

Service, Robert. *Lenin, A Biography.* Cambridge, MA, Harvard University Press, 2000.

Seth, Ronald. *The Russian Terrorists.* London, Barrie and Rockliff, 1966.

Hasegawa, Tsuyoshi. *The February Revolution: Petrograd, 1917.* Seattle and London, University of Washington Press, 1981.

Space Age Begins

Dornberger, Walter. *V-2.* New York, The Viking Press, 1954.

Von Braun, Wernher and Ordway III, Frederick I. *History of Rocketry & Space Travel.* Chicago, J.G. Ferguson.

Winter War 1939

Condon, Richard W. *The Winter War.* New York, Ballantine Books, 1972.

Engle, Eloise and Paaanen, Lauri. *The Winter W*ar. Harrisburg, PA, Stackpole Books, 1973.

Jakobson, Max. *Finland Survive*d. Helsinki, Otava Publishing.

Klinge, Matti. *A Brief History of Finland.* Helsinki, Otava Publishing,1981.

Klinge, Matti. *Let us be Finns, Essays in History.* Helsinki, Otava Publishing, 1990.

Linna, Vaino. *Under the Northern Star.* Beaverton, Ontario, Canada, 2001.

Mannerheim, C. G. E. *Memoirs.* Helsinki, Otava Publishing,1950.

Wiskari, Werner, *The Miracles of Finland's Freedom.* Finlandia Foundation, New York, 1993.

Soviet Communism Fails
Crozier, Brian. *The Rise and Fall of the Soviet Empire.* Rocklin, CA, Prima Publishing,1999.

Khrushchev, Nikita. *Khrushchev Remembers.* Little, Brown and Company, 1970.

Salisbury, Harrison E. *The 900 Days, The Siege of Leningrad.* New York, Avon Books, 1969.

General
Klinge, Matti, *the Baltic World,* Helsinki, Otava Publishing, 1994

Other Sources

The Internet was especially helpful in obtaining recent information. We accessed hundreds of Internet sites, too numerous to list. This quick reference to such sources as libraries and, museums around the world, and specialists interested in particular subjects was of great value. We were careful to cross check Internet facts since there is often no editing authority to prevent misinformation.

We've traveled to most of the places discussed in the book and collected information, brochures, and booklets while there. We took the photographs that appear in the book.

CPSIA information can be obtained at www.ICGtesting.com
Printed in the USA
236310LV00003B/58/A